Key Stage 3 Science

Spectrum

Biology

W0018907

Andy Cooke

Jean Martin

Series editors	Andy Cooke
	Jean Martin
Authors	Darren Beardsley
	Jenifer Burden
	Paul Butler
	Chris Christofi
	Andy Cooke
	Zoe Crompton
	Jean Martin
	Sue McCarthy

CAMBRIDGE
UNIVERSITY PRESS

University Printing House, Cambridge CB2 8BS, United Kingdom

Cambridge University Press is part of the University of Cambridge.

It furthers the University's mission by disseminating knowledge in the pursuit of education, learning and research at the highest international levels of excellence.

www.cambridge.org
Information on this title: www.cambridge.org/9780521549219

© Cambridge University Press 2004

First published 2004
9th printing 2013

Printed in Poland by Opolgraf

A catalogue record for this publication is available from the British Library

ISBN 978-0-521-54921-9 Paperback

Material in this book was previously published in *Spectrum Year 7 Class Book* (pp. 1–52), *Spectrum Year 8 Class Book* (pp. 1–50) and *Spectrum Year 9 Class Book* (pp. 1–49).

Cover design by Blue Pig Design Co
Page make-up and illustration by Hardlines Ltd, Charlbury, Oxford

Contents

Page

Introduction — v

Unit 7A Cells: the body's building bricks — 1

7A.1 What living things are made from — 1
7A.2 How microscopes helped to change our ideas — 2
7A.3 What cells are like — 4
7A.4 Different cells for different jobs — 7
7A.5 How new cells are made — 9
7A.6 The secret life of plants — 10

Unit 7B Reproduction — 13

7B.1 How a new life starts — 13
7B.2 The menstrual cycle — 18
7B.3 The uterus as home to the developing baby — 19
7B.4 Birth and care of the baby — 20
7B.5 How humans change as they grow — 22

Unit 7C Environment and feeding relationships — 25

7C.1 Habitats — 25
7C.2 Changing environmental conditions — 27
7C.3 Investigating woodlice — 29
7C.4 Seasonal change — 30
7C.5 Feeding relationships — 33
7C.6 Food webs — 35

Unit 7D Variation and classification — 37

7D.1 The same but different — 37
7D.2 The causes of variation — 40
7D.3 Describing living things — 42
7D.4 Sorting things into groups — 45
7D.5 Sorting plants and animals — 46

Unit 8A Food and digestion — 53

8A.1 Why we need food — 53
8A.2 A healthy diet — 58
8A.3 Getting nutrients out of your food — 59
8A.4 How your digestive system works — 61
8A.5 After digestion — 63

Unit 8B Respiration — 65

8B.1 How cells use food — 65
8B.2 How oxygen reaches your tissues — 66
8B.3 What happens to oxygen when it reaches the cells — 71
8B.4 What happens in your lungs — 72
8B.5 Comparing inhaled and exhaled air — 74
8B.6 Other living things respire too — 76

Unit 8C Microbes and disease   **79**

8C.1 Micro-organisms and how to grow them   79
8C.2 Micro-organisms and disease   83
8C.3 Protecting ourselves against disease   86

Unit 8D Ecological relationships   **91**

8D.1 Animals, plants and adaptations   91
8D.2 Interactions in a habitat   94
8D.3 How living things depend on each other   98

Unit 9A Inheritance and selection   **103**

9A.1 What information is passed from parents?   103
9A.2 Why are we similar but not identical?   105
9A.3 Differences between offspring   107
9A.4 The right breed for the right job   108
9A.5 How new varieties of plant are produced   110
9A.6 What is a clone?   112

Unit 9B Fitness and health   **115**

9B.1 Ideas about fitness   115
9B.2 Breathing in action   117
9B.3 The dangers of smoking   118
9B.4 Why your diet is important   120
9B.5 The use and abuse of drugs   122
9B.6 Fit for life   125

Unit 9C Plants and photosynthesis   **129**

9C.1 How do plants grow?   129
9C.2 Leaves and photosynthesis   131
9C.3 What happens to the glucose made in leaves?   133
9C.4 Roots, water and minerals   134
9C.5 Green plants and the environment   136

Unit 9D Plants for food   **139**

9D.1 Where does our food come from?   139
9D.2 How do fertilisers affect plant growth?   143
9D.3 Plants out of place   145
9D.4 Pests   147
9D.5 Producing more food   149

Scientific investigations   **152**

Glossary/Index   160
Acknowledgements   170

About *Spectrum Biology*

This *Spectrum* Class Book covers what you will learn about science and scientists in Key Stage 3 biology. It is split into twelve **Units**. Each Unit starts with a page like this:

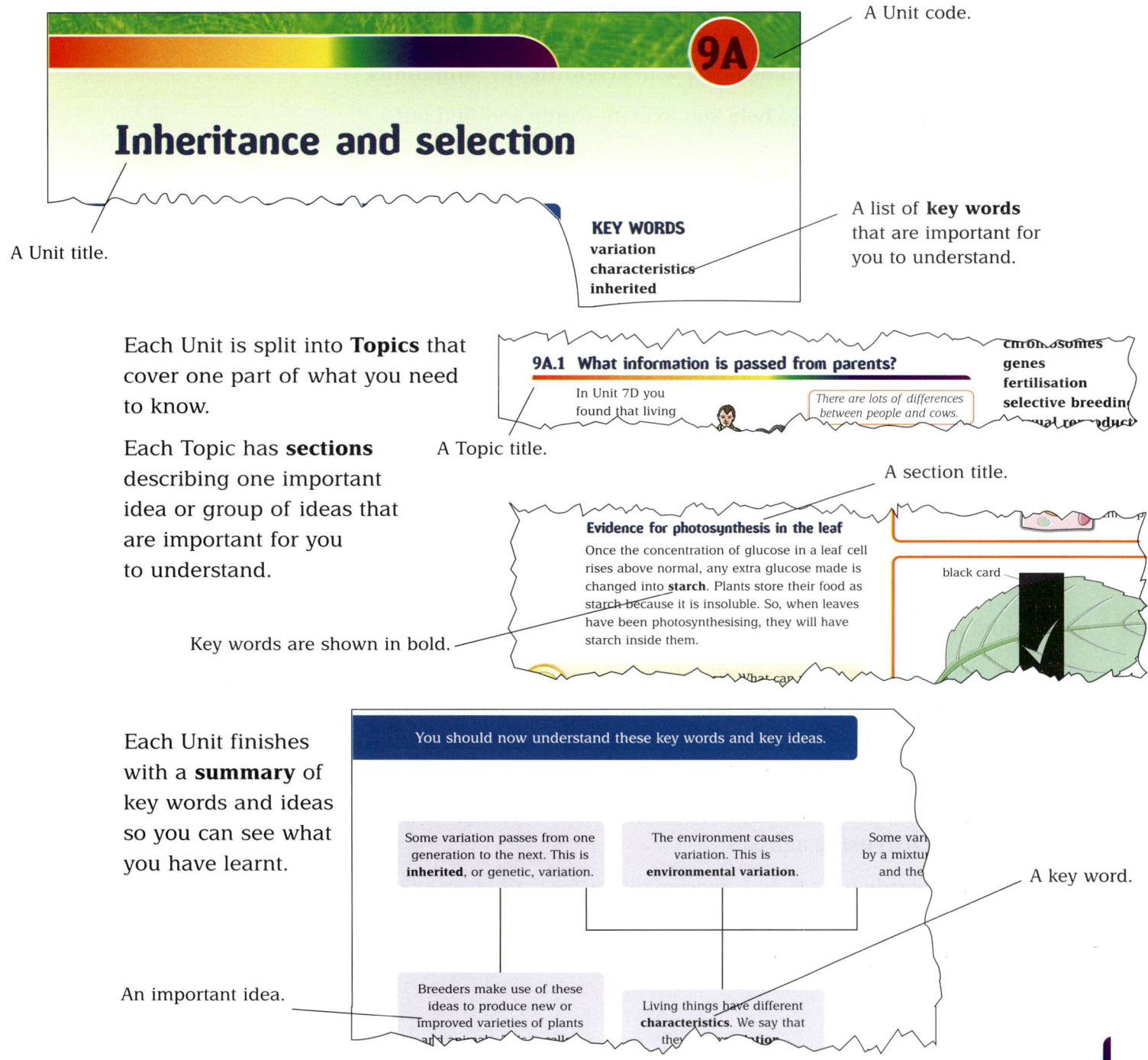

A Unit code.

9A

Inheritance and selection

A Unit title.

KEY WORDS
variation
characteristics
inherited

A list of **key words** that are important for you to understand.

Each Unit is split into **Topics** that cover one part of what you need to know.

9A.1 What information is passed from parents?

In Unit 7D you found that living

There are lots of differences between people and cows.

chromosomes
genes
fertilisation
selective breeding

A Topic title.

Each Topic has **sections** describing one important idea or group of ideas that are important for you to understand.

A section title.

Evidence for photosynthesis in the leaf

Once the concentration of glucose in a leaf cell rises above normal, any extra glucose made is changed into **starch**. Plants store their food as starch because it is insoluble. So, when leaves have been photosynthesising, they will have starch inside them.

black card

Key words are shown in bold.

Each Unit finishes with a **summary** of key words and ideas so you can see what you have learnt.

You should now understand these key words and key ideas.

Some variation passes from one generation to the next. This is **inherited**, or genetic, variation.

The environment causes variation. This is **environmental variation**.

Some var by a mixtu and the

A key word.

Breeders make use of these ideas to produce new or improved varieties of plants

Living things have different **characteristics**. We say that they

An important idea.

Icons

 Telling you where to look in the Class Book to help with activities.

 Asking questions about what you have just learnt.

 Asking questions that help you think about what you have just learnt.

 Asking questions that might need some research to answer.

At the end of the book

At the end of the book you will find:

- pages 152 to 159 to help you with **scientific investigations**;

- a **glossary/index** to help you look up words and find out their meanings.

Other components of *Spectrum*

Your teacher has other components of *Spectrum Biology* that they can use to help you learn. They have:

- a **Teacher file CD-ROM** full of information for them and lots of activities of different kinds for you. The activities are split into three levels: **support**, **main** and **extension**. Some of the activities are **suitable for homework**.

Also available by year:

- an **assessment CD-ROM** with an **analysis tool**. The CD-ROM has **multiple choice tests** to find out what you know before you start a Unit and for you to do during or after a Unit. It also has some end of year **SAT-style tests**.

And free on the web available at www.cambridge.org/spectrum:

- general guidance documents on aspects of the Science Framework;

- **investigation checklists**, **investigation sheets** – writing frames to help with structuring investigations, and **level descriptors** covering **Planning**, **Observation**, **Analysis**, **Evaluation** and **Communication**;

- **mapping grids** for the **Five Key Ideas**, **Numeracy**, **Literacy**, **ICT**, **Citizenship** and **Sc1**;

- **flash cards** for use as a revision aid or for card chases using the Years 7, 8 and 9 key words;

- **Five Key Ideas cards** for use as a revision aid and to build giant concept maps.

Cells: the body's building bricks

In this unit we shall be learning about some cells, tissues and organs in plants and animals.

KEY WORDS

organs
tissues
microscope
cells
nucleus
scale
cytoplasm
cell membrane
chloroplast
vacuole
cell wall

7A.1 What living things are made from

Aristotle lived in Greece over 2000 years ago. He was very interested in plants and animals and in how the human body works. Look at the drawing by Aristotle of some parts of the human body. We call these parts **organs**. The Greeks weren't the only people interested in how the body works. Old drawings and texts from China and the Middle East also show human organs. Some even show plant organs.

At first, information about organs came from operations and from cutting up dead bodies. Now we can look at X-rays and body scans, too.

1   Write down the names of <u>two</u> organs that you can see on:

a Aristotle's drawing;

b the scan.

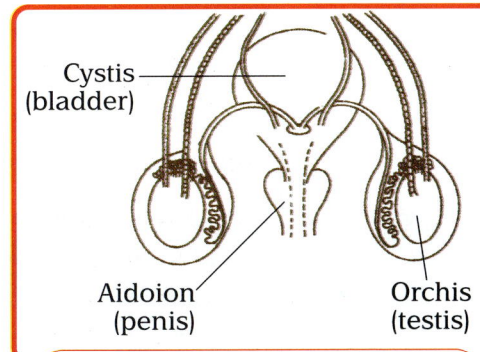

Aristotle's drawing. The names in brackets are the ones that we use.

A closer look at human organs

In the late 18th century, a French doctor called Xavier Bichat did hundreds of post-mortems. Post-mortems are operations carried out on dead bodies to find out what killed them. Bichat found that each human organ contains more than one kind of material. He listed 21 different kinds. Today, we call these materials **tissues**. Bichat wasn't able to see the detailed structure of these tissues because he didn't have a microscope.

2   Look at this picture of part of a thigh bone. Write down the names of <u>three</u> tissues in this bone.

3   What do we use to see what the cells in these tissues are like?

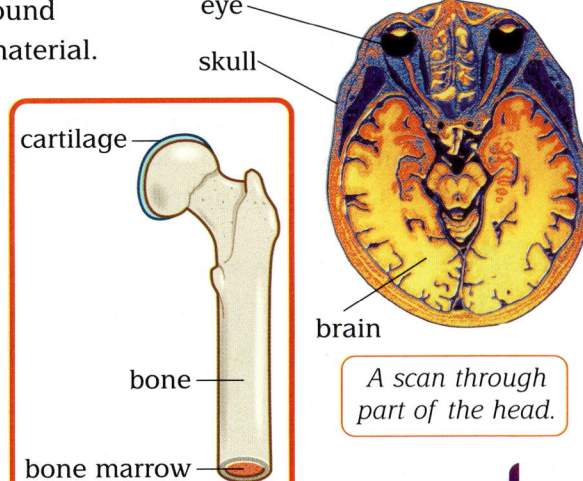

A scan through part of the head.

Part of a thigh bone.

7A.2 How microscopes helped to change our ideas

Microscopes were invented in the 16th century. The lenses of these microscopes were not very good, so the images were not clear. The first microscopes had only one lens. They were called simple microscopes.

It was not until 1590 that two Dutch spectacle makers, Hans and Zacharias Janssen, made a microscope with two lenses. We call this kind a <u>compound</u> microscope.

Later, an English scientist called Robert Hooke built a compound microscope. He used it to look at things that were too small to see with the naked eye. In 1665, he published the first book of drawings of these microscopic structures. One of the drawings was of a slice of cork.

Cork is the bark of a cork oak tree. Hooke's microscope showed that cork is made up of what look like tiny boxes. Hooke called these boxes **cells**.

In 1673, a Dutchman called Antonie van Leeuwenhoek found out how to make better lenses. He made a simple microscope with one of these lenses. His microscope made things look 200 times bigger than they really were. We say that it magnified things 200 times. Because his lens was so much better, the images were clearer than Hooke's. Leeuwenhoek published a book of drawings of microscopic creatures in 1683.

About 150 years later, a Scot called Robert Brown saw that there was something inside cells. He named this the **nucleus** in 1831.

Hooke's drawing of cork cells.

Leeuwenhoek's microscope

Onion cells, as seen using Robert Brown's microscope.

nucleus

By 1840, two German scientists called Matthias Schleiden and Theodor Schwann realised that all plants and animals were made of cells. They published this idea as a theory, called simply <u>cell theory</u>.

1   In one sentence, write down what you think that cell theory says.

2   Use the information on this page to draw a time-line for the invention of lenses and the microscope and the discovery of cells.

Scale drawings

When we draw what we see under a microscope, we draw things much bigger than they really are. We draw them to **scale**. We often use scale drawings in our lives, not just in science. Maps and plans are scale diagrams. They show places smaller than they really are. We call this <u>scaling down</u>. When we show things bigger than they really are, we are <u>scaling up</u>. You can show a scale in one of these ways:

× 20 |⊢— 1 mm —⊣|

3 a Why did Hooke draw the flea larger than life?

   b Is this scaling up or scaling down?

   c Adding a scale would make Hooke's drawing more useful. Explain why.

4 a How long is the ladybird in Leon's drawing?

   b How many times longer is the drawing than the real ladybird?

   c What is the scale factor of the drawing?

5 Draw the ladybird magnified 20 times. Remember to put a scale on your drawing.

6 Think about <u>two</u> jobs in which people draw things to scale. Explain why they need to use scale drawings.

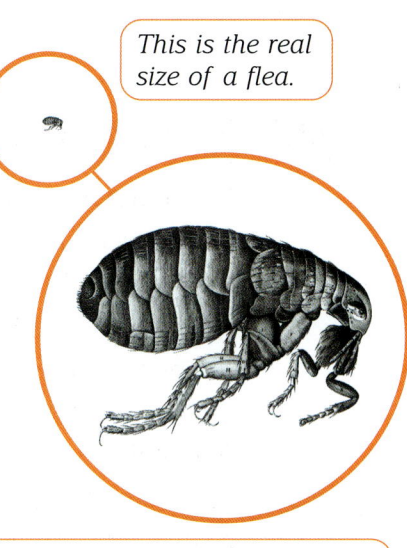

This is the real size of a flea.

Robert Hooke drew a flea bigger than it really is. This means you can see more detail.

This ladybird is 4 mm long.

Under a magnifying lens the ladybird looks three times as big, so the scale factor is ×3.

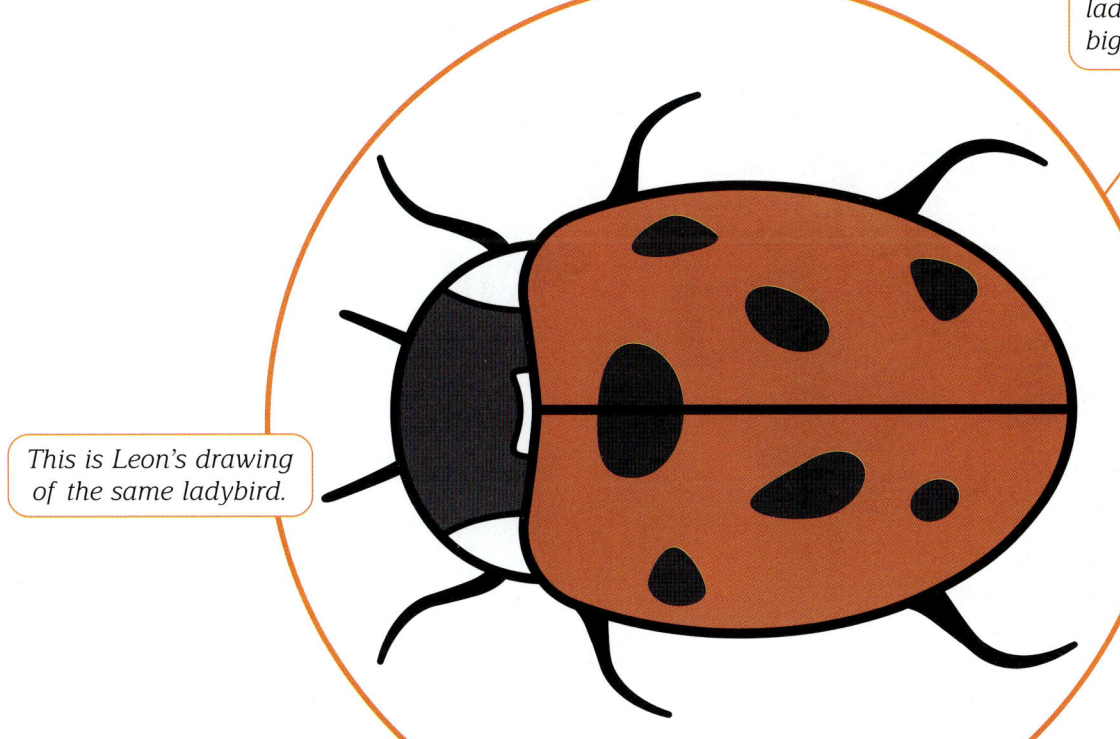

This is Leon's drawing of the same ladybird.

7A.3 What cells are like

Cells are very small

Remember that all living things are made of cells and that cells are so small that you need a microscope to see them. If you magnify cells a hundred times or more, you can see the smaller parts inside them. Not everything has got this type of detail. Many non-living things show no structure when you look at them under a microscope.

1 Look at the photos of thin layers from a candle and skin from a stick of rhubarb taken through a microscope.

   a What does the microscope view of the candle wax show?

   b What does the microscope view of the stick of rhubarb show?

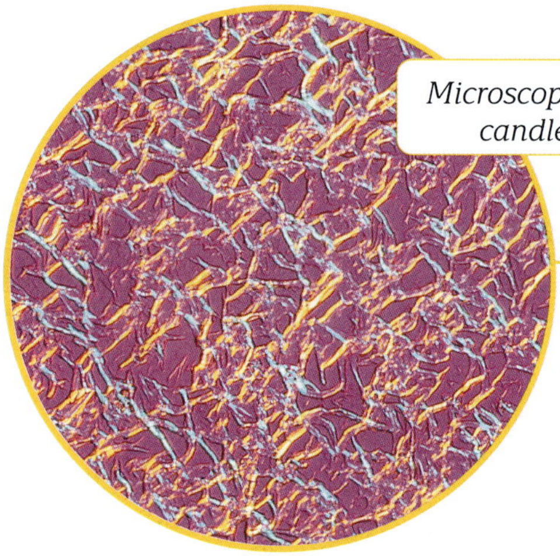

Microscope view of candle wax

Candle

Microscope view of rhubarb leaf stalk skin

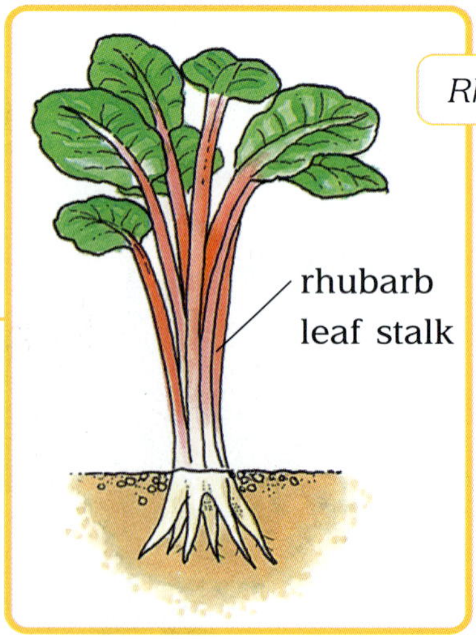

Rhubarb

rhubarb leaf stalk

2 Look at the microscope views of living and non-living things. Which ones do you think are of living things? Explain your answers.

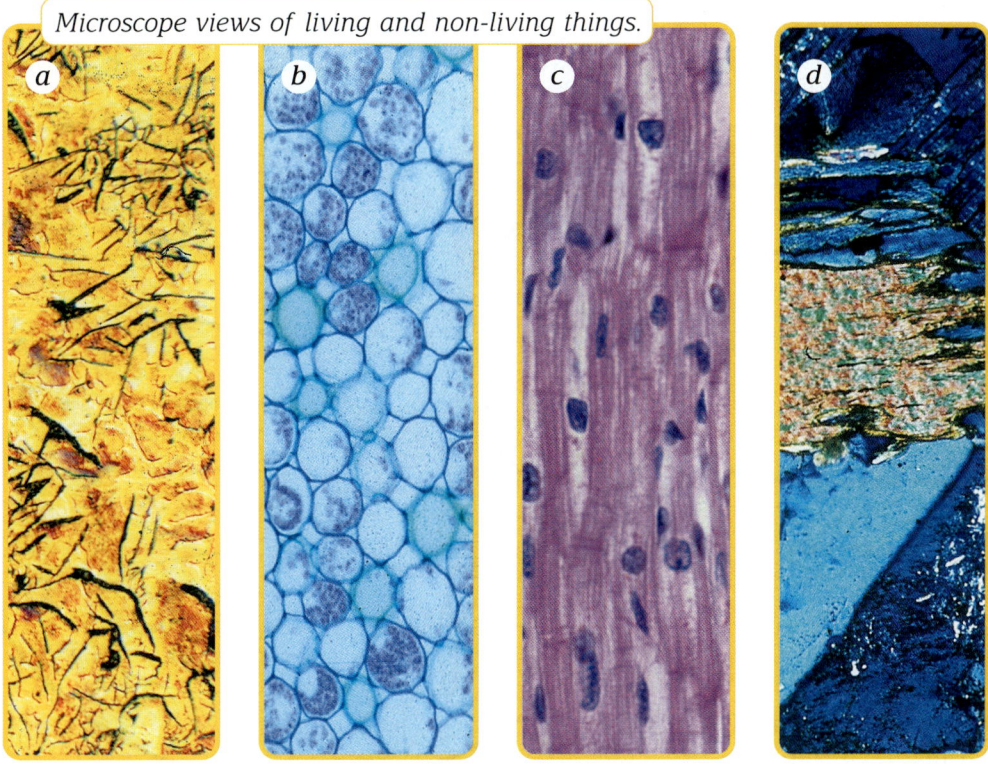

Microscope views of living and non-living things.

a

b

c

d

Cells are not all alike

All cells are very small, but they are not all the same size. In this square □ you could fit 2500 rhubarb skin cells or 10 000 human skin cells. Cells can be different shapes. Plant and animal cells look quite different under the microscope.

3 Which cells are bigger, rhubarb or human cells?

4 Look at the diagrams below.
Describe <u>two</u> differences between the plant and animal cells.

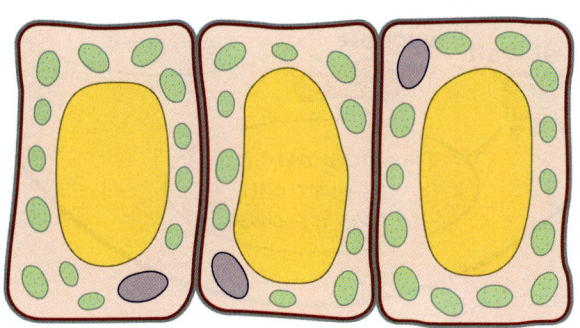

Plant cells

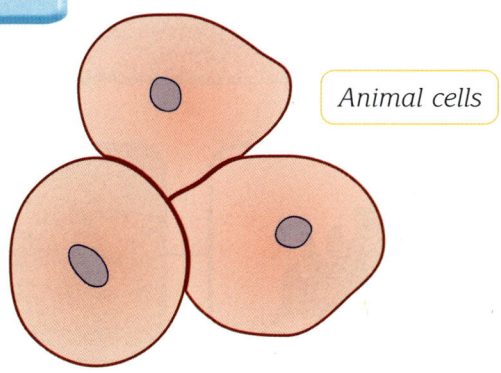

Animal cells

A closer look at animal cells

Cells are made of lots of different parts. Each part has a different job to do to keep the cell alive and working properly. Chris made a slide of some cheek cells. The picture shows what they looked like under the microscope.

5 Which part of a cell controls everything that goes on in the cell?

6 Why do you think a cell membrane is very thin?

Microscope view of cheek cells

Plant cells aren't quite the same

Chris also made a slide of a moss leaf. The picture below is what it looked like under the microscope.

7 Name the cell parts that plants have that animal cells don't have.

8 Which part controls what happens in a plant cell?

9 The roots of a plant are not green. Which part of a plant cell shown on the diagram is missing from root cells?

10 Write down one difference between these cell parts:

  a a nucleus and a chloroplast;

  b a cell wall and a cell membrane.

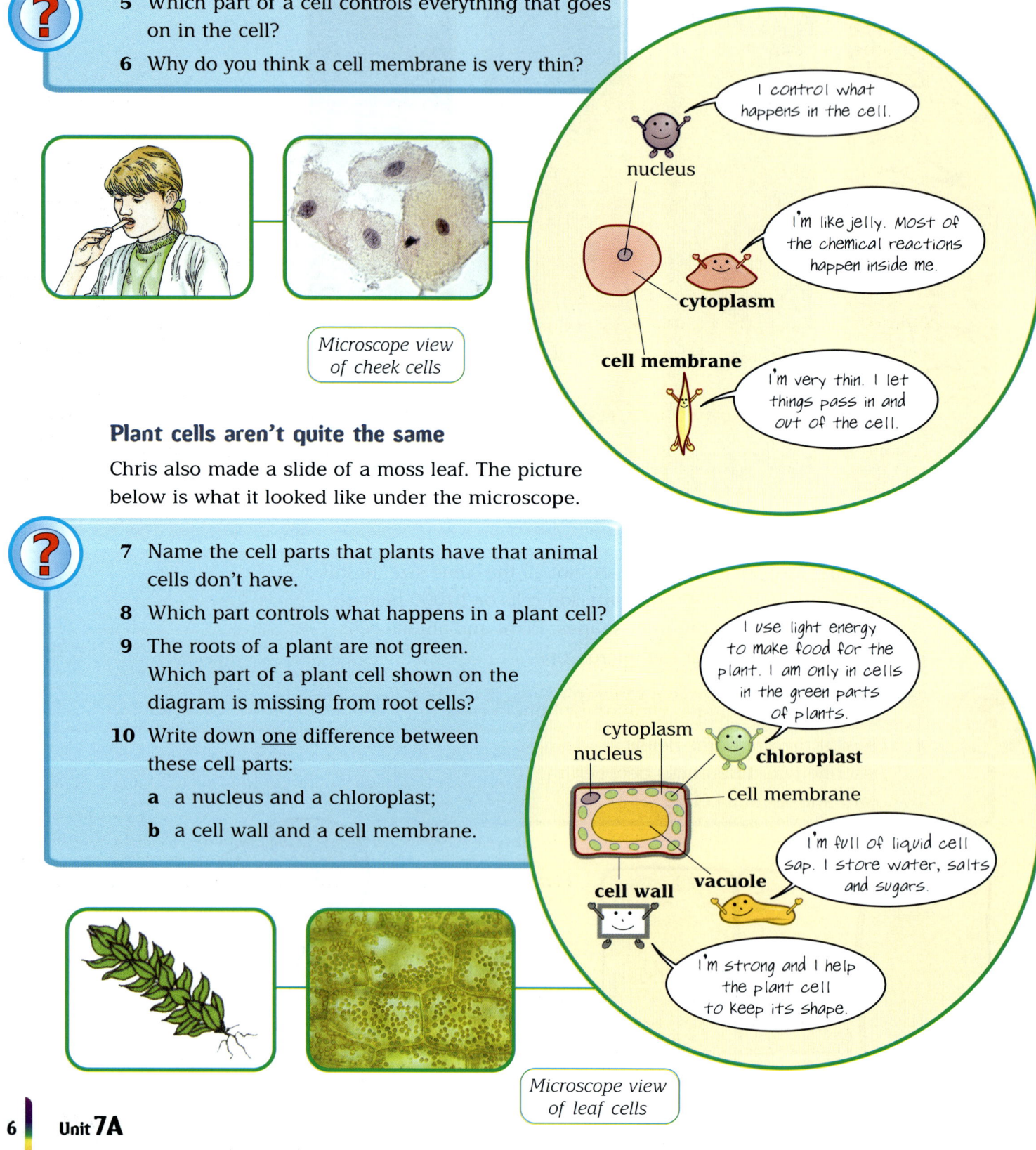

nucleus
I control what happens in the cell.

cytoplasm
I'm like jelly. Most of the chemical reactions happen inside me.

cell membrane
I'm very thin. I let things pass in and out of the cell.

cytoplasm
nucleus
chloroplast
I use light energy to make food for the plant. I am only in cells in the green parts of plants.

cell membrane

cell wall vacuole
I'm full of liquid cell sap. I store water, salts and sugars.

I'm strong and I help the plant cell to keep its shape.

Microscope view of leaf cells

7A.4 Different cells for different jobs

There are over a million different types of animals. They all have different shapes and sizes. But in all these animals there are only about 200 different kinds of cells. These cells are different because of the jobs they do, not because of the kind of animal they are found in.

This page shows some of the cells in animals and plants and the jobs that they do. For example, when you breathe in air you sometimes breathe in dust as well. This dust can clog up your lungs. Two kinds of cells in your breathing tubes stop this happening.

One kind makes the lining sticky with mucus. Dust gets trapped in this mucus. We call these cells <u>goblet cells</u> because of their shape.

The other kind has tiny hairs that carry the mucus and dust out of your lungs. A tissue that forms a skin or a lining is called an epithelial tissue and the hairs are called cilia. So we call these cells <u>ciliated epithelial cells.</u>

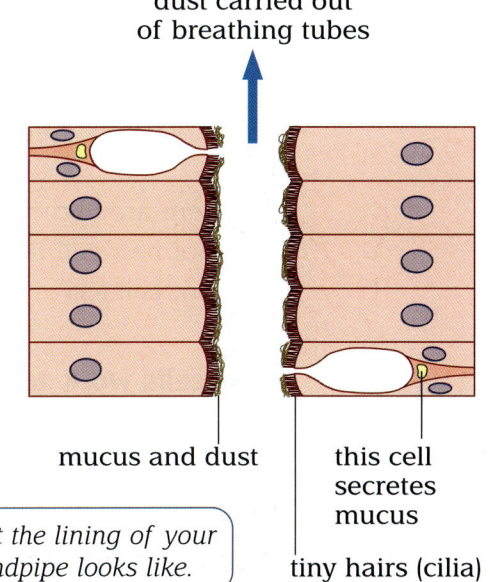

dust carried out of breathing tubes

mucus and dust

this cell secretes mucus

What the lining of your windpipe looks like.

tiny hairs (cilia)

 **1** How are ciliated epithelial cells different from other animal cells?

When you see, hear, smell, taste or touch anything you are using special cells. These special cells are called <u>nerve cells</u>. Nerve cells are very different from other animal cells because they are very long. They have to carry messages in the form of nerve impulses from one part of your body to another. Your brain and spinal cord can send and receive nerve impulses from all over your body.

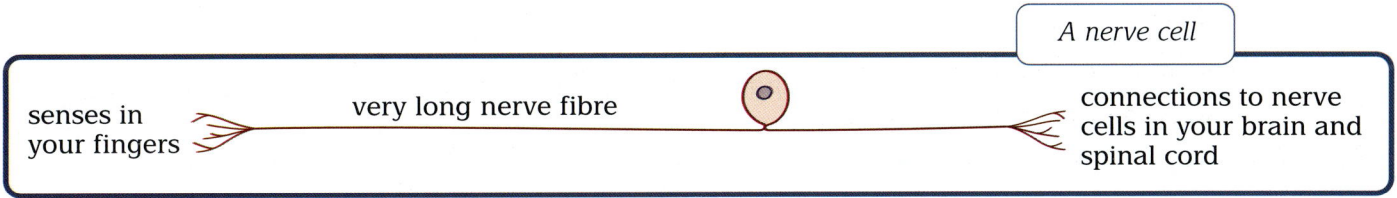

A nerve cell

senses in your fingers

very long nerve fibre

connections to nerve cells in your brain and spinal cord

 **2** How long is the nerve cell from your fingertip to your spinal cord? Hint: Measure the distance from your backbone to your fingertip.

The cells of your body need oxygen to stay alive. Special cells in your blood carry oxygen around your body. These special cells are called <u>red blood cells</u>. They are full of a chemical called haemoglobin which combines with oxygen. So the cells can carry oxygen to every cell in the body.

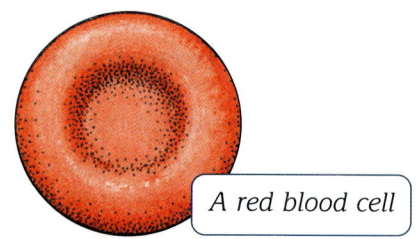

A red blood cell

3 The more haemoglobin there is in a red blood cell the more oxygen it can carry. Red blood cells do not have a nucleus. Why do you think this is?

It's not just animals that have special cells. Plants need water to stay alive. They take it in through special cells in their roots. These cells are called <u>root hair cells</u>.

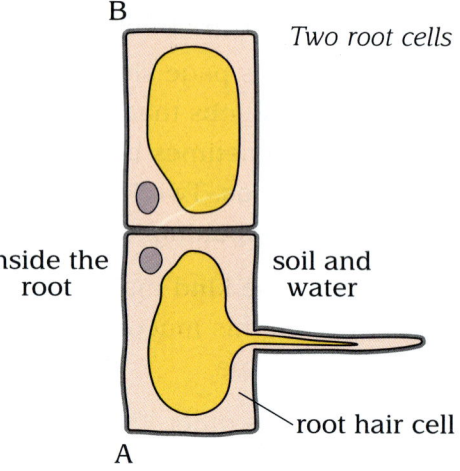

B

Two root cells

inside the root

soil and water

root hair cell

A

4 Here are two cells from a root. Why do you think the root hair cell (A) can take in more water than the other root cell (B)?

How cells work together

A house does not look like a living thing! However, the way the building materials of a house are grouped is similar to the way that cells in a living thing are organised. The bricks in a house are like the cells in a living thing. A group of bricks is called a wall. A group of similar cells is called a tissue. All the cells in a tissue are the same and work together to do the same job.

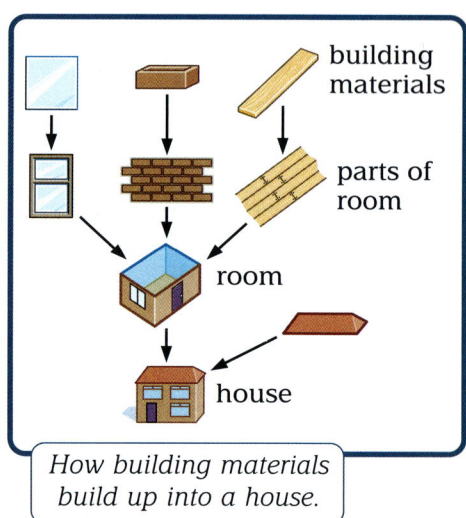

building materials

parts of room

room

house

How building materials build up into a house.

5 Muscle cells work together in muscle tissue. What do you think is the job of muscle tissue?

In a house, different groups of building materials are joined together to make the rooms. In a living thing, several tissues are joined together to make an organ.

There are many different rooms in a house, and each room is needed for a different reason. In a living thing there are many different organs, and each organ has a different job.

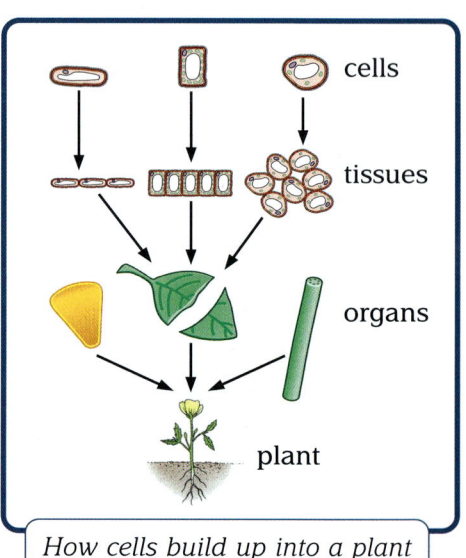

cells

tissues

organs

plant

How cells build up into a plant

6 The leaf of a plant is an organ. It is made of several different tissues. What job does the leaf do?

7 Why is a petal an organ?

8 **a** Can you think of some rooms in a house that are the same?

    b You have more than one of some organs in your body. Write down <u>one</u> example.

7A.5 How new cells are made

People used to think that living things sometimes appeared out of nowhere. They saw for themselves that maggots appeared in rotting meat, and Leeuwenhoek described tiny living animals in rotting things. So the idea seemed to be sensible. In the 19th century Louis Pasteur proved that this idea was wrong. He showed that living things come only from other living things.

Cells are the building blocks of life, and they don't just appear from nowhere either. In 1858, a German scientist called Rudolph Virchow suggested that new cells could only grow from cells that were already there. Now we know that new cells form only when existing cells divide.

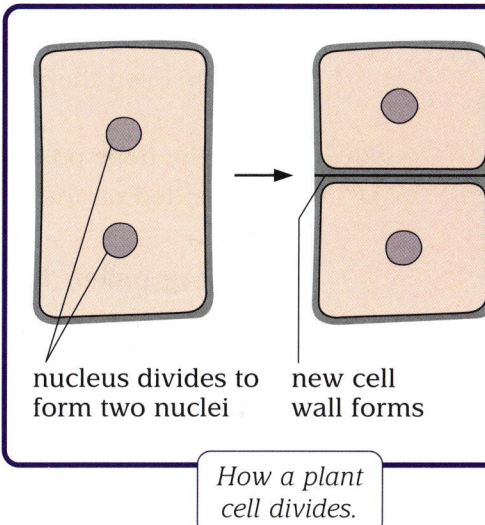

The cell cycle.

How a cell divides

The nucleus divides first, then the cell. As the new cells take in more materials, they grow. When they are big enough, the cells divide again. We call this the cell cycle.

1 Make a copy of the cell cycle diagram.
    Complete the labels on your copy.

When a plant cell divides, a new wall forms between the new nuclei. Some cells divide over and over again, but other cells become specialised to do particular jobs. Specialised cells don't divide again.

2 Think of <u>one</u> reason why a specialised cell can't divide.

nucleus divides to form two nuclei

new cell wall forms

How a plant cell divides.

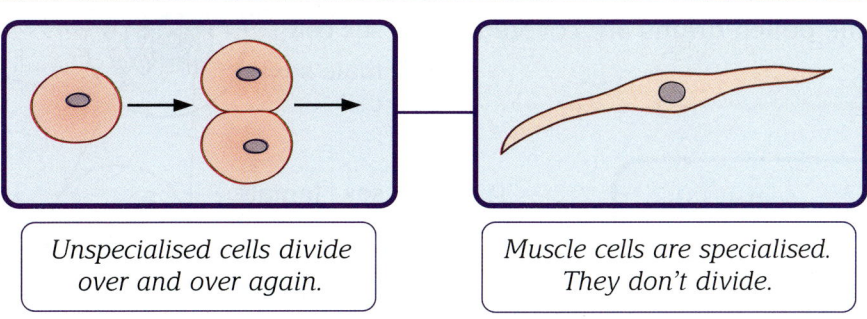

Unspecialised cells divide over and over again.

Muscle cells are specialised. They don't divide.

The nucleus controls how a cell develops

The nucleus of a cell holds all the information that tells a cell how to work and develop. Before it divides, the nucleus makes a copy of this information. One copy goes into each new nucleus. So the new cells are identical to the old ones.

3 Describe how information passes to new cells.

7A.6 The secret life of plants

A flower is the reproductive system of a plant. Its job is to make seeds which can grow into new plants. The flower has special sex cells to make seeds. Pollen contains the male sex cell, and the ovule contains the female sex cell. The pollen must travel from the male part of a plant to the female part of the same plant, or of another plant of the same kind.

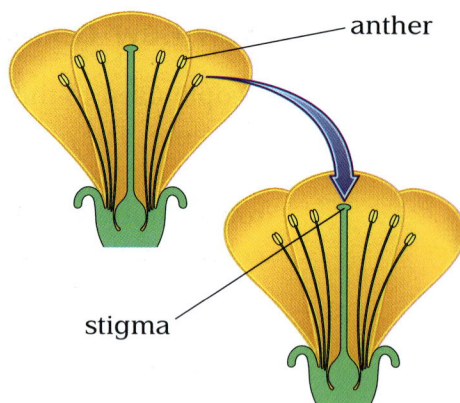

1 How do you think pollen gets from one flower to another?

2 Pollen contains the male sex cell of plants.
What is the male sex cell of humans called?

Pollen travels from an anther to a stigma. This is called pollination.

Once the pollen has reached the female part of a plant, the pollen grows a tube down to the ovule. The nucleus of the male sex cell travels down this tube to join with the nucleus of the ovule. Each nucleus contains half of the information to pass on to the new plant. When the two nuclei fuse, they make one complete nucleus in the first cell of the new plant. This first cell then grows and divides to make a seed.

3 Why does pollen need to grow a tube once it has landed on the stigma of a flower?

Growing pollen tubes

A pollen grain is very small. The male sex cell is inside. The outer wall of a pollen grain is strong, and in some plants it is spiky.

4 Why do you think some pollen grains are covered in spikes?

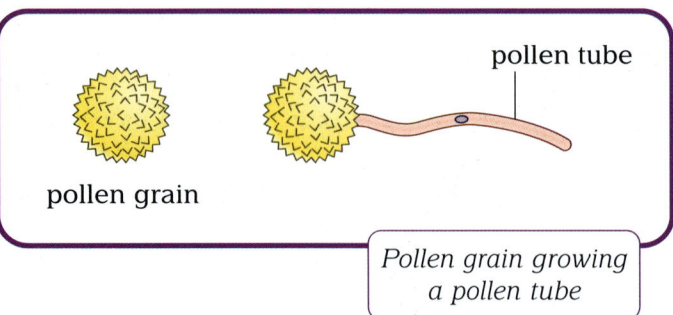

Pollen grain growing a pollen tube

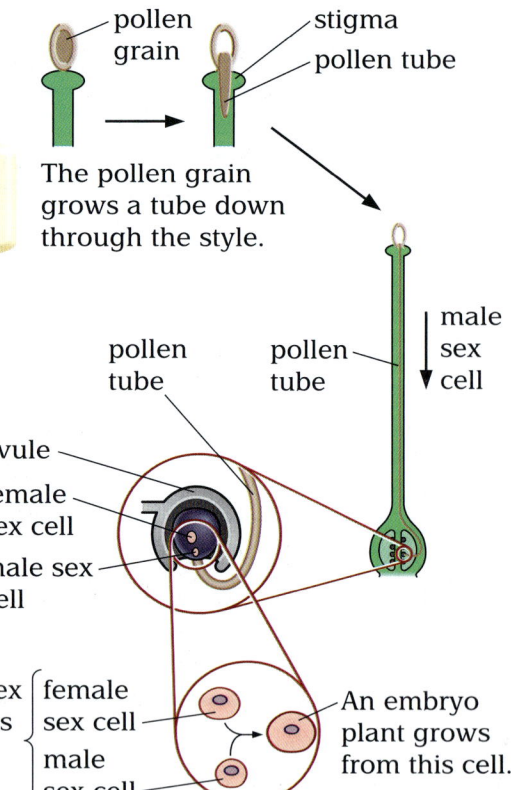

The pollen grain grows a tube down through the style.

The male sex cell fertilises the female sex cell.

Pollen tube growth and fertilisation

A pollen tube grows when a pollen grain sticks to the stigma of a flower and the nucleus of the male sex cell travels down this tube to reach the female sex cell. Sometimes it is possible to get pollen tubes to grow in sugary water.

Yasmin decided to do an experiment to grow pollen tubes. Look at the pictures to see what she did.

5 Look at the microscope slide. How many pollen tubes grew?

Yasmin tried the same experiment with pollen from a different flower. This time she used nasturtiums. She did not manage to get any pollen tubes to grow. She thought that the problem could be the concentration of the sugary water. She decided to investigate if the concentration of the sugary water affects how many pollen tubes grow.

6 Write a list of all the things that Yasmin needed to keep the same to make this a fair test.

7 Yasmin decided to make two slides for each sugar concentration. Why was this a good idea?

Yasmin collected some pollen grains from chickweed. She used a paintbrush to carefully pick up the pollen grains from a flower.

Next Yasmin put the pollen grains onto a microscope slide. Then she added a drop of sugary water to the slide. She left the slide in the dark for two hours.

Then she looked at the slide to see how many pollen tubes had grown.

Yasmin's view of the pollen grains down the microscope.

You should now understand the key words and key ideas shown below.

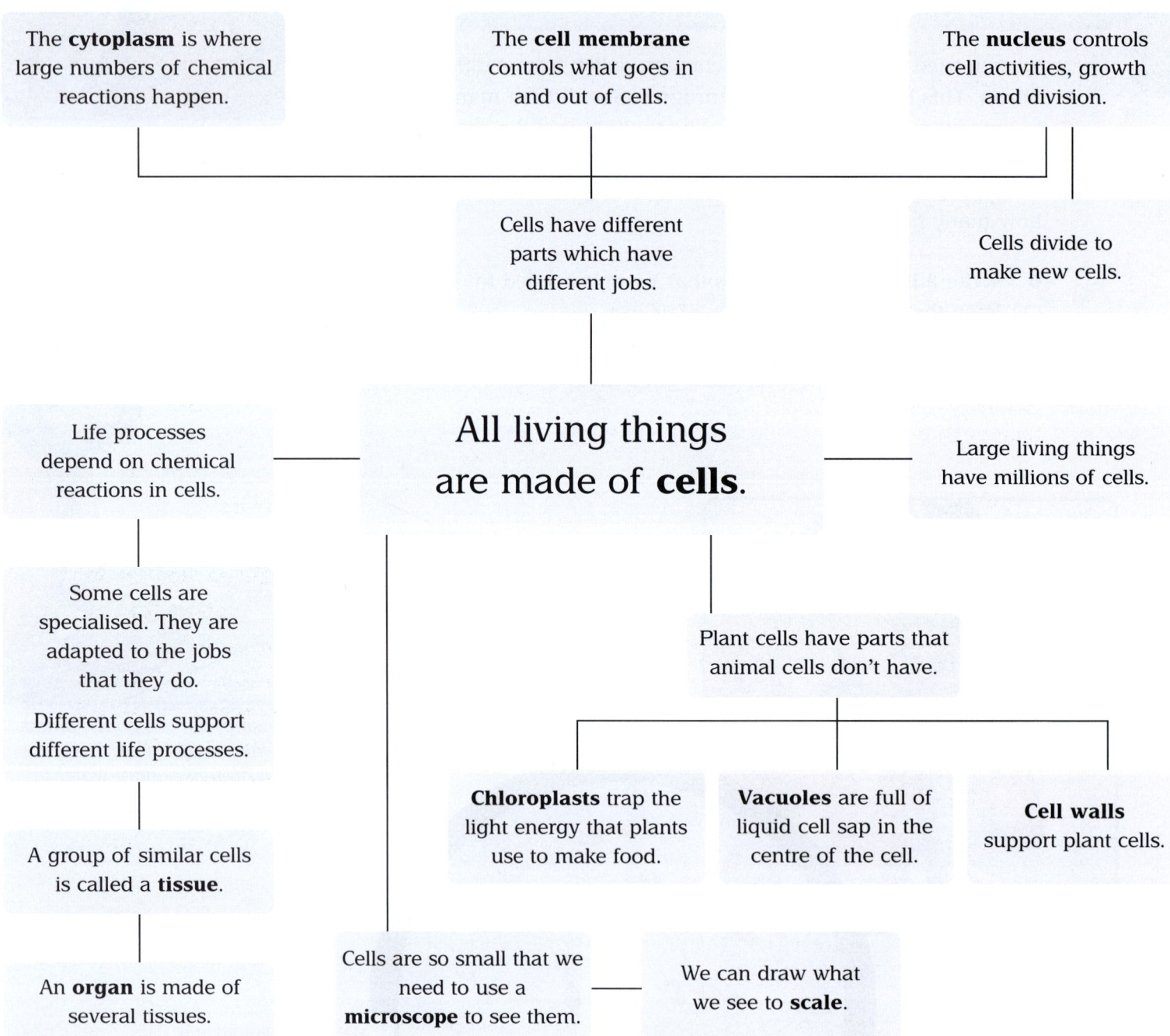

The **cytoplasm** is where large numbers of chemical reactions happen.

The **cell membrane** controls what goes in and out of cells.

The **nucleus** controls cell activities, growth and division.

Cells have different parts which have different jobs.

Cells divide to make new cells.

Life processes depend on chemical reactions in cells.

All living things are made of **cells**.

Large living things have millions of cells.

Some cells are specialised. They are adapted to the jobs that they do.

Different cells support different life processes.

Plant cells have parts that animal cells don't have.

A group of similar cells is called a **tissue**.

Chloroplasts trap the light energy that plants use to make food.

Vacuoles are full of liquid cell sap in the centre of the cell.

Cell walls support plant cells.

An **organ** is made of several tissues.

Cells are so small that we need to use a **microscope** to see them.

We can draw what we see to **scale**.

Reproduction

In this unit we shall be learning about reproduction and some of the different ways that humans and other animals make sure that their kind continues to exist.

7B.1 How a new life starts

All animals die. So they must produce young. They **reproduce** so that their kind survives.

In many animals, a new life starts when the nuclei of two **sex cells** join. One of these sex cells comes from the mother. The other sex cell comes from the father. We call this kind of reproduction <u>sexual reproduction</u>.

*A male sex cell. We call it a **sperm**. A sperm swims to reach an egg cell.*

*This female sex cell, or **egg cell**, is much bigger than the sperm cells around it.*

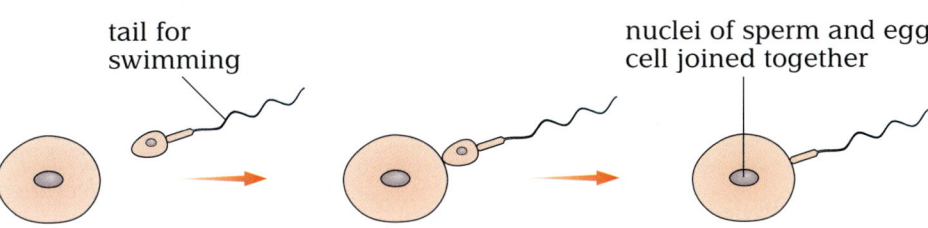

tail for swimming

nuclei of sperm and egg cell joined together

*A new life starts when the nucleus of a sperm joins with the nucleus of an egg cell. We say that the nuclei **fuse**. This fusing is called **fertilisation**.*

KEY WORDS

reproduce
sex cells
sperm
egg cell
fuse
fertilisation
uterus
testis
ovary
oviduct
ovulation
embryo
implantation
fetus
inherits
menstrual cycle
menstruation
placenta
amniotic fluid
mammary glands
adolescence
puberty
secondary sexual
   characteristics

1 What do we call male sex cells?

2 What do we call female sex cells?

3 A sperm is a specialised cell. What special feature helps it to reach the egg cell?

4 What is fertilisation?

Patterns of reproduction

Different animals fertilise their eggs in different ways. Male fish and male frogs fertilise the egg cells outside the female's body. We call this <u>external</u> fertilisation. The egg cells of birds and mammals are fertilised inside the female's body. We call this <u>internal</u> fertilisation.

Look at the pictures. The eggs of fish and frogs don't have shells. They would dry up if they were laid on land, so they are laid in water. Each egg contains only a little stored food.

Penguins are birds. They lay one or two eggs. Each egg contains lots of stored food.

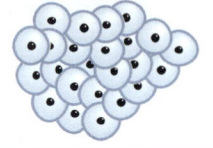

Most fish and frogs don't look after their eggs and young. They need to lay lots of eggs to make sure that a few survive.

Penguins look after their eggs and young.

Mammals are different again. Their young grow in a special organ inside the mother's body. We call this organ the **uterus**. After they are born, one or both parents feed and protect their young until they can look after themselves.

5   Shells protect the eggs of birds and reptiles. Write down <u>two</u> things that shells protect eggs against.

6   A large female fish like a cod can lay up to 7 million eggs. Explain, as fully as you can, why she needs to lay so many.

7   Each cod egg contains only a little stored food. Why do you think this is?

8   In some animals the eggs are fertilised inside the female. Why does this happen in:

   a birds;   **b** mammals?

9   The eggs of mammals have a good chance of developing and growing up. Eggs laid in water or on land have a smaller chance. Why is this?

Cats look after their young until they are old enough to find their own food and protect themselves.

Reproduction in humans

Humans are mammals. So:

- human eggs have no shell;

- fertilisation happens inside the mother's body;

- the young develop in the mother's uterus;`

- after they are born, the young feed on milk;

- one or both parents look after the young. Often other adults and older children help too.

Look at the diagrams.

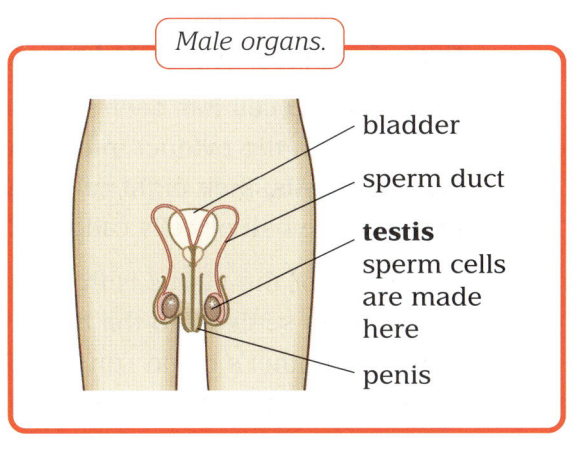

Male organs.

10 Write down the name of the organ that makes:

   a sperm;

   b egg cells.

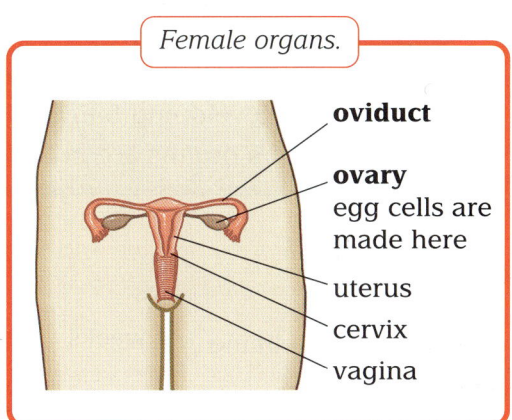

Female organs.

A woman releases an egg cell from one of her ovaries about once a month. This is called **ovulation**. Fertilisation can happen only as the egg cell travels down an oviduct. When sperm cells meet an egg cell, the sperm make a special chemical to break down the outer part of the egg cell. Then the nucleus of <u>one</u> sperm can join with the nucleus of the egg cell. We say that the egg cell is fertilised when this happens.

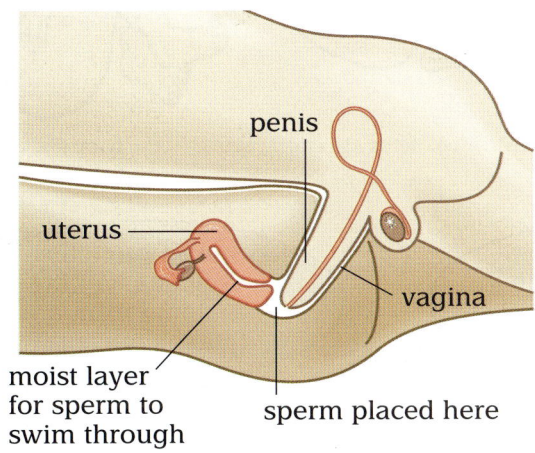

Over 200 million sperm cells travel from the testes through the penis and into the vagina.

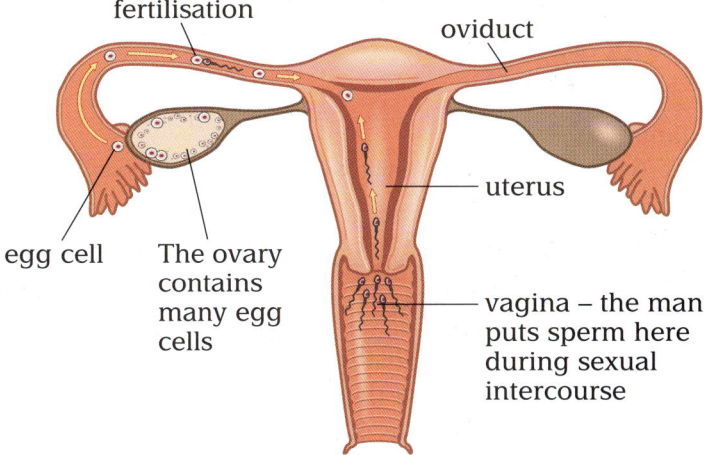

fertilisation

Note that the sperm and egg cells are really much smaller than the diagram shows. An egg cell is the size of a tiny speck of sand. You need a microscope to see sperm.

11 Where does fertilisation happen?

12 Write down a list of the parts that a sperm cell passes through on its way from the testis to the egg cell.

13 How do the sperm get from the vagina into an oviduct?

From fertilised egg to baby

Once the egg cell has been fertilised, it grows and divides as it travels down the oviduct into the uterus. First it forms two cells, then four cells, then eight cells. By the time it reaches the uterus, it is a whole ball of cells called an **embryo**.

The lining of the uterus is thick, with lots of blood vessels. The embryo settles into the lining. This is called **implantation**. Now the mother's blood can supply the embryo with the food and oxygen that it needs to grow.

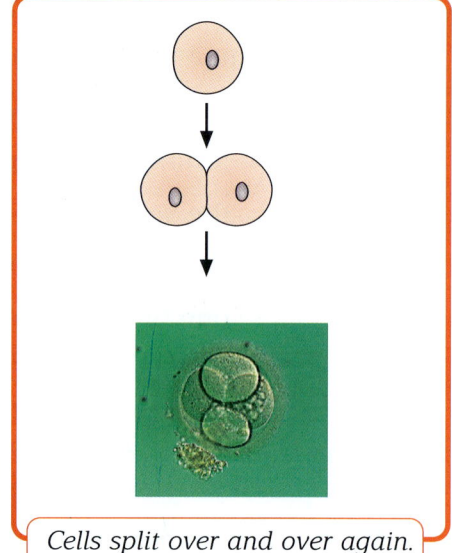

Cells split over and over again.

14 How long does it take for the ball of cells to reach the uterus?

15 What is implantation? Why is implantation important?

16 Before all its main organs have started to grow, we call the developing baby an embryo. Later, it looks like a baby but its organs are not fully developed. What do we call it then?

Growth of the embryo, fetus and baby after implantation. The pictures are not to scale.

Time since fertilisation

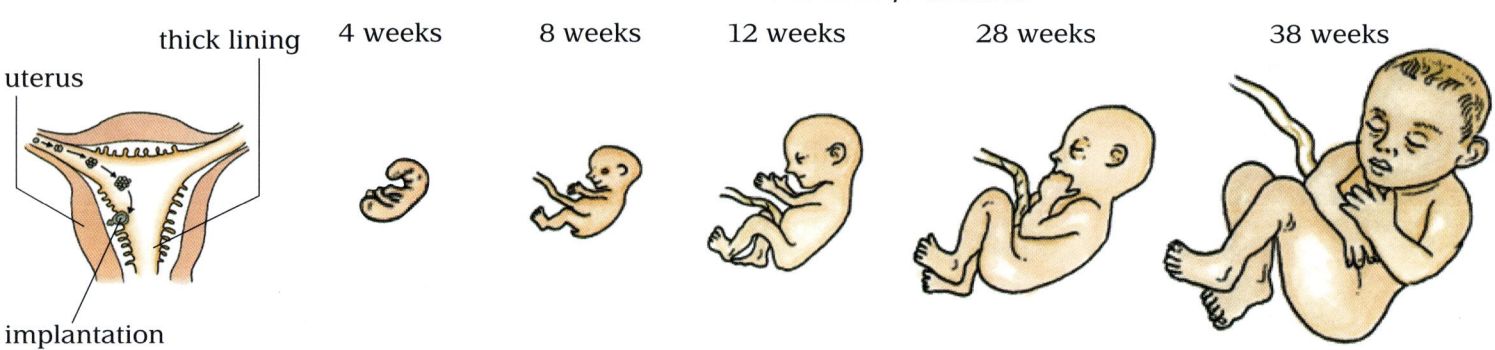

uterus — thick lining — 4 weeks — 8 weeks — 12 weeks — 28 weeks — 38 weeks

implantation after 5 days — embryo (1 cm) — **fetus** (3 cm) — fetus (12 cm) — fetus (34 cm) — baby (52 cm)

Why children are like their parents

The nuclei of the sex cells contain the pattern for a new life. So, the fertilised egg cell **inherits** part of the pattern from each parent. That is why parents, a child and its brothers and sisters have some features in common.

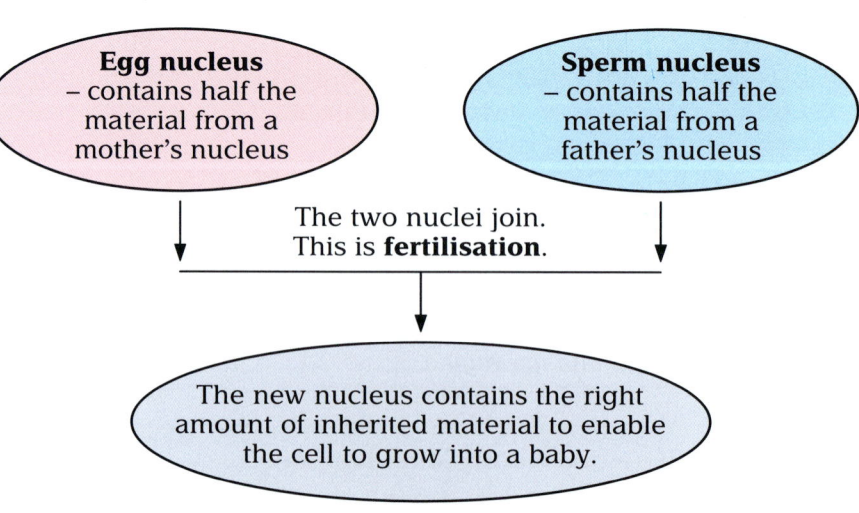

Egg nucleus – contains half the material from a mother's nucleus

Sperm nucleus – contains half the material from a father's nucleus

The two nuclei join. This is **fertilisation**.

The new nucleus contains the right amount of inherited material to enable the cell to grow into a baby.

Half of the inherited material came from the mother and half from the father, so the baby will have some features from each parent.

Some brothers and sisters are more alike than others

Twins are born at the same time. They can be identical or non-identical.

The twins in the first picture grew after two egg cells were fertilised by two different sperm. They inherited some of the same features from their parents, but they also inherited some features that are not the same.
So, they are <u>non-identical</u> twins.

The twins in the second picture grew after one fertilised egg cell divided to form two separate embryos.
They inherited the same pattern from their parents, so they are <u>identical</u> twins.

Non-identical twins

Identical twins

17 How much of the inherited material in the nucleus of a fertilised egg cell comes from the father?

18 Copy and complete the diagram below.

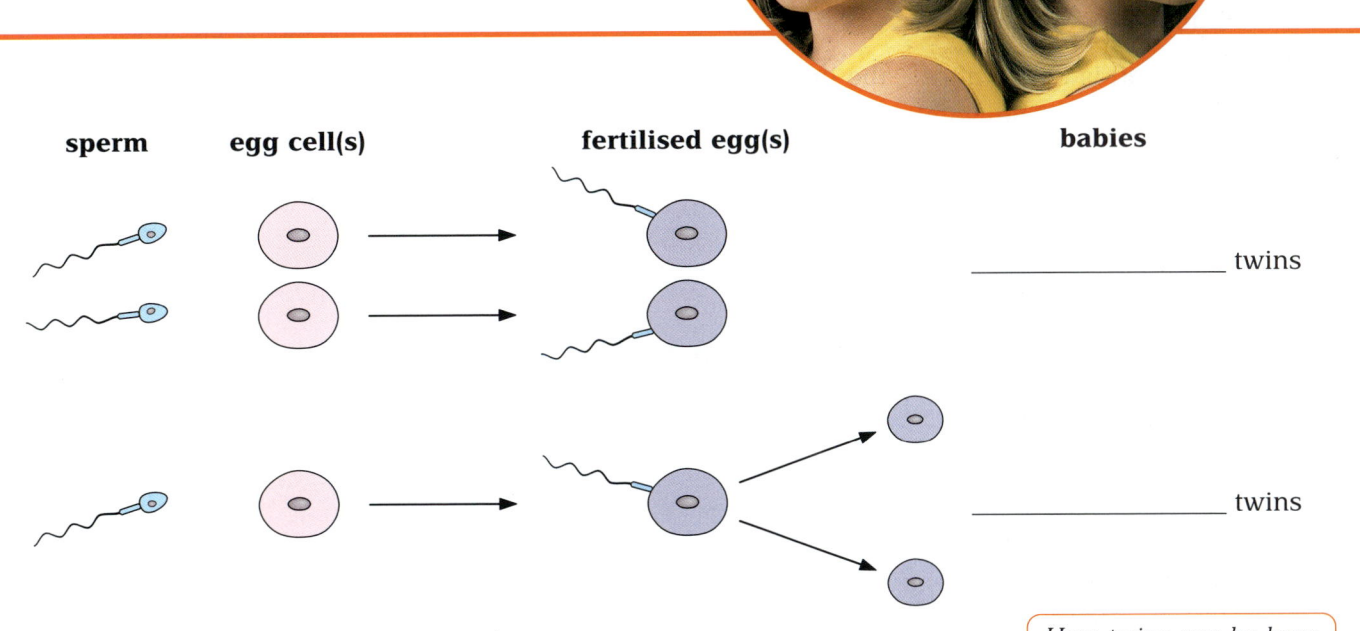

| sperm | egg cell(s) | fertilised egg(s) | babies |

_____ twins

_____ twins

How twins can be born

19 Are non-identical twins more alike than any other brothers and sisters? Explain your answer.

7B.2 The menstrual cycle

To survive and grow, an embryo has to be implanted in the lining of the uterus. For this to happen, the uterus lining must be ready for it. Timing is important. There is a cycle that links the release of an ovum (egg cell) to the development of the uterus lining. This cycle is called the **menstrual cycle**.

Each menstrual cycle lasts about a month.

1 Why does the lining of the uterus thicken every month?

2 An ovum is released about halfway through the cycle. Explain why this timing is important.

day
bleeding
ovum not fertilised so lining breaks down
uterus lining
ovum released from ovary
uterus lining thickens

The menstrual cycle. Days are numbered from the first day of bleeding.

Special chemicals called <u>hormones</u> control the menstrual cycle. These chemicals are so powerful they can even change how a woman feels at different times in the cycle.

If an egg is not fertilised, the lining of the uterus breaks down. The woman 'bleeds', or has a 'period'. We call this bleeding **menstruation**.

If an egg is fertilised and an embryo is implanted, the lining does not break down. Menstruation stops.

3 What do we call the time of the month when a woman is bleeding?

4 Where does the blood:

   a come from?

   b leave the woman's body?

5 Why does menstruation stop when a woman is pregnant?

7B.3 The uterus as home to the developing baby

The uterus has a thick muscular wall. As the fetus grows, the wall of the uterus stretches. A special organ called the **placenta** grows in the lining of the uterus.

In the placenta, the blood of the fetus and the blood of the mother are very close but <u>they do not mix</u>. So, substances can pass across the placenta between the blood of the fetus and the blood of the mother.

The fetus needs food and oxygen to grow. These substances pass across the placenta from the mother's blood. The fetus also needs to get rid of waste materials. These pass across the placenta into the mother's blood. The mother's body keeps the fetus at a constant temperature.

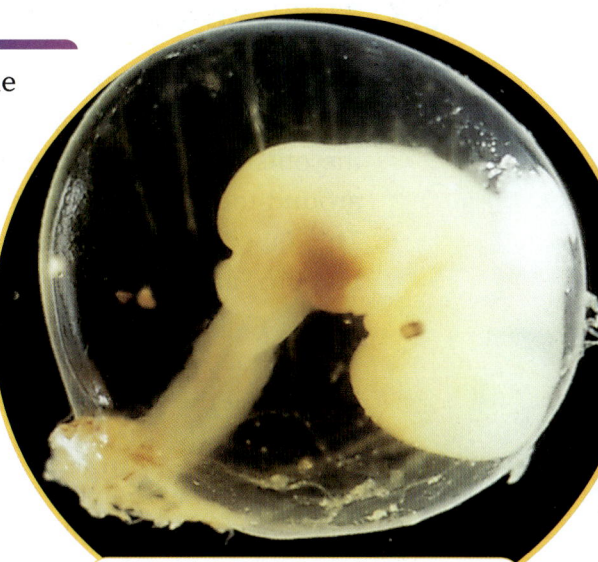

*There is a bag of thin skin around the embryo. This bag is full of a liquid called **amniotic fluid**. This fluid supports the embryo and protects it against shocks.*

1 Look at the pictures. Write down the job of

a the umbilical cord;

b the amniotic fluid.

2 Draw a diagram to show <u>two</u> substances passing across the placenta:

a from the mother to the fetus;

b from the fetus to the mother.

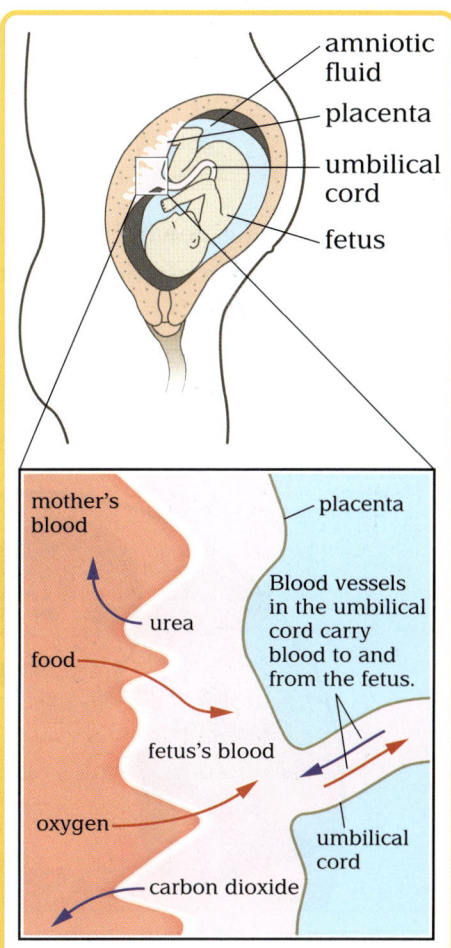

Sadly, harmful substances, such as alcohol and other drugs, can also cross the placenta into the fetus's blood. Some of them can harm the fetus as it grows.

- On average, babies born to mothers who smoke weigh less and have more health problems than babies born to non-smokers.

- A few babies are born addicted to alcohol or other drugs.

- Rubella (German measles) is a virus infection. If a mother gets it in the first three months of pregnancy, her baby may be born deaf and blind.

3 Write down <u>three</u> things that a pregnant woman should be careful to avoid. Explain your answers.

As the embryo grows, it becomes a fetus. The placenta supplies the fetus with food and oxygen and takes away waste materials.

7B.4 Birth and care of the baby

We call childbirth 'labour' because it is hard work. When a baby is born, it passes out of the uterus and through the vagina into the outside world. Before this can happen, a strong muscle around the opening of the uterus must relax and open up. This muscle is part of the cervix. When the baby is ready to be born, many strong contractions of the muscles of the uterus pull the cervix open. Once the cervix is open, the baby's head can go down into the vagina. Then the mother has to use the muscles of her abdomen, too. She has to push hard to get the baby out.

The next job is to make sure that there is no fluid in the baby's nose and mouth, so that it can take its first breath. A short time later, contractions of the uterus push the placenta out, too. We call this the afterbirth.

1   Write down <u>two</u> sets of muscles that contract to push the baby out.

2   What is the afterbirth?

3   The umbilical cord is clamped before it is cut. Why do you think the cord is clamped?

The newborn baby is cleaned, checked to make sure that there are no problems and then wrapped up to keep it warm.

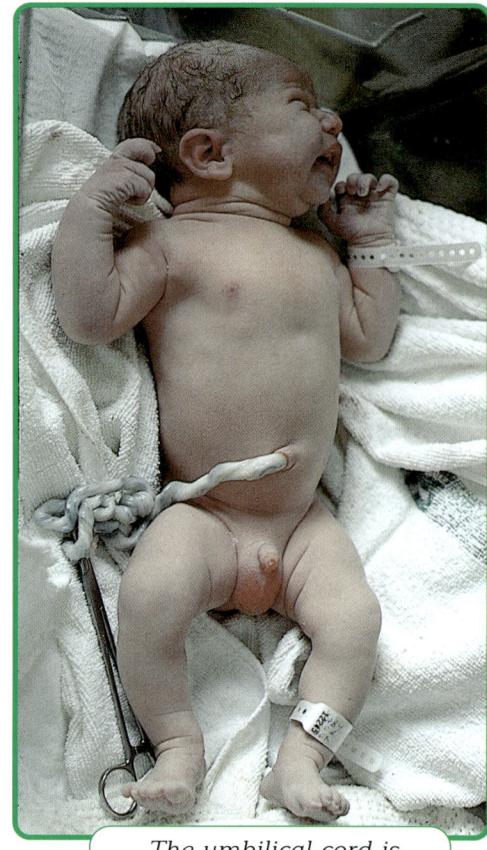

The umbilical cord is clamped before it is cut.

Baby care

Looking after a baby is also hard work. Human babies are entirely dependent on their parents and other adults.

Babies need protection against disease, accidents and animals.

Babies need to be kept clean.

The natural food for young mammals is milk. Milk is made in a mammal's **mammary glands**. The composition of milk is different in different mammals. Many human mothers prefer to feed their babies using their own breast milk. This milk contains substances that destroy some of the micro-organisms that cause infections in humans. So it also helps to protect the baby against these infections.

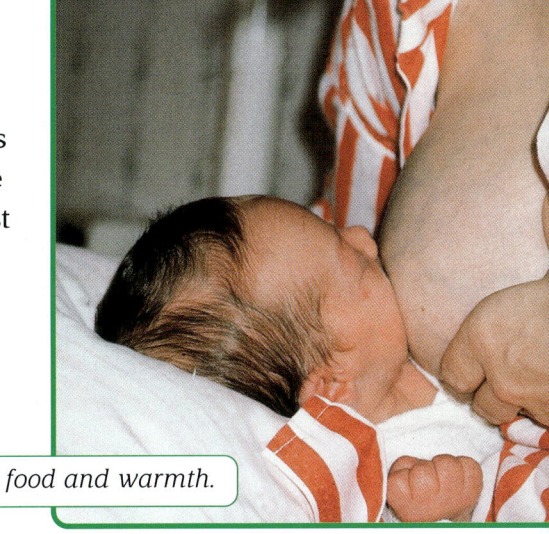

 **4** Look at the pie charts. Write down <u>three</u> differences between human milk and cow's milk.

Babies need food and warmth.

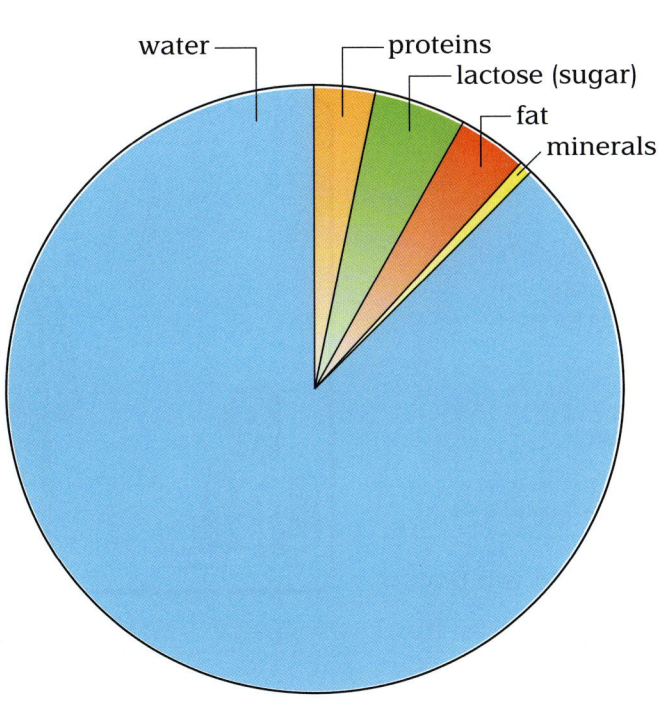

Cow's milk

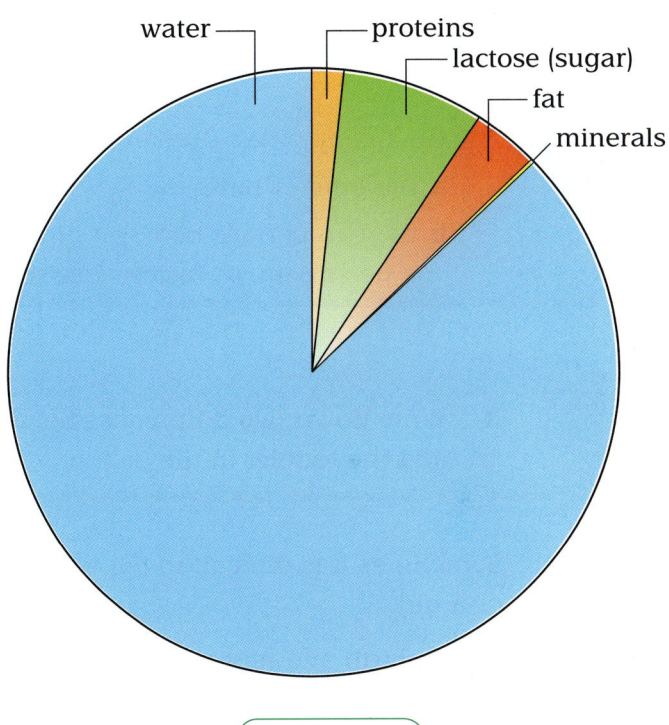

Human milk

5 Milk is sometimes called a 'complete food'. But some things that humans need in their diet are not in milk. Write down <u>one</u> of them.

6 Newborn babies don't control their body temperature. Why do you think this is?

Human children depend on adults for many years. Babies have to learn to control their bodies, to talk and to walk. Usually many adults and older children help to care for them and to teach them. Children also learn many things for themselves.

7B.5 How humans change as they grow

Some children grow up faster than others. But all children grow faster at certain times. Children also change as they grow.

This takes about 9 months.

fertilised egg starts to grow. → embryo → fetus → baby

adult → ... → adolescent ← child ← baby

This takes about 20 years.

The human life cycle

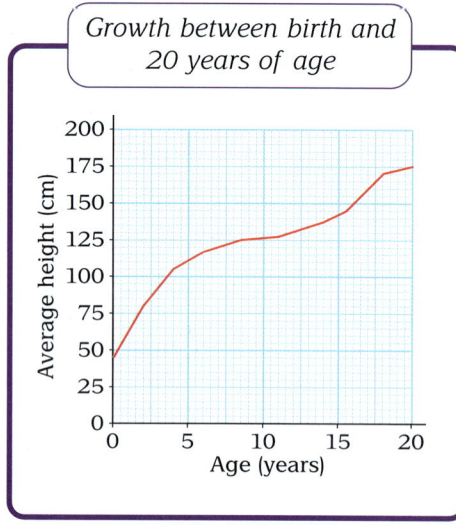

Growth between birth and 20 years of age

Average height (cm) vs Age (years)

1 On a copy of the human life cycle diagram, label:

a the time of birth;

b the two periods between birth and adulthood when a person grows fastest. Use the graph to help you.

2 Write down <u>two</u> differences between the baby and the toddler in the picture.

Children grow quickly from babies to toddlers.

Sometimes it is difficult to tell whether a young child is a boy or a girl.

Before birth and in the early years, a child's head grows faster than its body. Later, the body grows faster, and boys and girls start to look less alike.

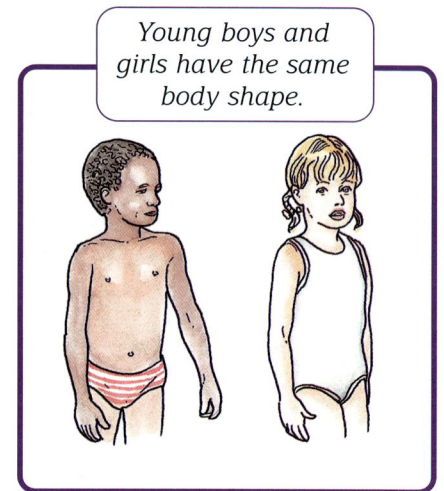

Young boys and girls have the same body shape.

A time of rapid growth and change starts in the early teens, at anything between nine and 16 years. Often the changes start earlier in girls than in boys. We call the time between childhood and adulthood **adolescence**.

At this time, a gland in the brain starts to make extra hormones. These are special chemicals that make cells grow and divide faster. They also make the testes and ovaries mature and produce sex hormones. At **puberty**, the mature testes and ovaries start to release sex cells.

3 To your diagram for question 1, add:

   a adolescence, the time between chidhood and adulthood;

   b puberty, the time when adolescents become sexually mature.

The testes and ovaries make different hormones. So boys and girls develop in different ways.

Body parts other than the sex organs develop special features. We call these features **secondary sexual characteristics**. When these develop, it becomes easier to tell a boy from a girl.

| Other changes during adolescence and puberty ||
Girls	Boys
Pubic and underarm hair grows.	Pubic and underarm hair grows.
Breasts grow.	Facial and body hair grows.
Ovaries start to release eggs.	Voice deepens.
Monthly periods (of bleeding) begin.	Testes start to make sperm.

4 **a** What are secondary sexual characteristics?

   b Write down <u>two</u> examples of secondary sexual characteristics.

5 Look at the pictures and the table. Write down <u>two</u> changes that happen during adolescence to:

   a both boys and girls; **b** girls only; **c** boys only.

Sex hormones also cause emotional changes. So adolescence is often a difficult time, especially as changes take place at different rates in different young people.

6 Why is there no need to worry if you start the changes of adolescence earlier or later than your friends?

Usually, men have broader chests and shoulders and more muscle than women.

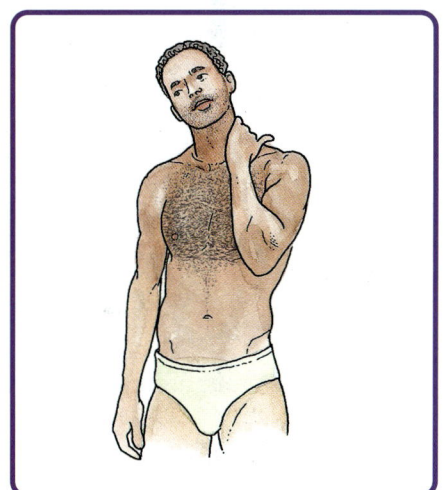

Women develop broader hips and breasts as they grow up.

You should know and understand the key words and key ideas shown below.

Key words

reproduce	uterus	implantation	amniotic fluid
sex cells	testis	fetus	mammary glands
sperm	ovary	inherits	adolescence
egg cell	oviduct	menstrual cycle	puberty
fuse	ovulation	menstruation	secondary sexual characteristics
fertilisation	embryo	placenta	

Key ideas

1 ● Living things produce young of the same kind as themselves. We say that they reproduce.

● Different animals reproduce in different ways.

2 ● In sexual reproduction, the nuclei of a sperm and an egg cell join, or fuse. We call this fertilisation.

● Sperm and egg cells are specialised to do their jobs.

● Sperm and egg nuclei contain inherited material from the parent that made them.

3 ● Women have a monthly cycle controlled by hormones. We call it the menstrual cycle. An egg cell is released and menstruation happens about once a month as part of this cycle.

● The menstrual cycle stops when a woman becomes pregnant.

4 ● A fertilised egg cell divides and grows to form an embryo. It is implanted in the uterus.

● When the embryo has grown all its main organs, we call it a fetus. The placenta supplies the needs of the fetus through the umbilical cord, and the amniotic fluid cushions it.

5 ● After it is born, mammary glands (breasts) produce milk for the baby.

● Human children are dependent on their parents and other adults for a long time.

6 ● The time between childhood and adulthood is called adolescence. Hormones control the changes that take place during this time.

● We call the time of sexual maturity puberty. This is when eggs and sperm are first released.

Environment and feeding relationships

In this unit we shall be learning how plants and animals are adapted to the places in which they live and to daily and seasonal change. We shall then study feeding relationships, including food chains and webs.

KEY WORDS
habitats
adapted
environmental conditions
nocturnal
seasons
climatic stresses
migrate
hibernation
camouflage
producers
herbivores
carnivores
predators
prey
food chains
consumers
food webs
compete

7C.1 Habitats

Habitats are places where plants and animals live. Your body is a habitat. Your skin is home to as many micro-organisms as there are people on Earth! Sometimes fleas, lice, flatworms and roundworms make their homes in or on your body.

A pond is a habitat with:

● fresh (not salty) water;

● a small temperature range;

● less light as you go deeper;

● less oxygen as you go deeper;

● a variety of food sources.

rock to hibernate under

It is damp and shady under plants.

eggs

newt tadpoles

insects and other small animals to eat

A pond is a watery habitat.

A great crested newt

A plant or animal's habitat provides the right conditions for it to survive. Each plant or animal has features that suit it to the conditions. We say that the plant or animal is **adapted** to these **environmental conditions**.

Look at the pictures of the newt tadpoles and the newt. The tadpoles are smaller than the adult newt, with no legs and with gills instead of lungs. They spend all their time in the water.

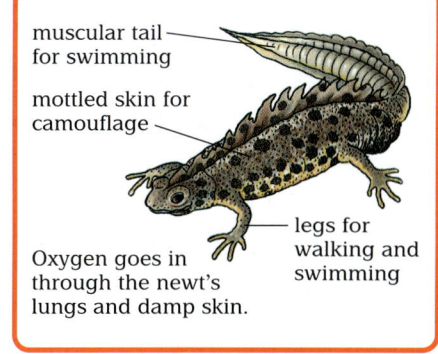

muscular tail for swimming

mottled skin for camouflage

legs for walking and swimming

Oxygen goes in through the newt's lungs and damp skin.

1 Draw a large copy of one newt tadpole. Label the ways that the tadpole is adapted to its habitat (to help you, look at the way the adult newt is labelled).

Plants need light to make food, so their leaves need to be near or above the surface of the water.

2 Look at the drawing. Explain how the duckweed and the water lily get enough light to grow.

Environmental conditions, such as the amount of light or water, are different in different habitats. So different habitats support different plants and animals.

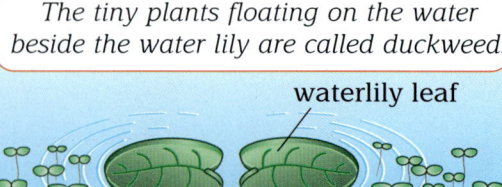

The tiny plants floating on the water beside the water lily are called duckweed.

waterlily leaf

long leaf stalk

Two land habitats	
Grassland	**Woodland**
Plenty of light	Trees shade the ground
Fairly large range of temperatures	Smaller range of temperatures
Exposed to the wind	Sheltered from the wind
Fairly dry soil	Damper soil
Less humid air	More humid air

Some animals shelter among plants, while others burrow in the soil	Animals live in trees and other plants, in leaf litter and in burrows

Some adaptations for burrowing are:

- a cylindrical or streamlined shape;
- strong legs and clawed feet;
- good senses of smell and vibration (although often the sense of sight is poor in these animals).

3 List the adaptations for burrowing of:

  a the earthworm;

  b the mole.

An earthworm has a long, thin body and slimy skin.

A mole has strong claws for digging.

4 Rabbits also burrow, but their legs are longer than those of moles and they see well to the front and side. Explain how longer legs and good eyesight help rabbits to survive.

5 The thrush can fly and has good eyesight. It sees in colour and is a good judge of distance. Its speckled feathers are good camouflage. These are useful adaptations for living in woodlands. Explain why.

A song thrush

7C.2 Changing environmental conditions

Conditions such as light and temperature are different in different habitats. These conditions also vary over a 24-hour period.

Marcus wanted to measure changes in temperature in the school greenhouse. He used a <u>datalogger</u> and a thermometer so that he could compare the results. A datalogger collects and records information.

Results for thermometer

1 Write down <u>two</u> problems of using:

  a a thermometer;

  b a datalogger.

The charts show Marcus's record of changes in temperature in the greenhouse. He can record daily changes in the amounts of light, sound and water vapour in similar ways.

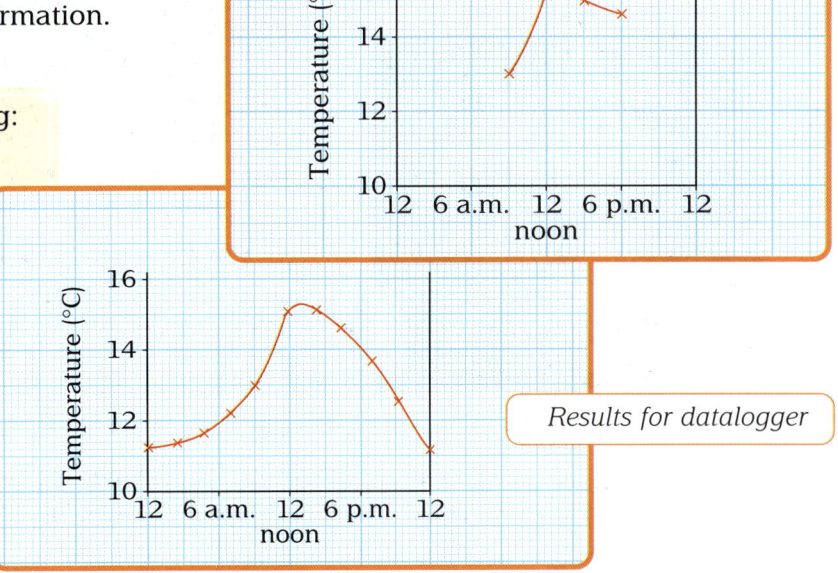

Results for datalogger

Like you, other animals are adapted to these daily changes. Some animals are up and about mainly during the day, others at night. Bats and owls are adapted to feed at night. We call them **nocturnal** animals. Some are active when it is getting light or getting dark. So you see different animals at different times.

The chart shows animals seen or heard in a school garden at different times of the day.

Before school	During school	After school	Getting dark	After dark
Squirrels	Butterflies	Butterflies	Sparrows	Bats
Sparrows	Bees	Bees	Midges	Foxes
Blackbirds	Sparrows	Squirrels	Bats	Owls
Rabbits	Kestrels	Sparrows	Foxes	Moths
		Kestrels	Mice	Earthworms

2 **a** When are foxes usually active?

 b When foxes are looking after cubs, they can be seen at any time. Why do you think this is?

3 Describe the different adaptations of bats and owls for hunting at night.

Light affects plants, too.

Owls hear well and can see in dim light.

Livingstone daisies open only in the sunshine.

This bat feeds on the nectar of banana flowers, which are open at night.

Bats send out sounds and listen for echoes using their sensitive ears. Bats that feed on flying insects have small eyes. Bats that feed on nectar have large eyes.

4 Why do you think the banana flower is light coloured, with scented nectar, and is open at night?

7C.3 Investigating woodlice

Science isn't just about what other people have found out. It is also about finding things out for yourself. You can ask questions. Then you can do investigations to find out the answers.

 **1** Woodlice are mainly found under things such as big stones and dead leaves. There are many possible reasons for this. Write down as many as you can think of.

You can test one of your ideas using a choice chamber. The woodlouse in the picture has a choice between dark and light.

 **2** The woodlouse is walking around the choice chamber. Where do you think it will stop? Explain your answer.

When you say what you think will happen, you are making a prediction. Scientists often make predictions. Then they test their predictions to see if they are right.

Even if the woodlouse stopped in the side that you predicted for a long time, you couldn't be sure that your prediction was correct for all woodlice. There are many different kinds of woodlice, and within each kind the woodlice vary.

You need to think about variation when you investigate an animal for yourself. You will also need to think about which environmental conditions you will vary and which you will keep the same.

 **3** Do you think that the three kinds of woodlouse in the picture will behave in <u>exactly</u> the same way? Explain your answer.

4 Write down some environmental conditions that you think affect woodlice.

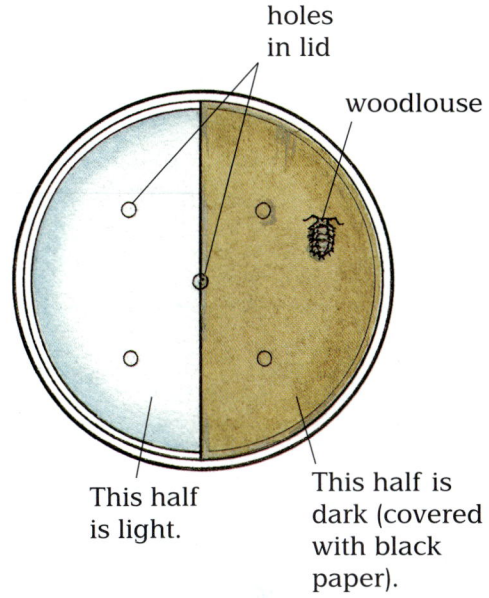

A woodlouse in a choice chamber

holes in lid

woodlouse

This half is light.

This half is dark (covered with black paper).

Three different kinds of woodlice

7C.4 Seasonal change

Environmental conditions change with the **seasons**. Plants and animals must be adapted to these changes to survive. In Britain, the cold and frost of winter are problems for many plants and animals. We call these difficult conditions **climatic stresses**. Climatic stresses are different in different parts of the world. In some places the problem is shortage of water; in other places it is high temperatures.

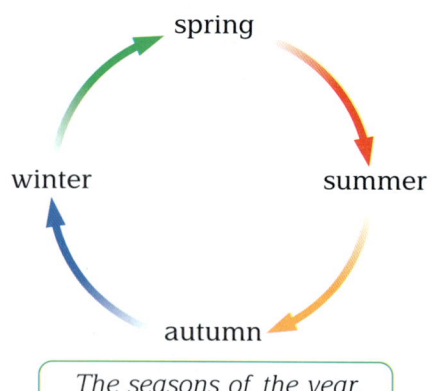

The seasons of the year.

There are fewer hours of daylight in winter.

 **1** The pictures show the same place in winter and summer. Write down <u>three</u> problems for plants and animals in winter.

Plants lose a lot of water from their leaves. When it is cold, they cannot take any more water in. Also, winter frosts damage some leaves. So, many plants get rid of their leaves before the frosts start.

Other trees keep their leaves all the year round. We say that they are <u>evergreen</u>. Their leaves have to be tough to withstand the cold. They also have a waxy surface so that they don't lose too much water.

 **2** Write down <u>two</u> advantages of having no leaves in winter.

3 Describe how the leaves of evergreens are adapted to surviving low temperatures and to keeping water in.

Pine needles aren't damaged by frost and snow.

Plants that lose their leaves can't make food in winter. We say that they are <u>dormant</u>. They use their stores of food to grow new leaves in spring.

iris   lily   dahlia

root tuber

stem

Some plants live through the winter as roots, stems or bulbs under the ground. All the parts above the ground die.

Some trees lose their leaves in autumn. We describe these trees as <u>deciduous</u>.

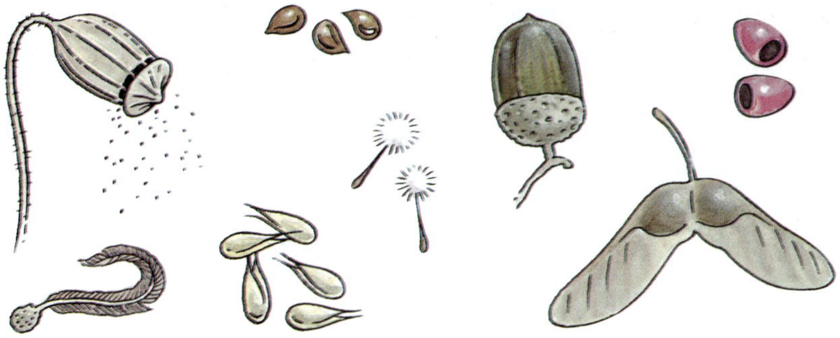

Plants can also survive the winter as seeds.

4   Deciduous trees store food in their roots and stems. Why do they need to do this?

5   Only underground parts of some plants survive the winter.

   a Suggest a reason why underground parts of plants are less likely to be killed than leaves.

   b Write down <u>one</u> plant that survives as an underground stem.

6   Find out <u>one</u> adaptation that seeds have to help them survive.

Problems for animals

The British winter brings problems for animals, too. It's cold and there isn't much food, because there are fewer leaves and insects about. Most of the insects that we see in summer live through winter as eggs or pupae. Both of these are hidden away.

Some birds fly south to warmer climates for winter. We say that they **migrate**. Other animals go into a deep sleep called **hibernation**. Their hearts slow down and their temperatures drop. Their bodies slow right down so that stored fat is used up very slowly through winter.

Some butterflies hibernate. Many survive the winter as pupae. Adults come out of the pupae in spring.

When it is winter in Britain, it is warmer in Africa and there are insects for swallows to eat.

During hibernation, hedgehogs use fat stored in their body.

 **7** Swallows migrate between Africa and Britain. Write down <u>two</u> ways they benefit from this.

Other animals stay active all the year round. In autumn, these birds and mammals store extra fat and grow a thicker coat of fur or feathers for insulation. Some change colour for better **camouflage**.

 **8** Explain, as fully as you can, how rabbits are adapted to survive winter.

9 Rabbits, swallows and hedgehogs all store up a lot of fat in their body to prepare for winter. Explain how this helps each of them to survive.

Rabbits get fatter and grow a thicker coat to prepare for winter.

7C.5 Feeding relationships

Plants make their own food. Plants are called **producers** because they produce the food. Animals feed on plants or on animals that have eaten plants so we call them **consumers**. Animals that are adapted to eating plants are called **herbivores**. Other animals are adapted to eating animal flesh. They are **carnivores**. Some carnivores hunt and kill living animals. These are **predators**. The animals that they hunt are their **prey**. Prey animals are adapted to escape or to hide from predators.

Predators		Prey	
	owl		snail
	fox		vole
	shark		antelope
	leopard		fly
	spider		rabbit
	eel		plaice
	mantis		greenfly

1 What is a predator?

2 Sort the predators in the table into groups of animals that:
- chase their prey; - ambush their prey; - build traps to catch their prey.

3 Write down <u>four</u> adaptations of predators.

4 Write down <u>four</u> adaptations of prey animals.

Food chains

A food chain shows what eats what.

This vole ⟶ is eaten by ⟶ this owl.

Food chains begin with green plants because only green plants make food. The arrows show the direction in which the food goes.

The arrows also show the way that energy is transferred along food chains. When they make food, green plants take energy from sunlight. When an animal eats a plant, the energy is transferred to the animal.

5 Food chains begin with green plants. Explain this as fully as you can.

6 In the food chain, grass ⟶ vole ⟶ owl, name the plant, the predator and the prey.

7 a Copy the diagram below. Alongside it draw your own food chain, this time using examples of real plants and animals. Don't forget to include the arrows to show the direction of energy transfer.

Predator	Carnivore	Consumer
Prey	Herbivore	Consumer
Green plant	Green plant	Producer

b Notice that the herbivore and the carnivore are both called consumers. The energy is transferred to the herbivore first. So we call it the <u>primary consumer</u>. The carnivore is the second animal to get the energy. So we call it the <u>secondary consumer</u>. Add primary and secondary to your copy of the diagram.

The vole eats plants, so we can add this to the food chain:

This grass

is eaten by

this vole,

which is eaten by

this owl.

7C.6 Food webs

Voles don't feed on grass alone, and owls don't just eat voles. Plants and animals belong to more than one food chain. So, we join food chains to make **food webs** for a habitat.

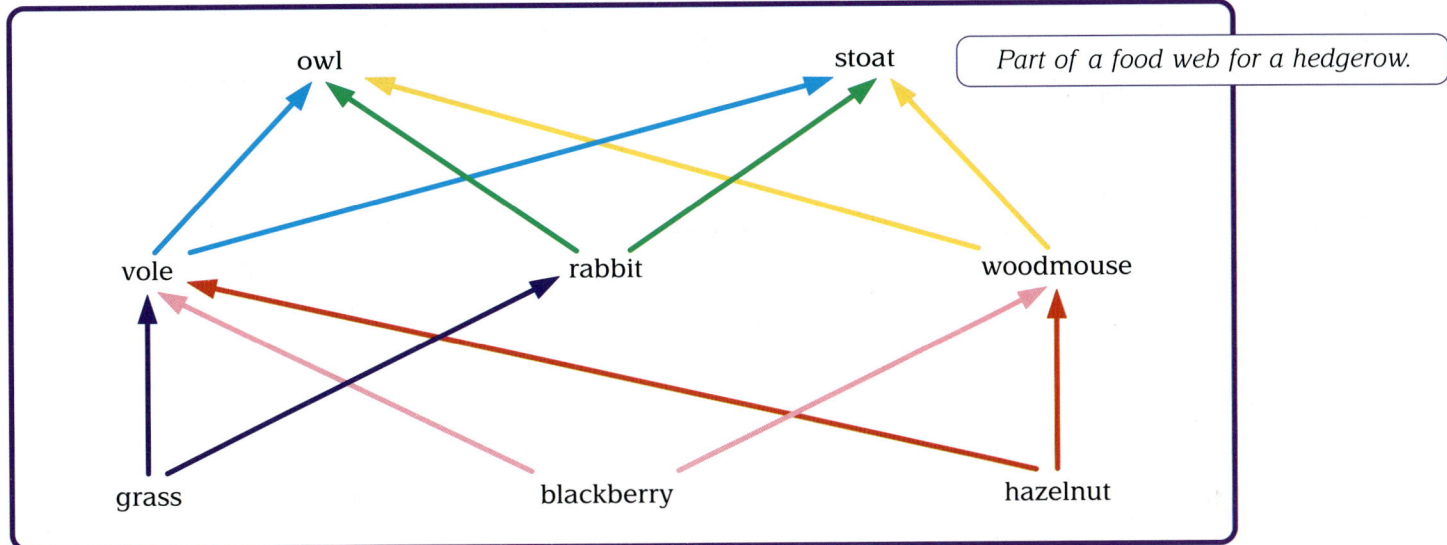

Part of a food web for a hedgerow.

1 **a** Make a copy of the food web. Add your name to it, with arrows to you from the things in it that you can eat.

   b Draw a large arrow next to your copy of the food web to show the direction of energy transfer.

2 Food webs are better than food chains for showing what happens in a habitat. Explain why.

Green plants are at the start of a food web. They transfer energy from sunlight into the web as food. So, if all the plants disappear, there is no food for the animals in the habitat.

A change in the number of animals also affects food webs. For example, the following things will happen if all the owls die.

- The population of animals that the owls usually eat will go up.

- Then there will be more food for stoats, and the population of stoats will go up.

- Rabbits, voles and mice **compete** for food. If there are too many of them, some won't get enough to eat. They will die.

3 **a** From the food web above, write down <u>two</u> animals that compete to eat rabbits.

   b Suppose all the rabbits catch a disease and die. Write down <u>two</u> effects that this would have on the food web. Explain your answer.

You should now have an understanding of these key ideas. You should also be able to spell and to know the meaning of the key words. The **key words** are in **bold** on this page.

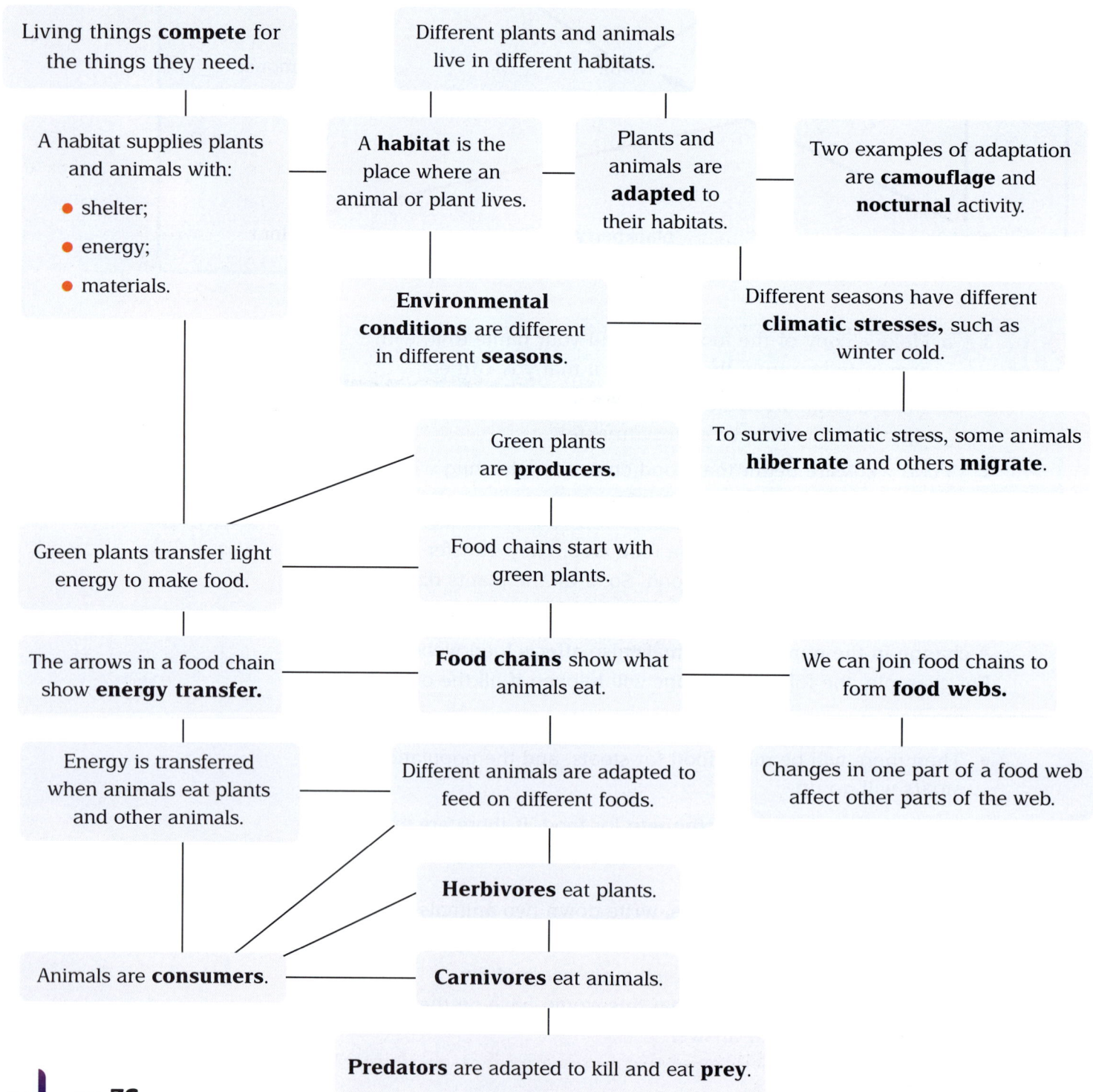

Living things **compete** for the things they need.

A habitat supplies plants and animals with:
- shelter;
- energy;
- materials.

Different plants and animals live in different habitats.

A **habitat** is the place where an animal or plant lives.

Plants and animals are **adapted** to their habitats.

Two examples of adaptation are **camouflage** and **nocturnal** activity.

Environmental conditions are different in different **seasons**.

Different seasons have different **climatic stresses,** such as winter cold.

Green plants are **producers.**

To survive climatic stress, some animals **hibernate** and others **migrate**.

Green plants transfer light energy to make food.

Food chains start with green plants.

The arrows in a food chain show **energy transfer.**

Food chains show what animals eat.

We can join food chains to form **food webs.**

Energy is transferred when animals eat plants and other animals.

Different animals are adapted to feed on different foods.

Changes in one part of a food web affect other parts of the web.

Herbivores eat plants.

Animals are **consumers**.

Carnivores eat animals.

Predators are adapted to kill and eat **prey**.

Variation and classification

In this unit we shall be studying some similarities and differences between species. We shall look at variation within species and consider the causes of it. We shall also look at how and why scientists sort living things into groups.

7D.1 The same but different

A **species** is one kind of living thing.

Members of a species:

- are very much alike (we say that a lot of their **characteristics** are the same);

- are different from members of other species;

- produce fertile offspring only when they breed with each other.

Humans all belong to the same species.

Humans are all similar. They can mate with each other and produce fertile offspring. So we say that they belong to the same species.

1   Why do we group all humans together as one species?
2   Write down <u>four</u> characteristics of all humans.

Variety is the spice of life!

Even though humans share many characteristics, there are differences between them. We say that they **vary**. We call the differences **variations**. Some of the differences are easy to see. Other differences are difficult or impossible to see.

3   Write down <u>three</u> differences between the people in the photograph.

4 Look at these pictures of girls. Write down <u>two</u> differences that you can see. Write down <u>one</u> difference that you cannot see.

All these girls have different blood groups.

Variations in other animals and plants

We have seen how humans vary. We can see variations in other animals, too. The dogs in the pictures below look different because they are different breeds. But they are all members of the same species.

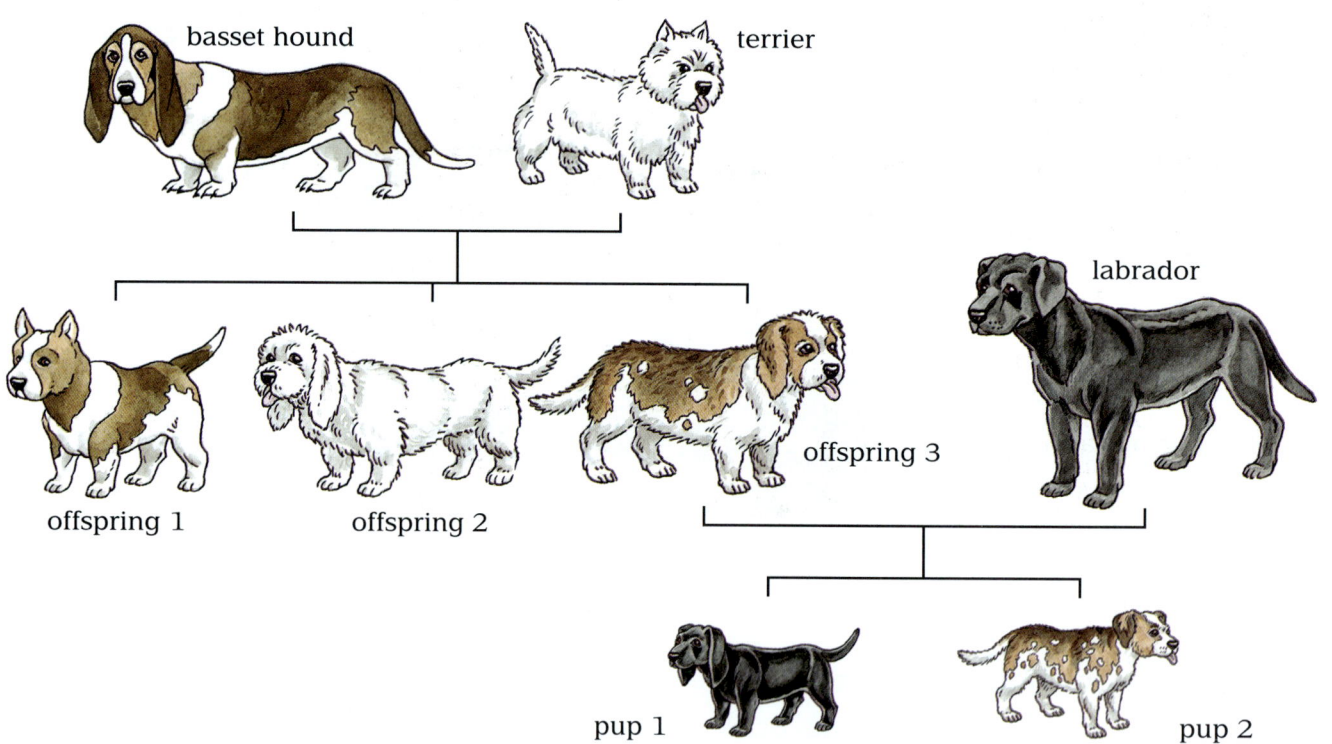

A family tree for a basset hound, a terrier, a labrador and their offspring.

5 Write down:

a <u>four</u> characteristics of dogs;

b how each of these characteristics varies.

6 How do you know that the breeds of dogs in the pictures belong to the same species?

Plants from the same species also vary. Corn is one species of plant. Its fruits are called cobs. Corncobs come in several different shapes, sizes and colours. We call these underline varieties of corn.

Corn is a species belonging to the grass family.

Look at the pictures of corncobs. We use different varieties for sweetcorn, animal food, popcorn, cornflour and cornflakes.

Different varieties of corncobs

7   Write down underline three variations between the cobs in the pictures.

8   Explain how we can prove that all the cobs belong to the same species.

7D.2 The causes of variation

Variations in a characteristic often run in families. They are passed from one generation to the next. We call them **inherited variations**. But not all variations are inherited. Some characteristics vary because of the environment in which a living thing develops. These variations are called **environmental variations**. Other variations have a mixture of inherited and environmental causes.

Emperor Maximillian (1459–1519)

Variations that run in families

The Habsburg family was one of the ruling families of Europe. Many members had a lip that was characteristic of the family. It is called the Habsburg lip.

Maximillian's grandson, Emperor Charles V (1500–1558)

 **1**   Look carefully at the pictures of the Habsburg family members. Describe the Habsburg lip.

Archduke Charles of Teschen (1771–1847)

 **2**   What other information would be useful to decide if this characteristic was inherited in the Habsburg family?

How we find patterns of inheritance

We can use a diagram to show how people are related to each other. We call this diagram a **family tree**. A family tree can also show how a characteristic is inherited. We can see if a characteristic passes from parents to children. A characteristic is inherited when we see a strong pattern in a family tree.

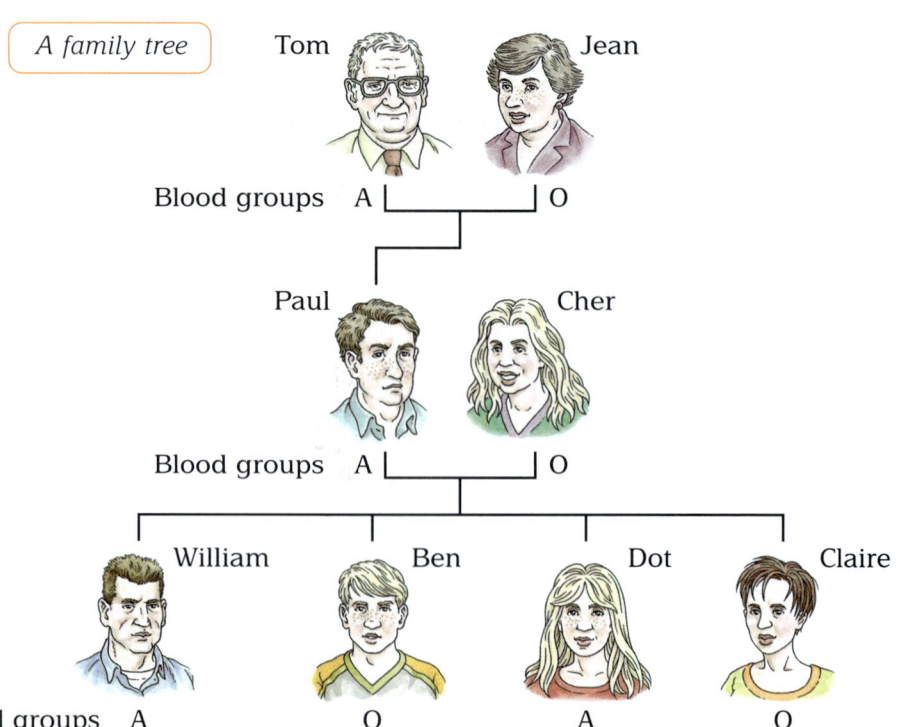

A family tree

Tom   Jean

Blood groups   A   O

Paul   Cher

Blood groups   A   O

William   Ben   Dot   Claire

Blood groups   A   O   A   O

3 Look at the family tree. How many generations does it show?

4 Write down <u>two</u> ways in which Paul is similar to his parents.

5 Write down <u>two</u> other characteristics that are inherited in this family.

6 For each statement, say whether it is TRUE or FALSE. In each case, write down <u>one</u> piece of evidence.

   a Boys always inherit characteristics only from their fathers.

   b Some characteristics seem to miss one generation.

   c Children are identical to their parents.

   d Children of the same family can be very different.

These pea plants grew in exactly the same environmental conditions.

Environmental variations

Environmental variations are not inherited. They develop as a result of what happens to an animal or plant during its lifetime.

7 The pea plants in the pictures inherited different characteristics. Explain how we know this.

This is how leeks grow. These leeks are all the same variety.

Leeks from the centre of the garden

Leeks from the edge of the garden

8 Write down <u>three</u> differences in the environment that could have caused the variation in the leeks in the picture.

Joan and Ellen are identical twins. Ellen had a serious illness when she was nine. So she did not grow as tall as her sister.

9 Look at the picture of the identical twins. Write down <u>two</u> characteristics of Joan and Ellen caused only by:

  a inheritance;

  b the environment.

10 Height is partly an inherited and partly an environmental variation. Use the information you know about Joan and Ellen to explain this.

7D.3 Describing living things

We have seen that there can be lots of variation between members of the same species. But there is more variation between members of different species. Gorillas have similarities to humans, but they also have key characteristics that are different from those of humans. So gorillas belong to a different species.

1 Look carefully at the pictures. Write down <u>three</u> differences between the human and the gorilla.

When you look for differences between a human and a gorilla, you have to look carefully. Careful observation is very important in science.

Books for identifying plants and animals use drawings and detailed descriptions to help us to tell one species from another. Descriptions in stories and poems don't have to be so accurate. They are sometimes about only one characteristic.

Gorilla

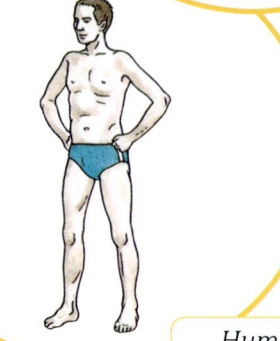

Human

2 Read the poem. Write down <u>three</u> animals that could fit the description in the poem.

> There once was a _____ called Nick
> whose movements were sudden and quick.
> He loved to pop out
> and cause people to shout
> but his wriggling legs made me sick!

3 Now read the description of the same animal below. What type of animal do you think it is now?

> Nick has eight legs.
> He has two parts to his body, a head and an <u>abdomen</u>.
> He has <u>spinnerets</u> that he uses to make silken threads.
> He has hard outer parts called an <u>exoskeleton</u> to protect him.
> Nick eats insects, so he is a <u>carnivore</u>.

4 a Write down <u>one</u> piece of information about Nick's structure that is in the poem.

b The description gives you more information about this part. Write down that extra information.

5 What does the poem tell you about Nick that is not in the description?

6 Make a list of the special words used in the description. Then match them with the definitions below.

a An animal that eats other animals.

b The tail end of the body, often swollen.

c A skeleton on the outside of a body.

d Tiny finger-like body parts that make silken threads.

Why details are important

Hoverflies and wasps look similar in many ways. However, wasps sting, but hoverflies don't. Many people like to see hoverflies in their gardens because hoverfly young eat the greenfly that damage their plants.

Hoverfly

Common wasp

 **7** Why is it useful to be able to tell the difference between a wasp and a hoverfly?

Scientific description of hoverflies	Scientific description of common wasps
Hoverflies have a head, a thorax and an abdomen.	Common wasps have a head, a thorax and an abdomen.
Hoverflies have six jointed legs.	Common wasps have six jointed legs.
Hoverflies have bright black-and-yellow markings on their abdomens.	Common wasps have bright black-and-yellow markings on their abdomens.
Hoverflies often feed on pollen and nectar from flowers.	Common wasps like sugary foods but mainly feed on meat.
Hoverflies can hover.	Common wasps do not hover.
Hoverflies have a margin on the edge of their wings.	Common wasps do not have a margin on the edge of their wings.
Hoverflies have large, round compound eyes.	Common wasps have crescent-shaped eyes.
Hoverflies do not have jaws.	Common wasps have jaws for biting.
Hoverflies do not have a sting.	Common wasps have a sting.

 **8** Look at the table. Write down <u>three</u> characteristics that hoverflies and common wasps share.

9 Write down <u>two</u> characteristics that would help you to tell the difference between a hoverfly and a common wasp.

 **10** Explain why looking at details is important when we describe animals such as these insects.

11 Look at the picture of a centipede and a millipede and use the words below to write a description of each one.

- **Jointed leg:** leg with more than one joint (or bend) along its length.
- **Segments:** sections along the body.
- **Antenna:** long, thin projection on the head.

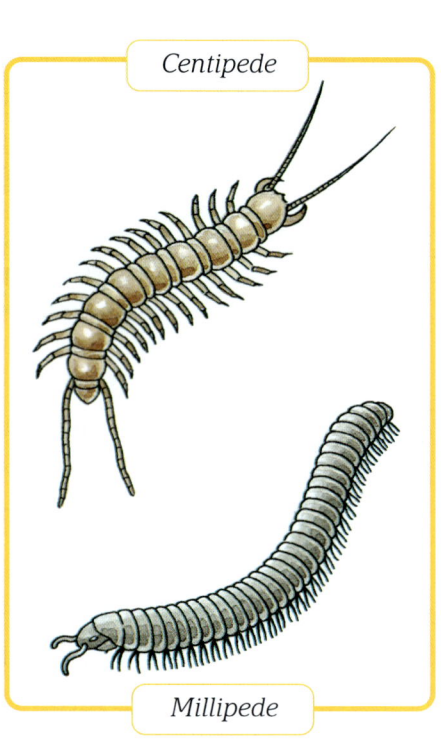

Centipede

Millipede

7D.4 Sorting things into groups

We often sort things into groups to make them easier to deal with. For example, the police have files containing millions of fingerprints. They use them to identify fingerprints found at crime scenes. If the fingerprints can be sorted into groups with similar characteristics, only one group of fingerprints needs to be checked, rather than all of them.

whorl

Whorls Loops Arches

1 Which file do you think the police will check to identify the fingerprint in the picture?

There are lots of ways of sorting living things. Some ways are more useful than others. We often start by sorting them into green plants and animals.

```
          living things
               |
    _____|_____
   |                       |
green plants           animals
```

2 You know from what you learned in Unit 7A that plant and animal cells are different. What else do you know about green plants and animals that helps you to fit them into their groups?

Then we sort these groups into smaller groups. These pictures show one way of sorting animals into groups.

eagle

sparrow

bat

owl

fly

These land animals can fly.

crab

shark

fish

octopus

whale

These animals live in water.

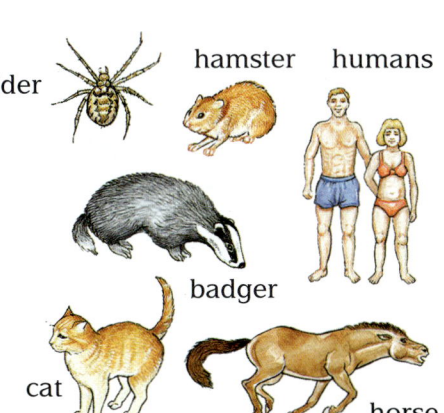

spider

hamster

humans

badger

cat

horse

These animals live on land.

3 Explain why these groups are not a very useful way of sorting these animals.

4 Write down <u>two</u> animals that are separated in these groups but that you think should be in a group together.

5 Sort the animals in the picture into <u>two</u> groups using a different characteristic.

7D.5 Sorting plants and animals

Scientists have named and described several million different species of plants and animals. They think that millions more will be discovered in the future. We can't learn about every one of them. So we sort them into groups with lots of characteristics in common. We call this sorting **classification**.

For example, birds have feathers, beaks and wings and they walk on two legs. So if we are told that an eagle is a bird, we already know a lot of things about it. You might see an animal that you haven't seen before, but you might know that it is a bird. So you look it up in a book about birds, rather than a book about all animals.

1 Write down <u>three</u> facts about an eagle.

2 What do we call it when we sort things into groups?

3 Why do we sort living things into groups?

Aristotle lived in Greece over 2000 years ago. He was the first person to use sets of characteristics of animals and plants to sort them into groups. Before Aristotle, people grouped animals into land and water animals or winged and wingless animals.

Aristotle saw that some ants have wings and others don't. So he realised that a simple grouping into winged and wingless animals doesn't work.

Aristotle (384–322 BC)

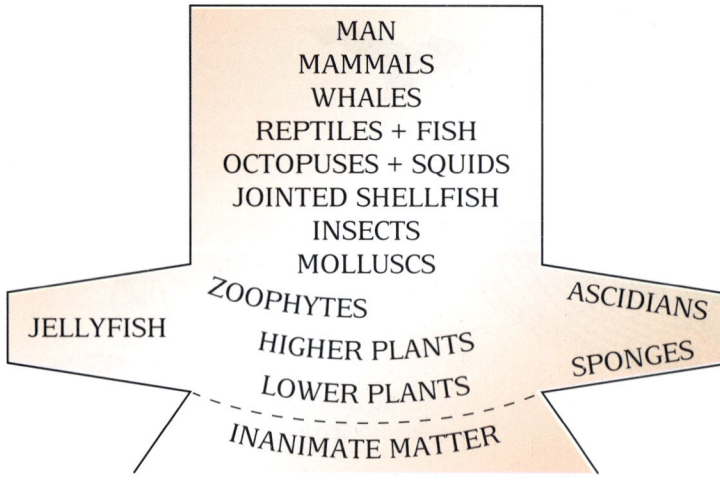

MAN
MAMMALS
WHALES
REPTILES + FISH
OCTOPUSES + SQUIDS
JOINTED SHELLFISH
INSECTS
MOLLUSCS
ZOOPHYTES
JELLYFISH
HIGHER PLANTS
ASCIDIANS
SPONGES
LOWER PLANTS
INANIMATE MATTER

Aristotle's classification system.

4 Why do you think Aristotle used sets of characteristics for his classification system?

Now we sort living things into groups that have lots of characteristics in common. Scientists all over the world use the same system. When they find a new animal or plant, they look at similarities and differences between it and known animals. Then they fit it into a group. Sometimes they have to change the groupings a bit.

5 Look at the pictures of the eagle, the bat and the dragonfly below. Write down <u>one</u> similarity and <u>one</u> difference between the eagle and the bat.

Bat

Dragonfly

Eagle

Birds have feathers, but other animal groups don't. So feathers are a useful characteristic for identifying an animal as a bird. Birds, bats and many insects fly. But bats and insects are very different from birds. So flying is not a useful characteristic for classifying animals.

6 Some characteristics are more useful than others for classifying. Look at the pictures of the eagle, the bat and the dragonfly. Having feathers is a better characteristic than flying to tell birds apart from other animals. Why is this?

7 Why is it useful for all scientists to use the same classification system?

Classifying animals

Some animals have skeletons made of bone inside their bodies. Scientists classify all these animals in a group called **vertebrates**. We sometimes call them <u>animals with backbones</u>.

 **8** The skeletons of different vertebrates have lots of characteristics in common. Write down <u>three</u> similarities between the skeletons of the human and the mole in these pictures.

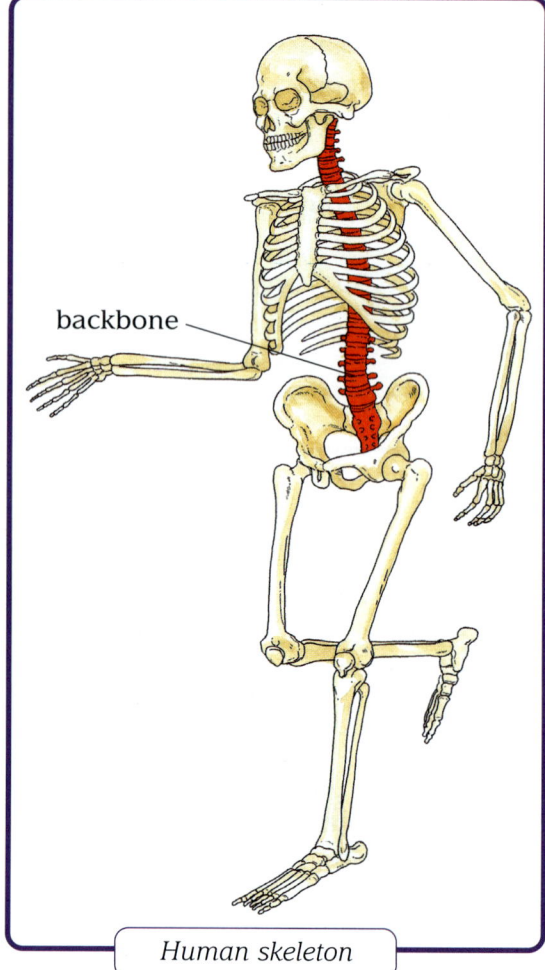

backbone

Human skeleton

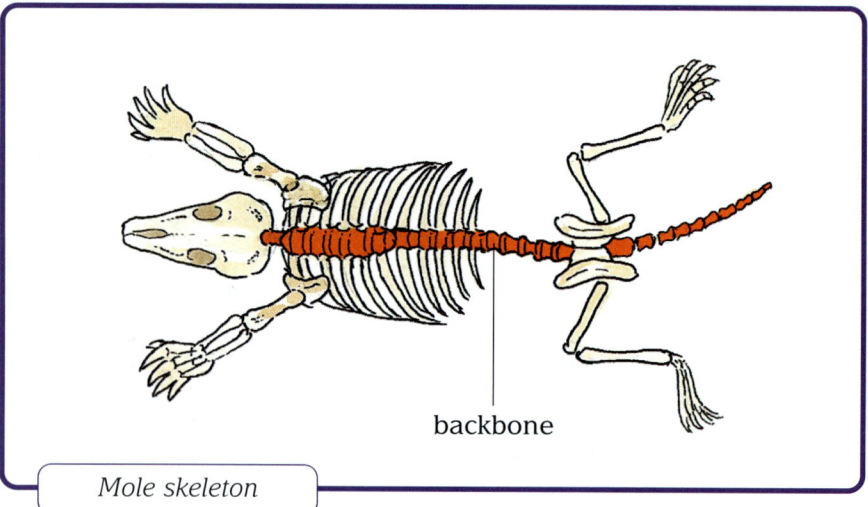

backbone

Mole skeleton

Animals without backbones are called **invertebrates**. Some of them have hard body parts, but these are different from vertebrate skeletons.

A snail is an invertebrate with a shell.

A crab is an invertebrate. Its jointed skeleton is on the outside of its body.

 **9** Describe the hard body parts of <u>two</u> invertebrates.

Vertebrates

There are about 60 000 different species of vertebrates that we know about, so we divide them into smaller groups.

Vertebrates

Fish **Amphibians** **Reptiles** **Birds** **Mammals**

e.g. e.g. e.g. e.g. e.g.

goldfish frog adder golden plover chimpanzee

Goldfish have scales, gills and fins. They have a streamlined shape. Their eggs have no shells.

The adder is a reptile. It has a dry scaly skin and it eggs have tough shells.

Chimpanzees are mammals. They have hair and feed their young on milk.

Frogs have moist skin with no scales. Their eggs have no shells. They are amphibians.

The golden plover has feathers and lays eggs with hard shells.

10 Look carefully at the diagram and pictures above. Write down <u>one</u> characteristic that all these animals share.

11 What makes mammals different from the other groups of vertebrates?

12 Write down <u>two</u> differences between amphibians and reptiles.

13 Newts are amphibians. From this information only, write down <u>two</u> things that you know about newts.

Invertebrates

Over nine tenths of all species of animals don't have bones. They are classified as invertebrates. We divide them into groups, too.

Invertebrates

Jellyfish e.g. sea anemone	Molluscs e.g. snail	Flatworms e.g. planarian and tapeworm	True worms e.g. earthworm	**Arthropods** e.g. spider
jelly-like body, stinging cells	shell, one muscular foot	flat body, not divided into segments	round body, divided into segments	hard parts on outside, jointed legs, segmented body

14 Write down <u>one</u> characteristic that all invertebrates share.

15 Look carefully at the diagram. The planarian and the earthworm are in different groups. Write down <u>two</u> differences between them.

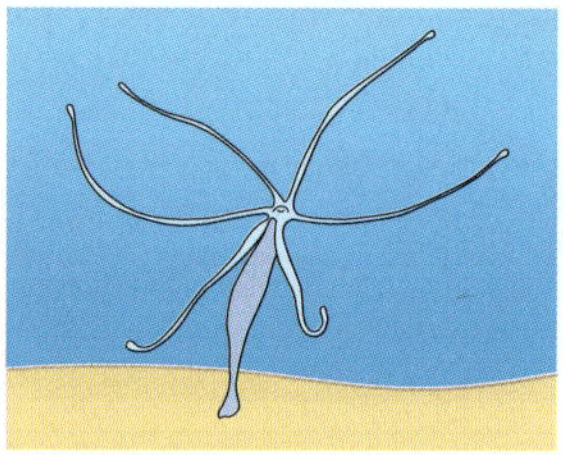

Hydra

Snail

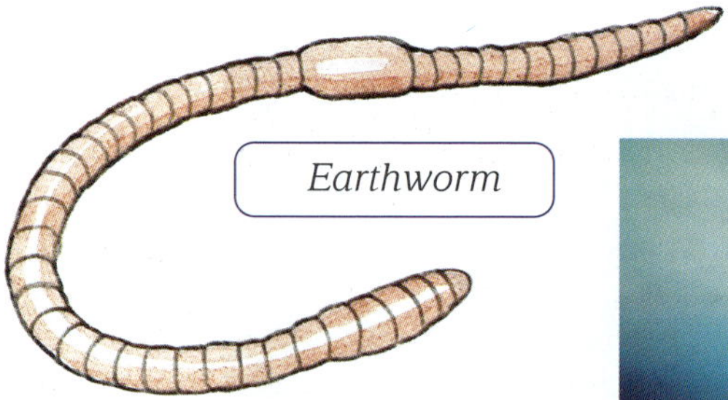

Earthworm

Jellyfish

Spider

Tapeworm

Planarian

16 The hydra and the jellyfish belong to the same group of invertebrates. Write down <u>two</u> characteristics that they share.

17 The ragworm is in the same invertebrate group as the earthworm. Explain why these animals are classified in the same group.

Ragworm

More groups

All the groups that we have studied so far are very big. So we divide them into smaller groups. More than three quarters of all animal species are arthropods. We divide these animals into four main groups.

Crab

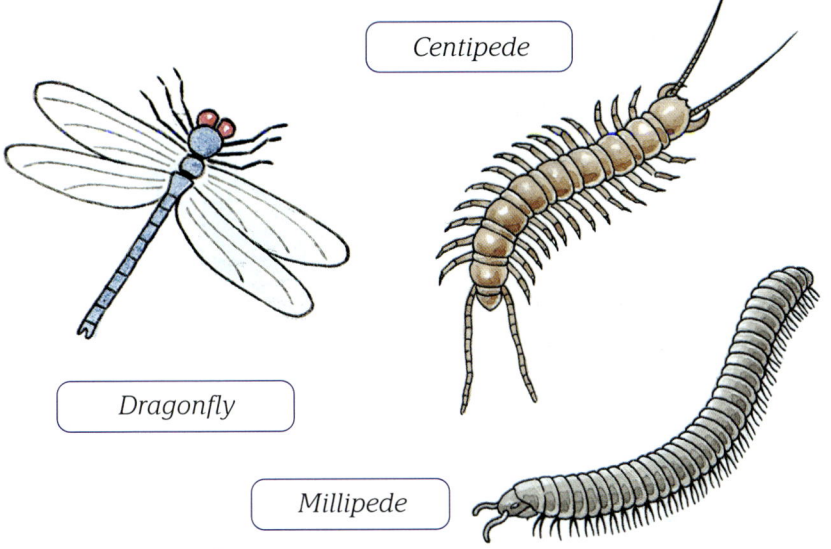

Centipede

Dragonfly

Millipede

Lobster

Fly

Erigone

 **18** Look carefully at the pictures of arthropods.
Write down <u>two</u> characteristics that all arthropods share.

19 What <u>two</u> characteristics could you use to split this big group?

Arthropod group	What do they look like?
Crustaceans	Two pairs of antennae; five or more pairs of legs
Insects	Three pairs of legs; one or two pairs of wings
Spiders	Four pairs of legs; no antennae
Myriapods (many legs)	Long body divided into segments; legs on every segment

 **20** Look carefully at the pictures and the table.

a Which invertebrate group do these animals belong to?

dragonfly   centipede   crab   *Erigone*

b Explain why you chose the group you did for each animal.

You should now understand the key words and key ideas shown below.

Key words

species

characteristics

vary

variations

inherited variations

environmental variations

family tree

classification

vertebrates

invertebrates

fish

amphibians

reptiles

birds

mammals

arthropods

Key ideas

- A species is one kind of living thing.

- Members of a species breed with each other to produce fertile offspring.

- Members of a species have a lot of characteristics in common.

- Individuals of the same species vary.

- Variations that pass from parents to offspring are called inherited variations.

- Differences caused by the conditions in which the plant or animal lives are called environmental variations. They are not passed on to offspring.

- Sorting things into groups is called classification. We put living things with the same characteristics in a group.

- We divide large groups into smaller groups.

- Scientists all over the world use the same classification system. This means that they all know which animals or plants they are writing about.

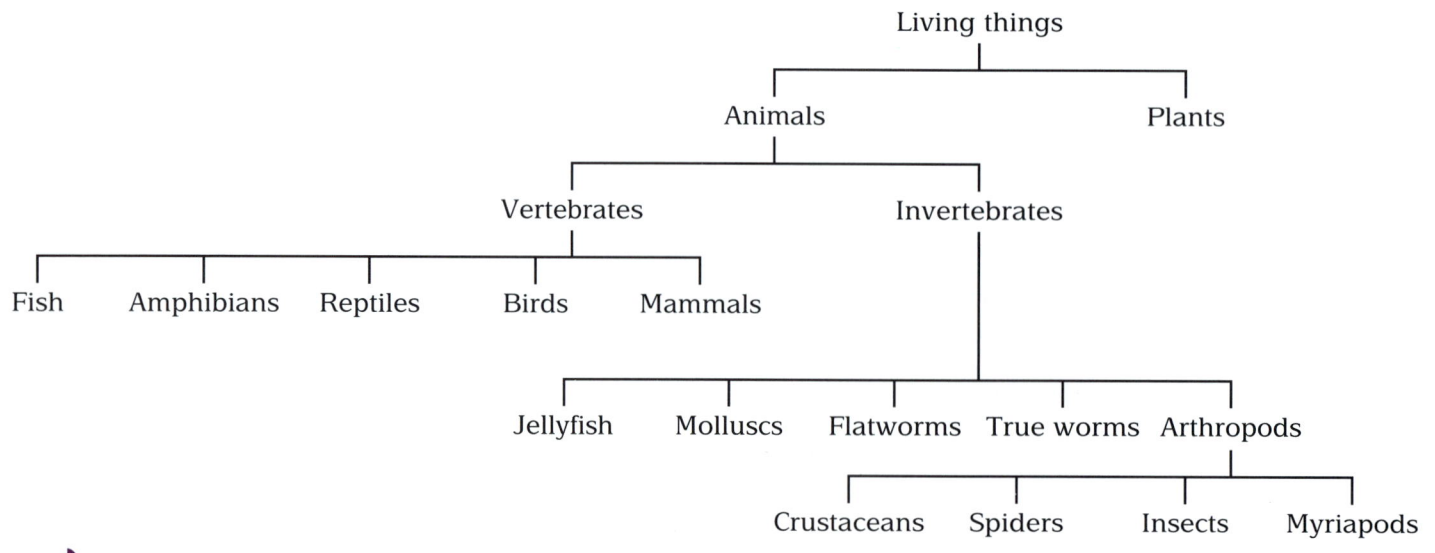

Food and digestion

In this unit we shall be learning about different food groups and what we need for a balanced, healthy diet. We shall also be learning about how our bodies break down food and use it for growth, repair of damage, and as an energy source.

KEY WORDS
grow
repair
energy
nutrients
proteins
carbohydrates
fats
vitamins
minerals
water
fibre
absorb
digestion
faeces
enzymes

8A.1 Why we need food

We need food to survive. A healthy person who stops eating can live for only about 40 days.

Food gives us the raw materials that our bodies use…

… *to* **grow**

… *for* **repair**

… *to get* **energy** *for:*
• *growth and repair;*
• *moving;*
• *keeping warm.*

1 Look at the pictures. Write down:

  a <u>two</u> reasons you need to make new cells;

  b <u>three</u> uses for energy in your body.

We call the food substances that our cells use **nutrients**. They are:

● **proteins**, for making new cells;

● **carbohydrates** and **fats** for energy;

● small amounts of **vitamins** and **minerals**.

2 Find out a use of <u>one</u> vitamin and <u>one</u> mineral in your body.

We are what we eat

Proteins are the main raw materials for making new cells. So proteins are particularly important at times when we are growing quickly.

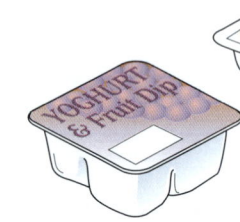

Taribo has a healthy diet.

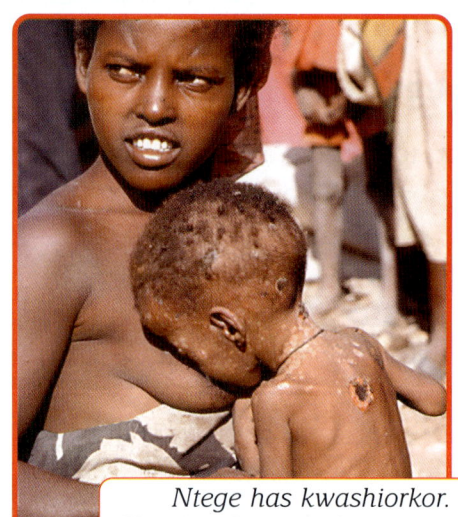

Ntege has kwashiorkor. Kwashiorkor is a disease caused by a lack of proteins in his diet.

3 Write down <u>two</u> differences between the children in the photographs.

4 Write down <u>two</u> foods that will improve Ntege's health if he can get them.

5 Some children don't eat enough protein foods. Will this have any long-term effects on them? Explain your answer.

6 On average, a pregnant woman needs 76 g of protein per day. A woman who is not pregnant needs less.

  a Explain why a pregnant woman needs extra protein.

  b Find out how much protein a woman normally needs.

When we cut ourselves some cells are damaged, some die and others are lost when we bleed. Our bodies have to make more cells to repair the wound and to replace the lost and damaged cells. Cells in our bodies are continually dying and being replaced by new ones. For example, a red blood cell lasts for only about four months. New red blood cells are made all the time to replace those that are worn out.

Look at the photographs. The wound is gradually healing up. Eventually, there will be no sign of it.

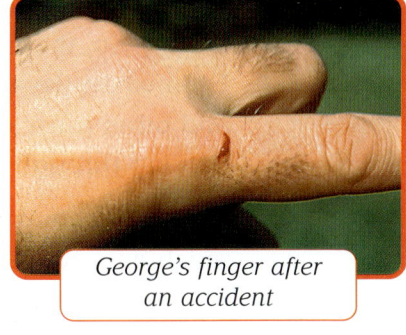
George's finger after an accident

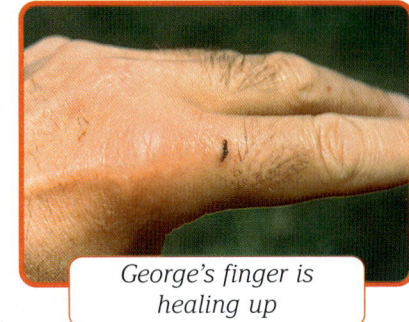
George's finger is healing up

7 Explain what is happening to make the wound on George's finger heal up.

8 Wounds take longer to heal if the person doesn't eat enough protein foods. Why is this?

We eat for energy too

We need energy for:

- growth and repair of cells;
- moving;
- keeping warm.

We need raw materials <u>and</u> energy from our food to make and repair cells. So energy as well as proteins are important when we are growing. We release this energy from the carbohydrates and fats in our food.

Carbohydrate foods

starchy

sugary

9 Write down <u>four</u> energy foods that you eat.

10 Lack of energy foods affects a child's growth. Why is this?

11 Explain the effects of a lack of energy foods on adults who are no longer growing.

Fatty foods

Muscles contract to make us move. To contract, muscles need energy. So, the more we move around, the more energy we need. Even when we are not moving around, our hearts are beating and other muscles are helping us to breathe and to keep food moving through our digestive system.

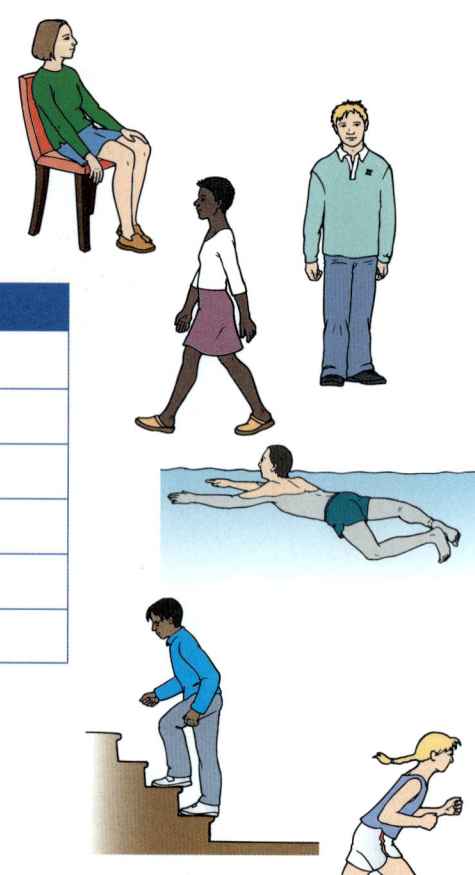

The table shows how much energy we need for different activities. We measure energy in kilojoules (kJ).

Activity	kJ/hour
Sitting	63
Standing	84
Walking	750
Swimming	1800
Walking upstairs	4184
Sprinting	5183

12 When we are sitting still, what do our bodies use energy for?

13 Between which <u>two</u> activities in the table does a person getting dressed fit? Explain your answer.

14 Adam is a distance runner. On the day before a race, he eats lots of carbohydrate foods.
Why do you think he needs to do this?

15 Why do we need more energy when standing up than sitting down?

Mini but mighty

We also need small amounts of vitamins and minerals. Although the amounts that we need are very small, they are very important for our health.

In the 1740s two-thirds of sailors died from a disease called scurvy. When they were away from land for a long time, they didn't eat any fresh fruit or vegetables. So they didn't have any vitamin C in their diet, and lack of vitamin C causes scurvy.

Minerals such as calcium and iron are also important.

Calcium is a raw material for making bones and teeth, and iron is needed to make red blood cells.

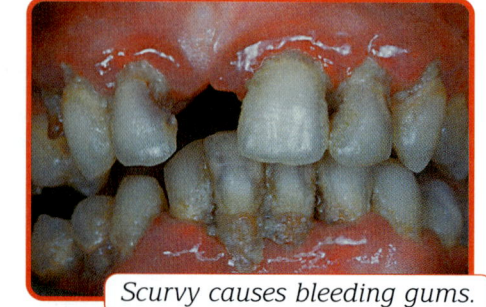

Scurvy causes bleeding gums.

16 Look at the photograph. Describe some effects of scurvy.

17 Write down <u>one</u> food that contains:

   a vitamin C;

   b vitamins A and D and the mineral iron;

   c calcium.

The label shows some of the nutritional information from a packet of Sugary Puffs.

18 What is the main nutrient in Sugary Puffs?

19 Which mineral is found in Sugary Puffs?

20 Write down <u>one</u> vitamin in Sugary Puffs.

21 Find out the effects of lack of each of the two B vitamins.

NUTRITIONAL INFORMATION	
TYPICAL VALUE per 100 g	
Energy	1620 kJ
Protein	6.5 g
Carbohydrates	86.5 g
(of which sugars)	49.0 g
Fat	1.0 g
Fibre	3.0 g
VITAMINS	
Thiamin (B1)	1.0 mg
Riboflavin (B2)	1.0 mg
MINERALS	
Iron	8.0 mg

Foods containing vitamins and minerals

fish

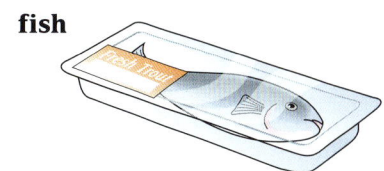

vitamins A, D

milk

vitamins A, D; calcium

vegetables

vitamins A, B, C

egg

vitamins B, D

liver

vitamins A, D; iron

wholemeal bread

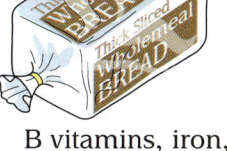

B vitamins, iron, calcium

Fibre and water are important too

Most foods contain a large amount of **water**. If you have eaten a watermelon, you will know how watery food can be. Even your body is about two-thirds water.

Fruit and vegetables contain a lot of **fibre**. Fibre is the cellulose of plant cell walls. Our bodies can't break it down, so it goes right through the digestive system. It is not a nutrient because our cells do not use it. But it gives the muscles of the digestive system something to push against, helping to move food along more easily. Without it, you'd be very constipated! In fact, fibre and water make up a large part of the bulk of your food.

22 Explain why you need water and fibre in your diet.

8A.2 A healthy diet

A balanced, healthy diet contains the correct amount of each food group. We can get a balanced diet in all sorts of ways. Many people in richer countries like the USA and the UK get a lot of their protein from meat. Most people in poorer countries like India and China rely on cereals and beans for their proteins.

A West Indian meal of rice, fish and vegetables.

1. In the West Indian meal, the rice is the main energy source. What provides most of the protein?
2. In the Chinese dish, the prawns provide most of the protein. What is the main energy source?
3. Which part of the European meal contains most of the proteins and fat?

A Chinese meal of noodles, prawns and vegetables.

Every meal that you eat does not have to be balanced. It is what you eat over several meals that matters. You can find out the amount of each group in a packaged food by looking at the label.

4. Which of the foods on the graph contains the most:
   a water?   b protein?
5. What is the main nutrient in potatoes?
6. Which nutrients in the graph are missing from cod?

A European meal of meat, potato and vegetables.

An analysis of the main nutrient content, water and fibre in four foods

A healthy, balanced diet is different for different people. The amount of each nutrient we need depends on:

- our age;
- whether we are male or female;
- our body size;
- the activities and jobs that we do.

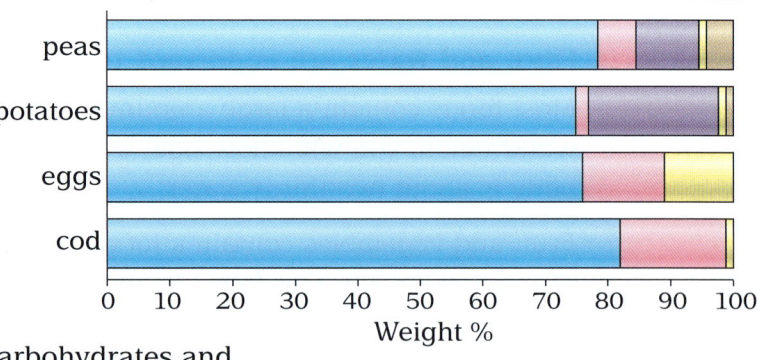

A person doing building work needs more carbohydrates and fats for energy than a person working at a desk all day.

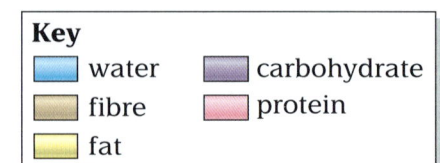

Key
- water
- carbohydrate
- fibre
- protein
- fat

7. What do the following people need to eat?
   a Mmapula, a 13-year-old girl living in South Africa.
   b Steve Carr, who plays professional football for Spurs.

8. Janet is breastfeeding her baby. Find out what she should eat and drink.

8A.3 Getting nutrients out of your food

The nutrients in your food have to pass into your blood. We say that you **absorb** them. The particles of vitamins, minerals and some sugars such as glucose are small enough to be absorbed. The large, insoluble molecules of fats, proteins and some carbohydrates are not. So you have to break them down into smaller molecules. We call this process **digestion**. It happens in your digestive system. After digestion, the small molecules pass into your blood and are transported to your cells.

 **1** Write down <u>three</u> substances that you can absorb without digesting them.

Modelling what happens in your digestive system

In science, we sometimes use models to help us understand how things work. We can use this model of the gut to find out which substances can pass into the blood and which can't.

 **2** What part of the diagram represents the blood?

3 What does the visking tubing represent?

 **4** Later, there is glucose in the water around the visking tubing, but no starch. Explain why.

starch and glucose solutions

water

visking tubing

boiling tube

Look at the diagram of what happens in your gut.

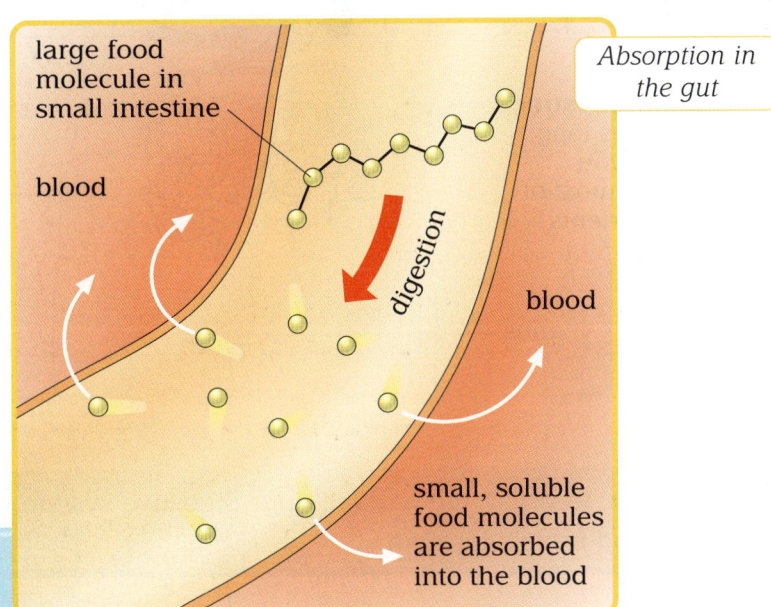

large food molecule in small intestine

blood

digestion

blood

Absorption in the gut

small, soluble food molecules are absorbed into the blood

 **5** Which kind of molecules:

a can pass into your blood?

b cannot pass into your blood?

Explain your answers.

Your digestive system

The food's journey through your digestive system starts in your mouth and ends when it passes out through your anus as **faeces**. The journey is 8 to 9 metres long and usually takes between 24 and 48 hours to complete.

If food goes through too quickly, it is not broken down into the nutrients that you need. If the surface area of your digestive system is not large enough, you will not be able to absorb all the nutrients.

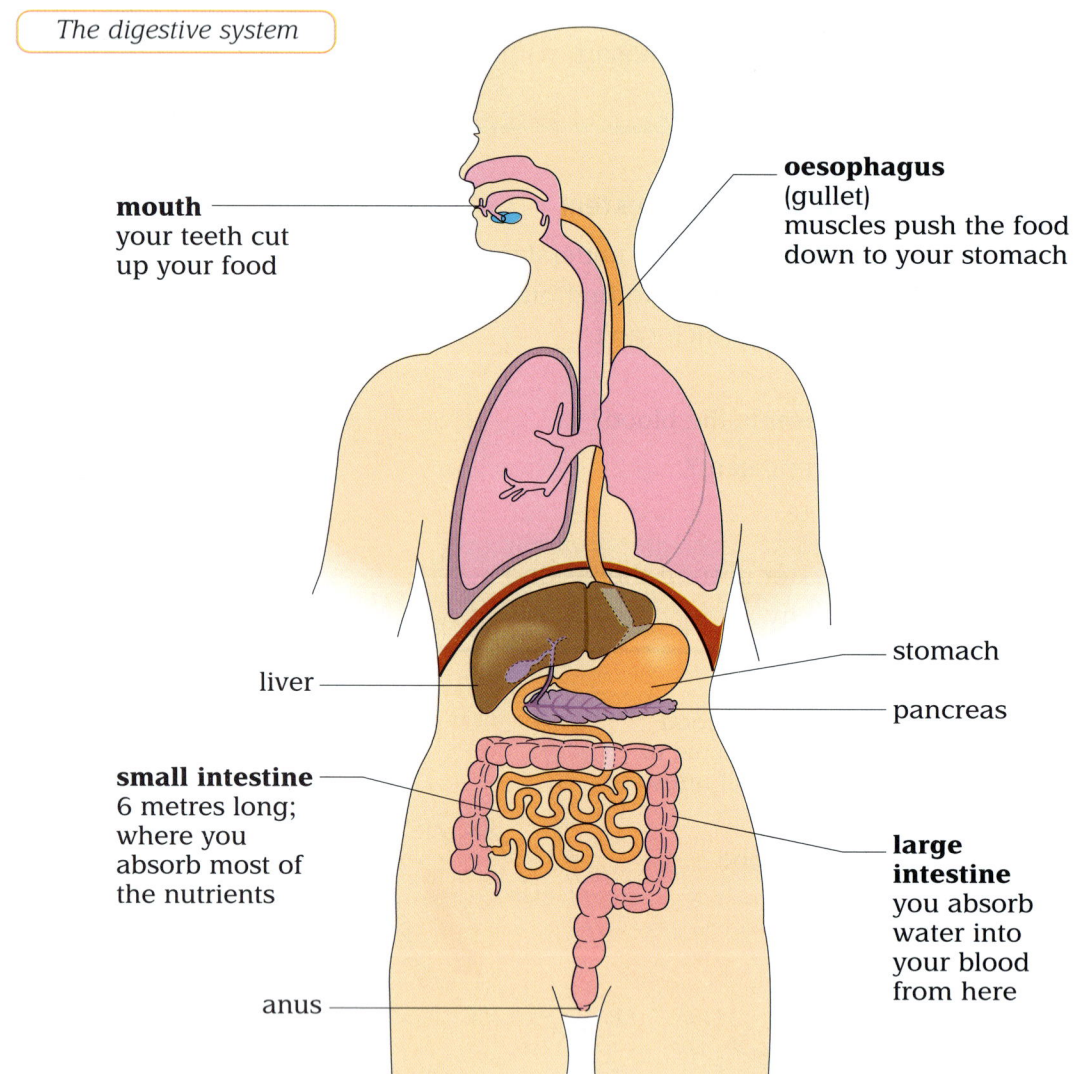

The digestive system

mouth
your teeth cut
up your food

oesophagus
(gullet)
muscles push the food
down to your stomach

liver

stomach

pancreas

small intestine
6 metres long;
where you
absorb most of
the nutrients

**large
intestine**
you absorb
water into
your blood
from here

anus

6 List, in order, the parts of your digestive system that your food travels through.

8A.4 How your digestive system works

Over 3000 years ago, the Ancient Greeks described many of the organs of the digestive system. They found out about the different organs by dissecting dead bodies, sometimes in public places.

In the 1760s, an Italian priest called Lazzaro Spallanzani did experiments on his own body to find out about the digestion of food. He swallowed wooden blocks with holes containing meat and collected them when they passed out of his anus. He discovered that the food in the wooden blocks had disappeared. Spallanzani also made himself vomit and showed that the liquid vomit dissolved away meat. Sometimes he swallowed food on a piece of thread and pulled the food out before it was fully digested.

Lazzaro Spallanzani

1 a What happened to the meat in the wooden blocks that Spallanzani swallowed?

   b Where did this happen?

We now know that Spallanzani's meat disappeared because **enzymes** had broken it down. We know that cells in some parts of our digestive systems release these chemicals and that they break down large molecules of food into smaller ones.

Large insoluble molecules

fat

starch

protein   amino acids

using enyzme

using enyzme

Small, soluble molecules

glycerol   fatty acids

sugars

2 Write down the names of the molecules produced by the breakdown of:

   a fat;

   b starch.

3 Proteins break down into amino acids. Draw a diagram to show what the protein in the diagram looks like when it is broken down.

Now look at the gut model again.

4 What kind of substance can you put in the visking tubing to break down the starch into sugar?

5 What happens to the sugar that is made?

6 Your saliva breaks down starch. What does this tell you about your saliva?

7 Think carefully of ways in which the model is different from a real small intestine. Write down your answers.

starch and glucose solutions

water

visking tubing

boiling tube

Scientists continue to research what happens to food in the digestive system. They have found out that different enzymes break down different foods, and that different enzymes work best in different conditions. For example, some work best in acidic conditions, others in alkaline.

Often the research is done to find out more about illnesses. One way is to give a patient a harmless liquid containing a barium compound to drink. The barium shows up on an X-ray photograph as it moves through the digestive system. Doctors can even look inside the stomach using an endoscope.

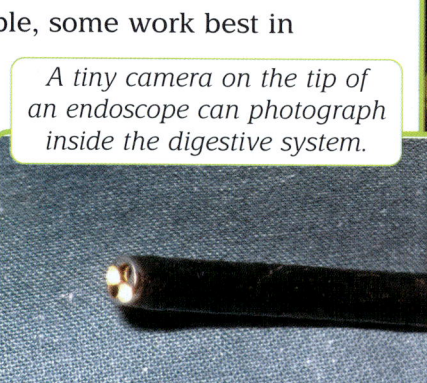

A tiny camera on the tip of an endoscope can photograph inside the digestive system.

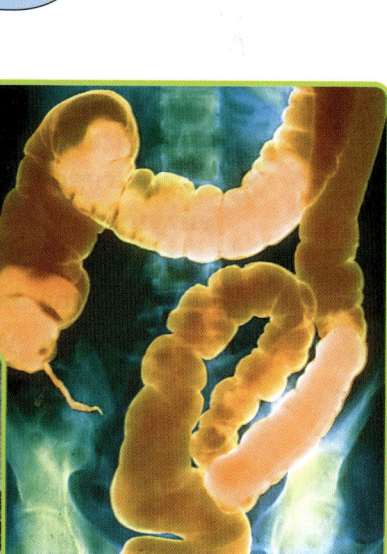

An X-ray of the large intestine after a barium meal

8 Write down <u>two</u> things that scientists have found out about enzymes.

9 Find out:

a the connection between an endoscope, fibre optics and a stomach ulcer;

b <u>one</u> reason why doctors take X-rays of a patient's digestive system.

8A.5 After digestion

Every cell of the body needs nutrients. Cells need them for growth, repair and as an energy source. So the bloodstream carries the nutrients absorbed in the small intestine to all parts of the body. They are carried in solution in the blood plasma – the liquid part of blood.

 **1** Write a list of nutrients that can pass into your blood.

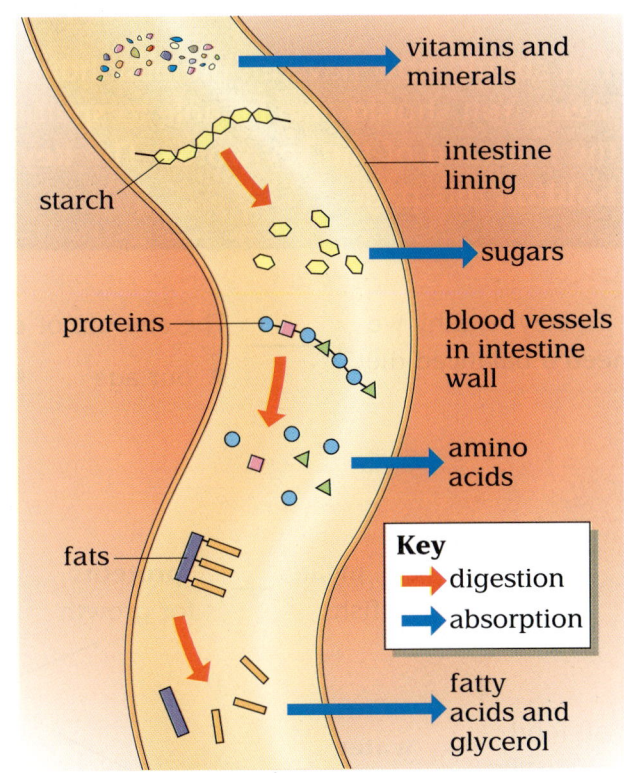

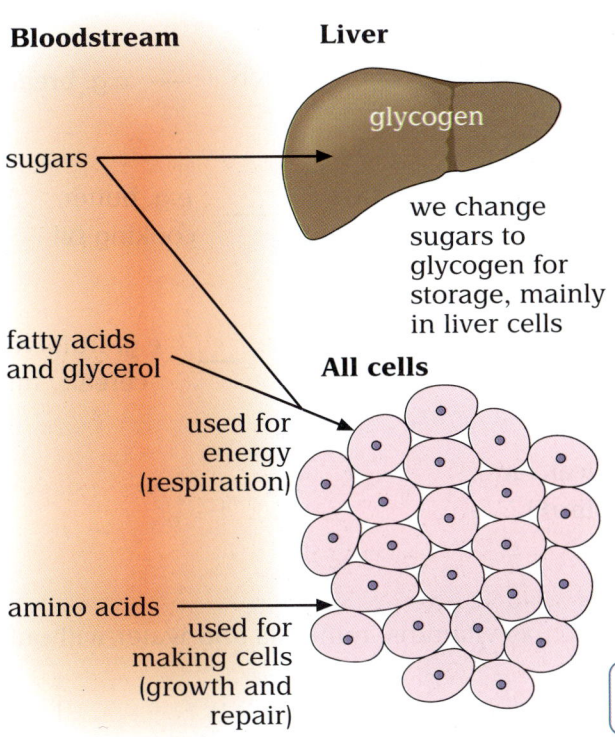

What happens to the products of digestion

 **2** Describe <u>two</u> things that can happen to sugars after they pass into the blood.

 **3** Write down <u>one</u> kind of cell that uses lots of sugars. Explain your answer.

Remember: All the undigested food, including fibre, is got rid of in faeces. We say that we <u>egest</u> it. Faeces are mainly fibre, water and bacteria.

You should now have an understanding of these key ideas. You should also be able to spell and to know the meaning of the key words. The **key words** are in **bold** on this page.

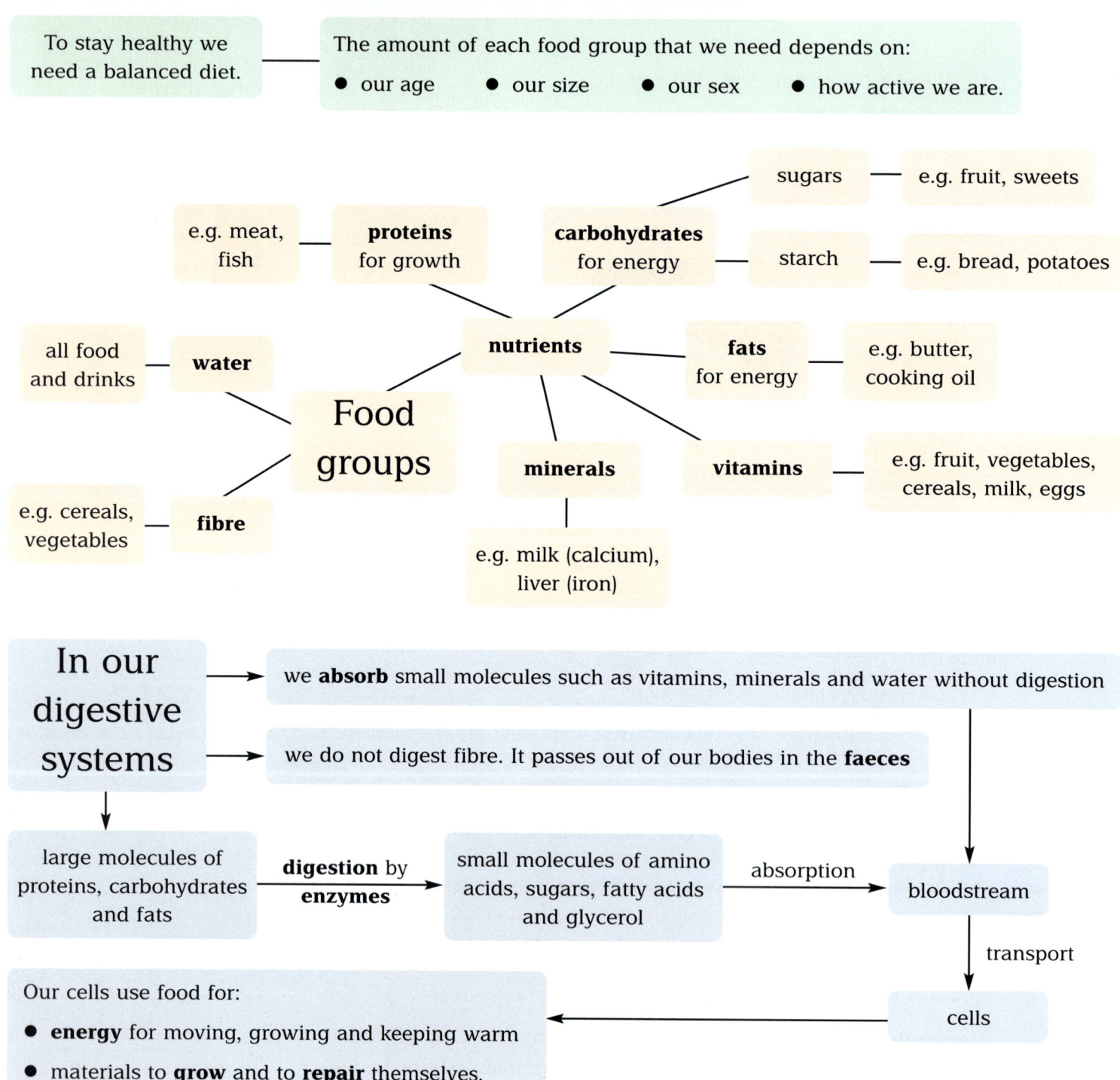

To stay healthy we need a balanced diet.

The amount of each food group that we need depends on:
- our age
- our size
- our sex
- how active we are.

Food groups

- e.g. meat, fish — **proteins** for growth
- all food and drinks — **water**
- e.g. cereals, vegetables — **fibre**

nutrients

carbohydrates for energy
- sugars — e.g. fruit, sweets
- starch — e.g. bread, potatoes

fats for energy — e.g. butter, cooking oil

vitamins — e.g. fruit, vegetables, cereals, milk, eggs

minerals — e.g. milk (calcium), liver (iron)

In our digestive systems

→ we **absorb** small molecules such as vitamins, minerals and water without digestion

→ we do not digest fibre. It passes out of our bodies in the **faeces**

large molecules of proteins, carbohydrates and fats → **digestion** by **enzymes** → small molecules of amino acids, sugars, fatty acids and glycerol → absorption → bloodstream → transport → cells

Our cells use food for:
- **energy** for moving, growing and keeping warm
- materials to **grow** and to **repair** themselves.

Respiration

To stay alive we must get energy from our food. In this unit, we shall be learning about food that our cells use as a source of energy, and how cells release the energy stored in this food.

KEY WORDS
glucose
amino acids
blood
moving
growing
keeping warm
energy
respiration
oxygen
aerobic
carbon dioxide
water
breathing
diffusion
heart
arteries
capillaries
veins
lungs
gas exchange

8B.1 How cells use food

You absorb digested foods such as **glucose** and **amino acids** into your **blood**. Your blood transports them to all the cells of your body. All cells use food as a source of materials to grow, and for energy. You use energy for **moving**, **growing** and **keeping warm**.

You need glucose for energy, and amino acids to make proteins for new cells.

your body needs new cells to repair damage

skin cells have to be replaced as they get worn away

Gail's muscle cells use up more glucose to release extra energy when she runs.

1 Write down <u>one</u> food that provides energy for cells.

2 Write down <u>two</u> reasons why you need to make new cells.

3 Write down <u>one</u> time when your muscle cells need more glucose than normal.

4 People doing sports often use high energy drinks. A slice of bread contains just as much energy as 200 cm³ of the drink.

Why is the energy in the drink more useful than the energy in the bread <u>during</u> exercise?

This is a high-energy drink. It contains a lot of glucose. High energy drinks are advertised for sports players.

How cells release energy from glucose

Glucose supplies your cells with **energy**. It is a type of sugar.

You could say that glucose is your body's fuel. In a machine like a car, fuel is burnt in oxygen to release the energy.

Your cells also use oxygen to release energy from their fuel. But the glucose doesn't burn. Chemical reactions in your cells break down the glucose and release the energy a bit at a time. We call this **respiration**. Respiration takes place in every cell in your body. Your cells normally use **oxygen** from the air when they respire. So we call this **aerobic** respiration.

fuel

oxygen

ENERGY

Releasing energy from fuels

This is the word equation for respiration:

glucose + oxygen → **carbon dioxide** + **water** + energy

The word equation doesn't show that the glucose breaks down a bit at a time. It just shows the reactants and the products.

5 What is respiration?

6 Write down:

    a <u>two</u> things that cells need for respiration;

    b how these things get to your cells;

    c <u>two</u> waste substances that are produced in respiration.

8B.2 How oxygen reaches your tissues

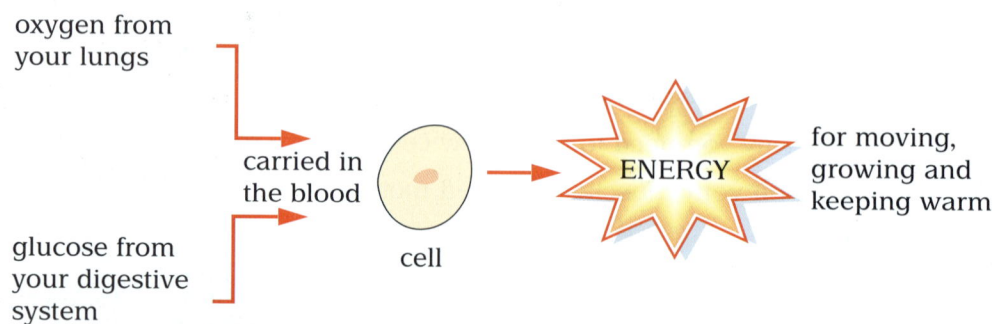

oxygen from your lungs

glucose from your digestive system

carried in the blood

cell

ENERGY

for moving, growing and keeping warm

1 Why do we take oxygen into our bodies?

All your cells use oxygen to release energy from glucose. Air contains oxygen. You take air in and out of your lungs. This is called **breathing**. Some of the oxygen from the air in your lungs passes into your blood. Your blood then carries the oxygen to your tissues.

Oxygen and glucose pass out of the blood into the tissue fluid (a liquid that surrounds all cells). Then they pass into the cells. Cells use the oxygen to release energy from the glucose. The more energy your cells use, the more oxygen and glucose they need.

 **2** Draw a flow diagram to show how oxygen gets from the air to the cells in the body.

 **3** Why do all the tissues in the body need blood vessels near them?

 **4** Some parts of the body have a better blood supply than others. Explain why the following organs need to have plenty of blood vessels:

a the muscles;

b the lining of the uterus of a pregnant woman.

More about exchanges

Substances are passing in and out of your blood and your cells all the time. In *Spectrum Chemistry* Unit 7G, you learnt how substances <u>diffuse</u> from where they are in <u>high</u> concentrations to where they are in <u>low</u> concentrations. Substances pass in and out of cells by **diffusion**.

In your tissues, oxygen and glucose diffuse into your cells; carbon dioxide diffuses out of your cells into the tissue fluid.

In your lungs, oxygen goes into your blood and carbon dioxide leaves it and goes into the air in the lungs. When you breathe out, you get rid of this extra carbon dioxide.

 **5** Write down <u>two</u> materials that diffuse:

a from your blood to your cells;

b from your cells into your blood.

6 Why do you need tissue fluid?

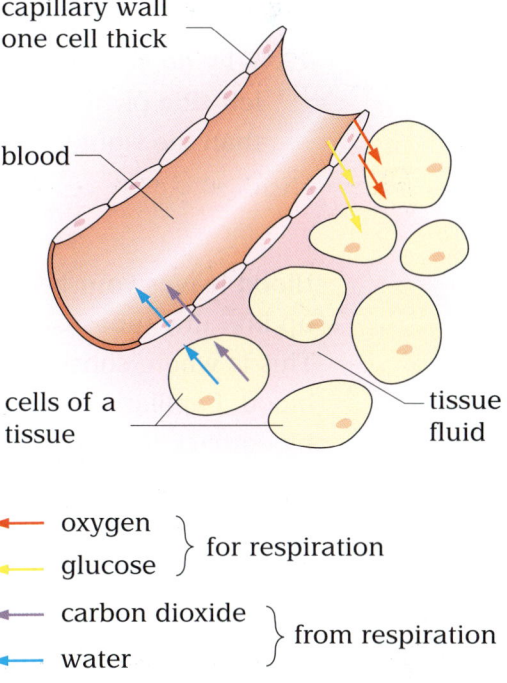

Exchange of materials between cells and the blood

capillary wall one cell thick

blood

cells of a tissue

tissue fluid

→ oxygen } for respiration
→ glucose

→ carbon dioxide } from respiration
→ water

Your heart

Your **heart** is a muscular pump that squeezes blood to move it around your body. It is divided down the middle by a wall of muscle. The left side pumps blood to the whole body. At the same time, the right side pumps blood to the lungs. Because of this, we say that it acts like a double pump.

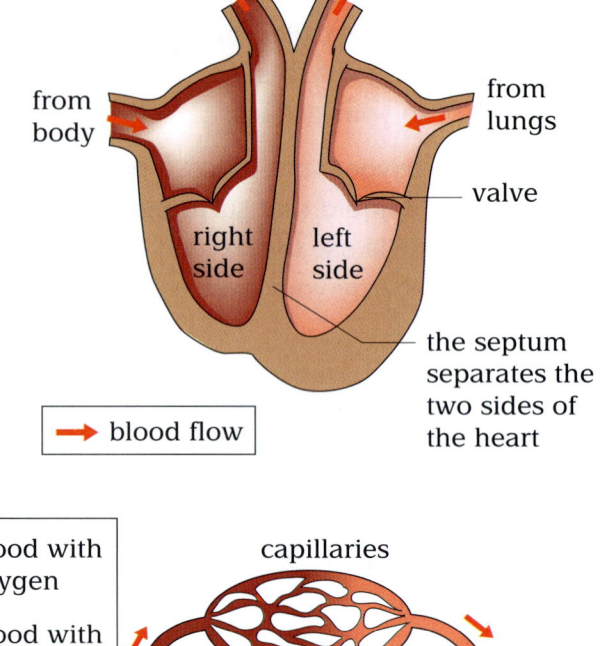

The human heart

to lungs to body

from body

from lungs

valve

right side left side

the septum separates the two sides of the heart

→ blood flow

7 What is your heart mainly made from?

8 Why does your heart need lots of glucose and oxygen?

The right side of your heart pumps blood to the lungs to pick up oxygen. The blood then goes back to the left side of your heart. The left side pumps blood rich in oxygen to the rest of your body.

9 Look at the diagram. Write down, in order, the parts that the blood goes through. Start and finish at the right side of the heart.

10 How many times does blood pass through your heart each time it does a full circuit of your body?

11 Why do you think the wall of the left side of the heart is thicker than the right side?

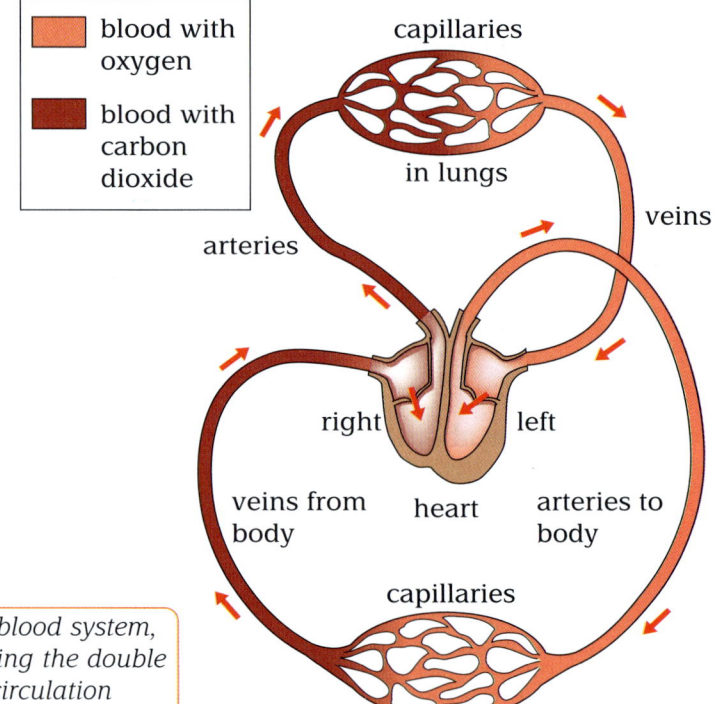

blood with oxygen

blood with carbon dioxide

capillaries in lungs

capillaries

veins

arteries

right left

veins from body heart arteries to body

The blood system, showing the double circulation

Blood leaves your heart in **arteries**. Arteries split up into tiny tubes called **capillaries** in your tissues. This is where substances go in and out of your blood. Capillaries join up to form **veins** that take blood back to your heart.

12 Write down <u>one</u> reason why substances pass in and out of capillaries easily.

13 There are blood capillaries close to all the cells in all your organs, including your lungs. Why is this?

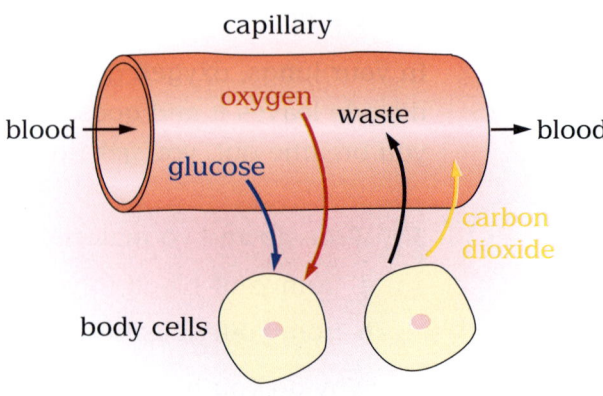

capillary

blood → oxygen waste → blood

glucose carbon dioxide

body cells

No cell is far from a capillary.
Capillary walls are only one wall thick.

Exchanging substances at the capillaries

The story of blood circulation

In Ancient Greek and Roman times, people thought that blood was one of four liquids that made up the body, and that the heart was where our emotions came from. They knew that blood moved out of the heart in blood vessels, but they thought the blood moved back and forth like the tides in the sea. They also believed that the body used up blood and that fresh blood was made from food, drink and air.

From Ancient times up to the Middle Ages, some of the knowledge of the body and how it worked was based on dissection – cutting up bodies to examine the parts. People didn't know that the heart was a pump or that blood was used for transport.

In the 17th century, scientists were trying to find things out by doing experiments. William Harvey was a British scientist who discovered that blood circulates around the body.
He observed the hearts of many different types of animals.
He compared the working of hearts and pumps. He also took measurements of the amount of blood leaving the heart.

William Harvey is often credited with the discovery of circulation. He showed that blood flows from the heart in arteries and back to the heart in veins.

 **14** How was the way that Harvey investigated the heart different from what was done in Ancient Greece and Rome?

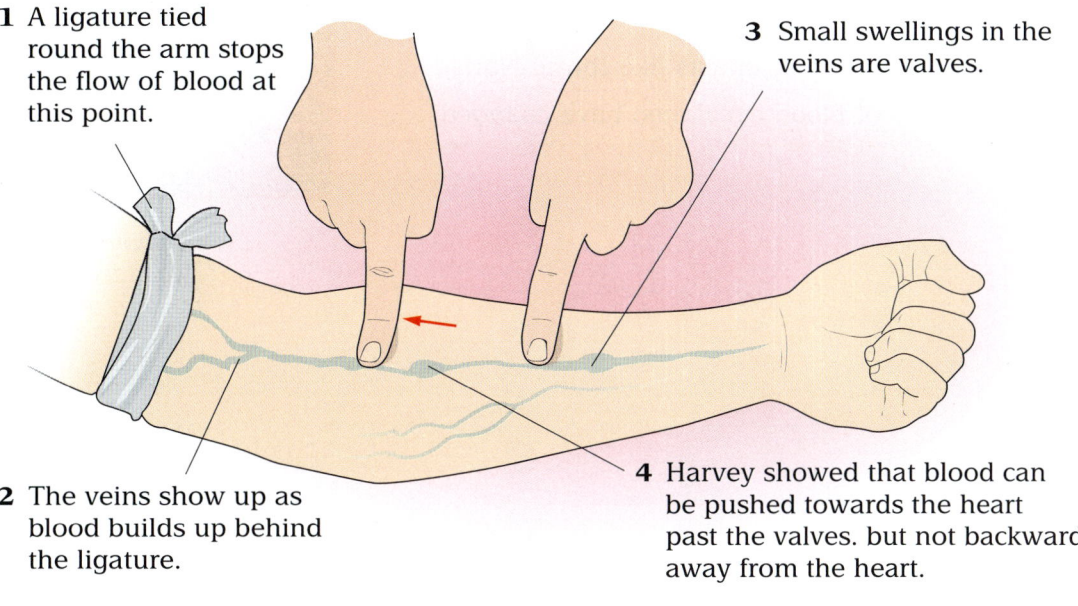

1 A ligature tied round the arm stops the flow of blood at this point.

2 The veins show up as blood builds up behind the ligature.

3 Small swellings in the veins are valves.

4 Harvey showed that blood can be pushed towards the heart past the valves. but not backwards away from the heart.

Harvey's experiment showed that blood circulates round the body in one direction.

Although Harvey worked out how blood moves around the body, he was not able to see the tiny blood vessels that link the arteries and veins together. We call them capillaries. They were discovered some years later by an Italian scientist called Marcello Malpighi. Capillaries are about 0.01 mm wide.

15 Why could Harvey not identify capillaries?

16 What technology was needed before capillaries could be discovered?

17 Draw a simple diagram to show what Harvey and Malpighi found.

18 What have modern scientists learnt from Harvey about studying the human body?

19 A lot more people were involved in the story of blood circulation than just Harvey and Malpighi.

    a Find out about the contribution made by one of the following to the story of blood circulation:

      ● The Chinese

      ● The Ancient Greeks (including scientists like Galen and Erasistratus)

      ● Islamic science (including scientists like Ibn-al-Nafis).

    b Explain how our ideas of blood circulation have changed.

Marcello Malpighi found the capillary connection between arteries and veins that completes the circulation.

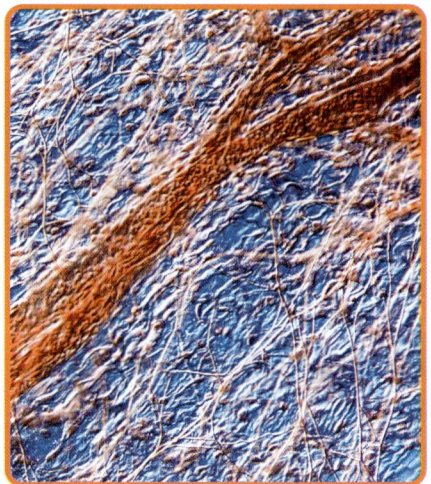

This photo of capillaries was taken using a modern microscope.

8B.3 What happens to oxygen when it reaches the cells

Aerobic respiration is a chemical reaction.
It happens in every cell.

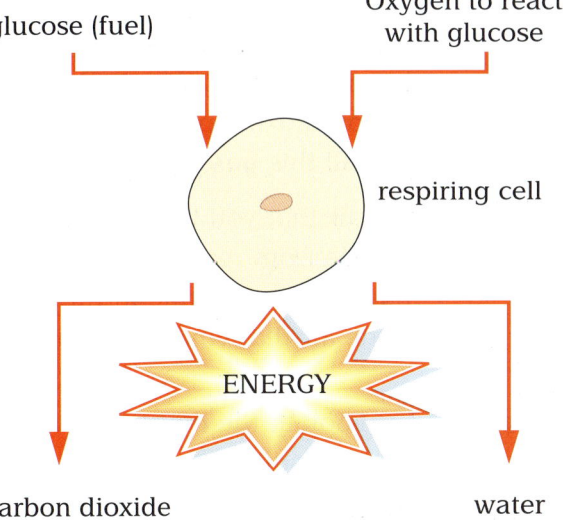

glucose (fuel)

Oxygen to react
with glucose

respiring cell

ENERGY

carbon dioxide

water

1 Write down the word equation for respiration to remind yourself of what happens.

2 How do you think the amount of energy available is affected if there isn't enough:

a glucose?

b oxygen?

An aerobics exercise class

3 Look at the photograph. Are the people using more or less energy in the aerobics class than when they are walking along the street? Explain your answer.

4 Why do you think this exercise class is called 'aerobics'?

Sometimes there isn't enough oxygen in the air

This climber is working at 4500 m above sea level. At high altitudes like this the air molecules are more spread out. The climber is taking in less oxygen than normal with each breath. So his blood cannot supply his cells with all the oxygen they need.

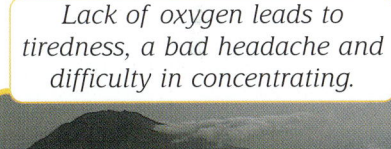

Lack of oxygen leads to tiredness, a bad headache and difficulty in concentrating.

5 What are the symptoms of altitude sickness?

6 The climber's cells are not getting enough oxygen. Explain why this makes him feel tired.

At high altitudes, the air in a passenger aeroplane is kept pressurised. This means that the amount of oxygen in the air is similar to that near the ground.

7 If the amount of oxygen in the air drops slightly, pilots notice that their judgement and ability to concentrate is not as good. Why do you think this is?

8B.4 What happens in your lungs

You get the oxygen you need from the air. You breathe air in and out of your **lungs**. In your lungs, oxygen from the air diffuses into your blood. At the same time, waste carbon dioxide passes from your blood into the air. We call this **gas exchange**.

The air that you breathe out contains the waste carbon dioxide from respiration. So there is <u>less</u> oxygen and <u>more</u> carbon dioxide in the air that you breathe <u>out</u> than in the air that you breathe <u>in</u>.

1   Look at the diagram. Draw a flow chart to show the route air takes to get into your lungs.

2   What happens during gas exchange?

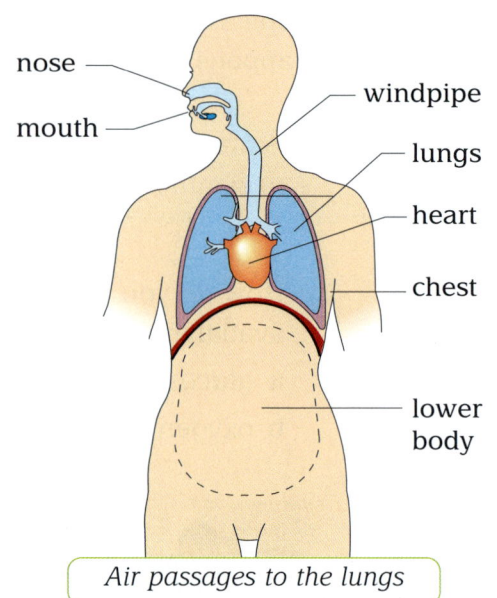

Air passages to the lungs

How gas exchange happens

Inside the lungs are millions of tiny air sacs called alveoli. Alveoli give the lungs a spongy feel and a very large surface area.

The walls of alveoli are only one cell thick. The very large number of capillaries surrounding the alveoli give the lungs their pink colour. Capillaries also have walls just one cell thick. So gases can pass quickly between the air in the alveoli and the blood.

Blood in the capillaries carries oxygen away continuously from the alveoli to supply the body cells. It also continuously brings waste carbon dioxide from the body cells to the alveoli. This prevents carbon dioxide building up in your blood and poisoning you. You breathe out the carbon dioxide.

3   Write down <u>two</u> reasons why it is important that gas exchange happens very quickly.

4   In what way are lungs arranged so that they have a large surface area?

5   Why does a large surface area help gas exchange happen quickly?

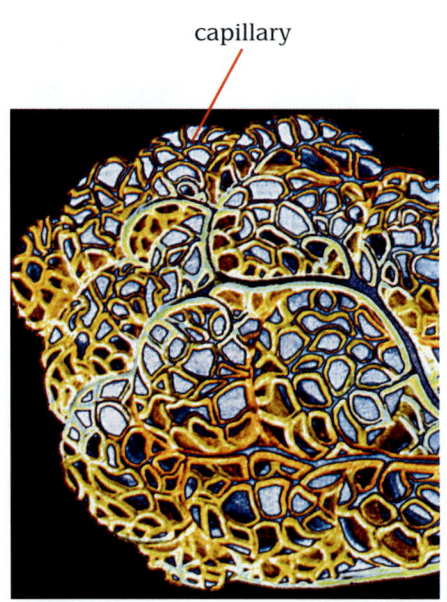

Alveoli in the lungs

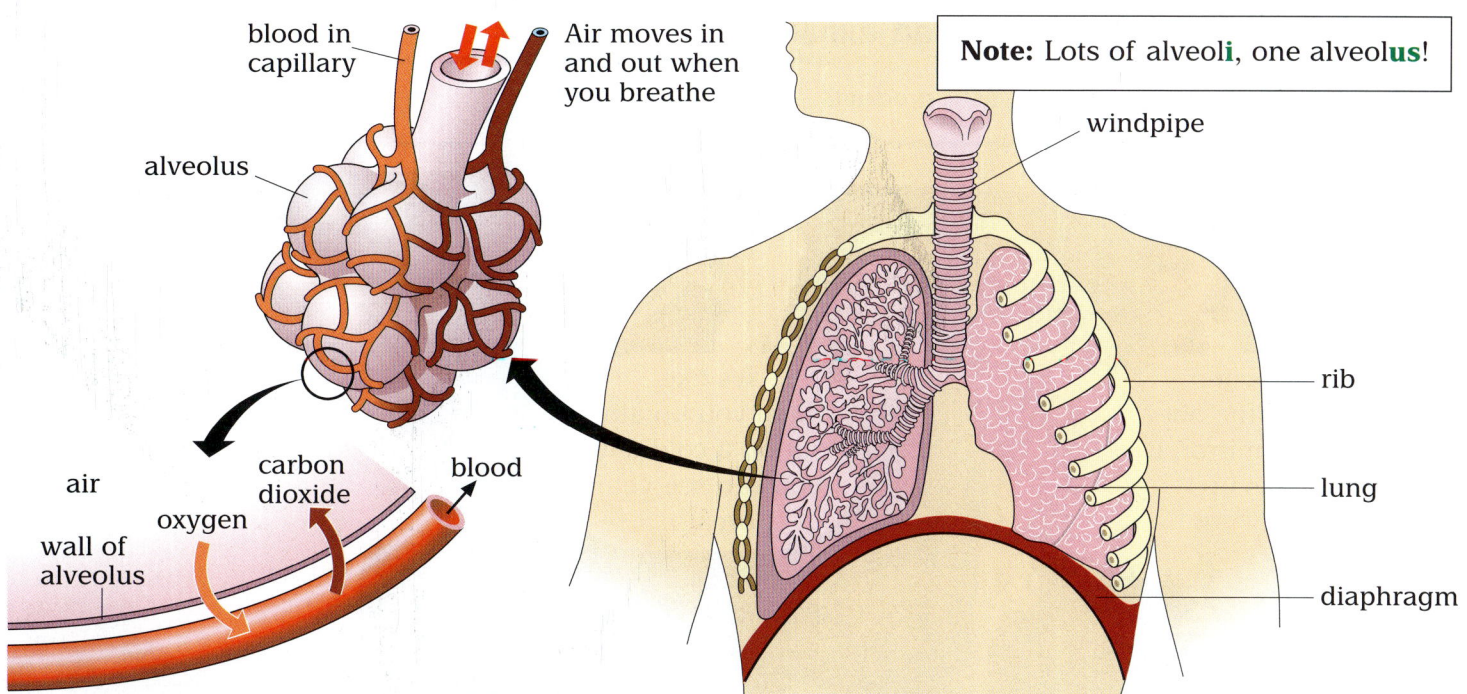

blood in capillary

Air moves in and out when you breathe

alveolus

Note: Lots of alveol**i**, one alveol**us**!

windpipe

rib

lung

diaphragm

air

wall of alveolus

oxygen

carbon dioxide

blood

6   Why do thin walls help gas exchange happen quickly?

7   Why can substances pass in and out of capillaries easily?

8   Why does having a lot of capillaries around the alveoli help gas exchange?

Smoking affects gas exchange

Smokers often cough because tobacco smoke irritates their breathing system. Coughing damages alveoli. The more they are damaged, the smaller the surface area of the lungs. This makes gas exchange more difficult.

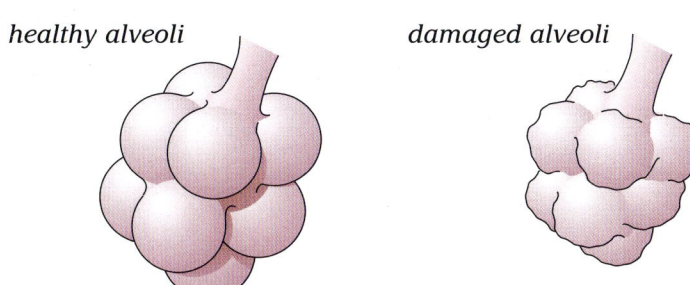

healthy alveoli   *damaged alveoli*

9   How does the loss of alveoli affect the rate of gas exchange? Explain your answer.

10   Describe <u>one</u> feature of alveoli that makes them suitable for gas exchange.

8B.5 Comparing inhaled and exhaled air

Respiration makes waste products.

Look, when you breathe out onto this mirror, it steams up.

It's like when you breathe out on a cold day, you can see your breath.

1   What is the liquid on the mirror?

2   Where does it come from?

3   Why does water vapour show up in exhaled air on a cold day?

All cells make waste products when they respire. The waste products of aerobic respiration are carbon dioxide and water. Carbon dioxide is poisonous so you get rid of it in the air you exhale (breathe out).

Comparing the amounts of carbon dioxide in inhaled and exhaled air

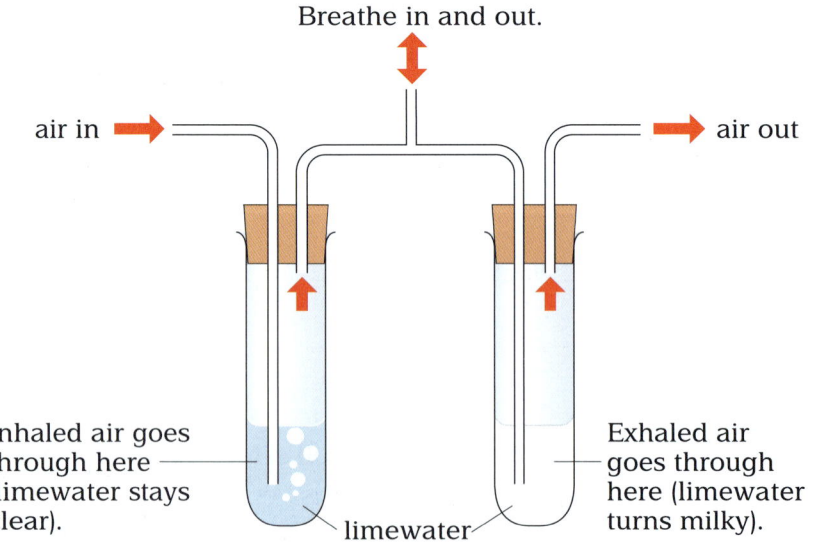

Breathe in and out.

air in ➡

air out ➡

Inhaled air goes through here (limewater stays clear).

Exhaled air goes through here (limewater turns milky).

limewater

4   What are the two waste products from aerobic respiration?

Peter did an experiment to compare the amounts of gases in air breathed in and out. Look at his results.

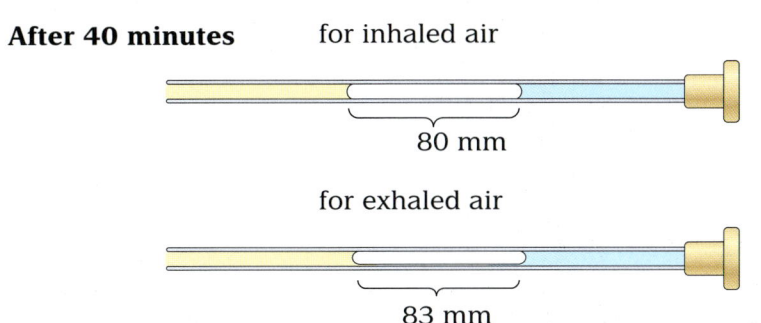

At the start

alkaline pyrogallate (absorbs oxygen)

original volume of air minus CO_2

screw for drawing up liquid

100 mm

After 40 minutes

for inhaled air

80 mm

for exhaled air

83 mm

5 **a** Which contains more oxygen – inhaled or exhaled air?

b Explain why this is.

Gas	Air breathed in (%)	Air breathed out (%)
Oxygen	21	17
Carbon dioxide	0.03	4
Nitrogen	79	79
Water vapour	Varies	Saturated

6 Which gas is more abundant in exhaled air than inhaled air?

7 Where was this extra gas made?

This athlete is measuring the gases in his exhaled air.

8 The amount of water vapour in inhaled air varies. Why is this?

9 The runner in the photograph is making more carbon dioxide than he does when he is asleep. Explain why that is.

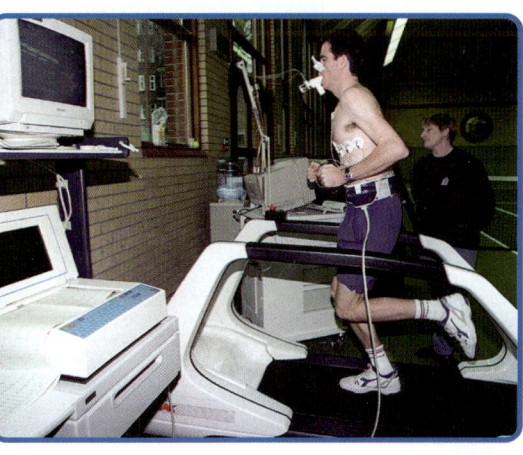

8B.6 Other living things respire too

The cells of <u>all</u> living things need to release energy to carry out their life processes. Most of them use oxygen and produce carbon dioxide. Carbon dioxide production is a good way of finding out if respiration is happening.

When you breathe in and out through limewater, you find that the air you breathe out contains a lot more carbon dioxide than the air you breathe in. But you can't ask a seed or a woodlouse to breathe in and out! The diagrams show what you can do.

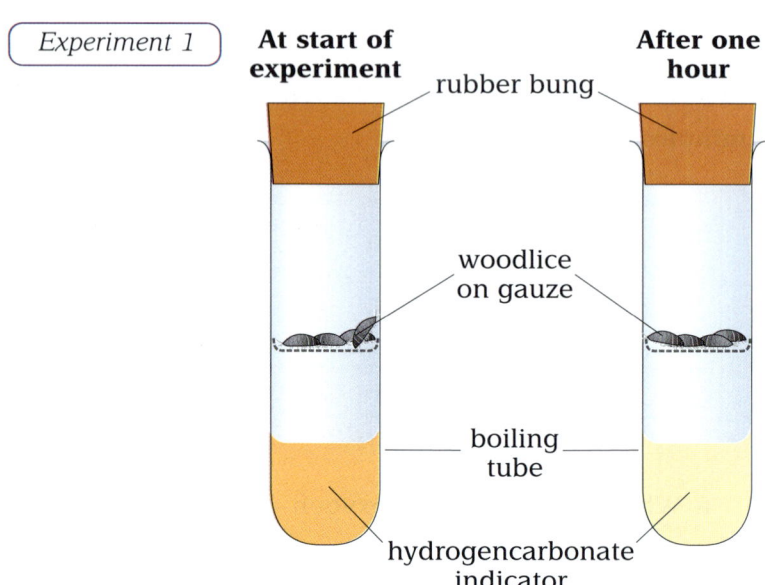

Experiment 1

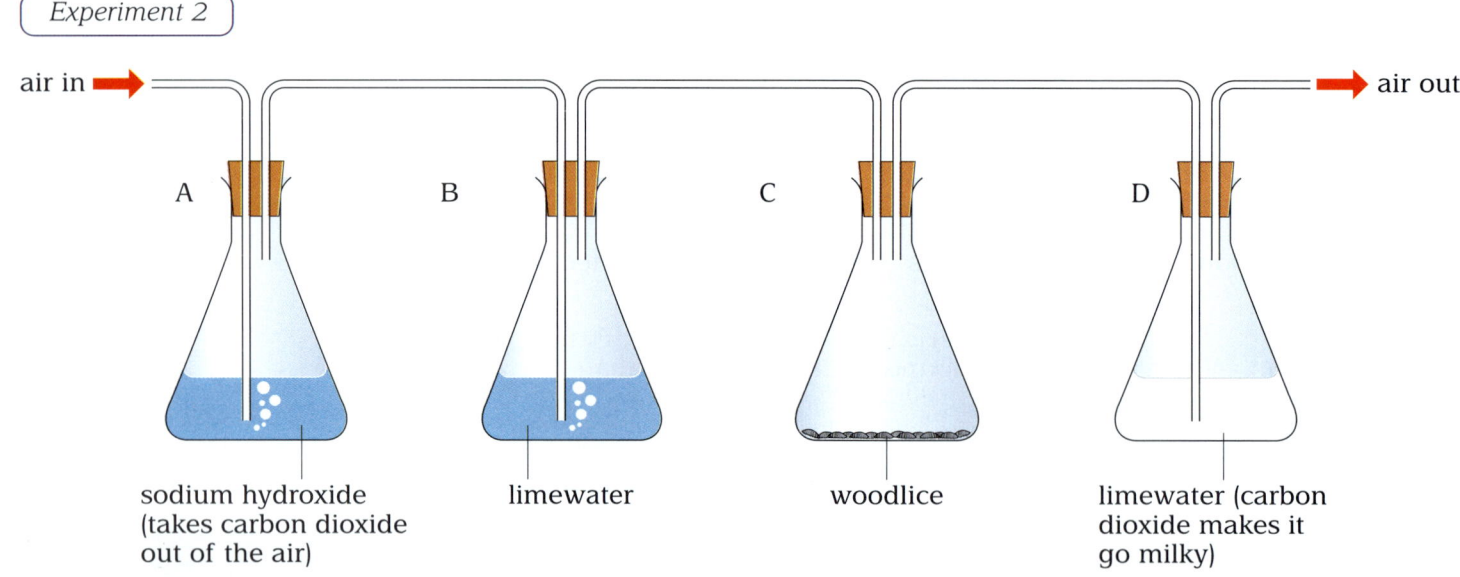

Experiment 2

air in ➡

air out ➡

A — sodium hydroxide (takes carbon dioxide out of the air)

B — limewater

C — woodlice

D — limewater (carbon dioxide makes it go milky)

1 **a** Write down <u>two</u> substances that you can use to detect carbon dioxide.

b Describe the change to each substance when carbon dioxide is present.

2 In experiment 2, the woodlice breathe in air that has no carbon dioxide in it. How do you know?

3 The change in the limewater shows that there is carbon dioxide in the air going through flask D.
Where did it come from?

In experiment 2, the first flask of limewater (flask B) shows that the air reaching the woodlice has no carbon dioxide in it.
We need flask B, to show that the carbon dioxide in flask D can have come only from the woodlice and anything living in or on them.

In experiment 1, we use one tube with and one tube without woodlice. Then we can say that the woodlice cause any change. We call the second tube the <u>control</u>. Without the control, we can argue that something else might have caused the change. Carbon dioxide could have leaked into the tube. Light or temperature differences, or anything else, could have caused the change.

4 Describe the results of experiment 1.

5 What can you conclude from experiment 1?

6 Katie did an experiment like this with maggots. But she didn't use a second tube. The indicator changed colour. Her teacher told her that she couldn't conclude that maggots produced carbon dioxide. Why is this?

When you design experiments using living things, remember to:

- use more than one living thing, because living things vary;

- use a control, then any change can be caused only by the variable that you are testing – it can't be caused by light, or temperature, or any other variable;

- vary only one thing at a time.

Remember that all living things respire.

   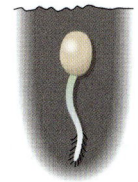 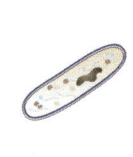  

lion   dandelion   oak tree   germinating   bacterial   killer whale   yeast cell
                                     seed   cell

You should now understand the key words and ideas shown below.

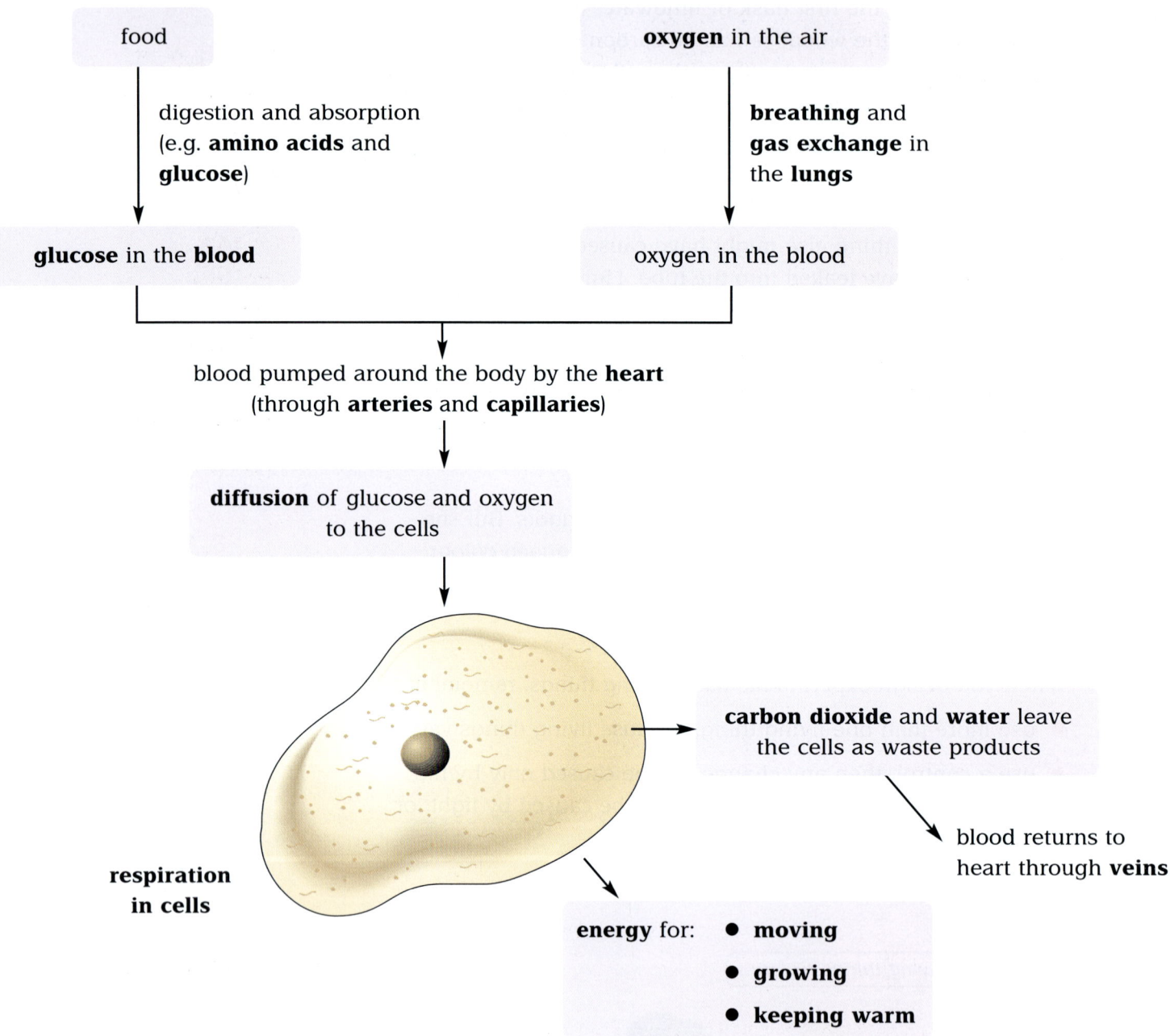

food

oxygen in the air

digestion and absorption (e.g. **amino acids** and **glucose**)

breathing and **gas exchange** in the **lungs**

glucose in the **blood**

oxygen in the blood

blood pumped around the body by the **heart** (through **arteries** and **capillaries**)

diffusion of glucose and oxygen to the cells

carbon dioxide and **water** leave the cells as waste products

blood returns to heart through **veins**

respiration in cells

energy for:
- **moving**
- **growing**
- **keeping warm**

The word equation for **aerobic** respiration is:

glucose + oxygen → carbon dioxide + water + energy

Microbes and disease

In this unit we shall be learning about some micro-organisms and how we grow them to make useful products. We shall also find out about micro-organisms that cause disease and how our bodies fight disease.

KEY WORDS
micro-organisms
viruses
bacteria
fungi
disease
infection
immunity
antibiotic
vaccine
immunisation

8C.1 Micro-organisms and how to grow them

Types of micro-organisms

Some living things are so small that we can only see them through a microscope; we call these tiny living things **micro-organisms** or microbes. They include **viruses** and **bacteria** and some **fungi**.

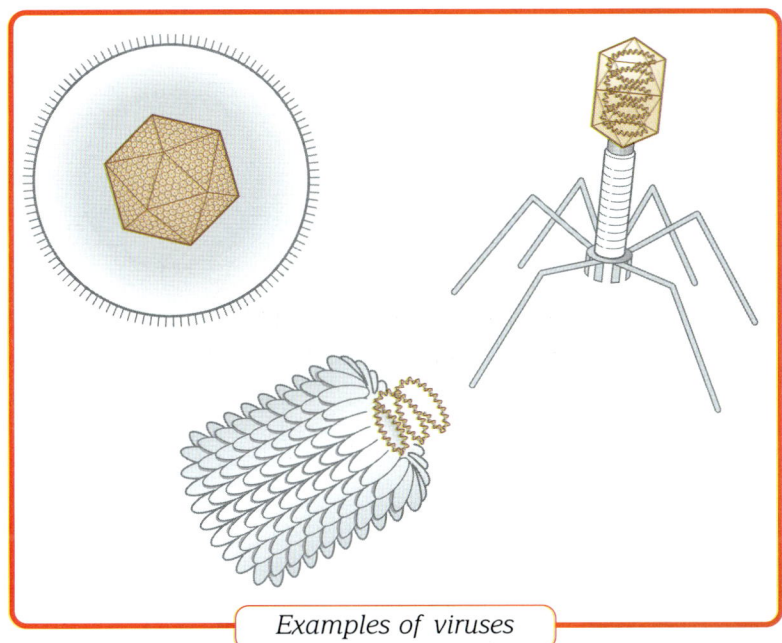

Examples of viruses

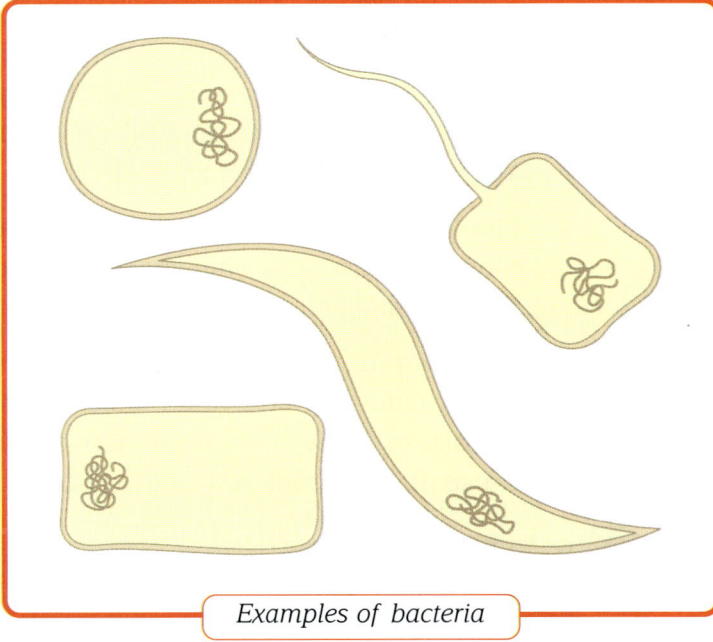

Examples of bacteria

There are lots of different types of micro-organisms. Although they are very small, they have a huge effect on our lives.
Micro-organisms are an essential part of life on Earth and do many vital jobs. They also cause many problems, including **disease**.

1   Write down <u>three</u> different types of micro-organism.

Here are two micro-organism fact files:

FACT FILE: Viruses

Average size:	0.0001 mm
Structure:	A strand of genetic material wrapped in a protein coat.
Found:	Viruses can reproduce only inside living cells.
Uses:	To kill pest animals.
Diseases:	Common cold, influenza (flu), measles, AIDS, yellow fever, rabies. Viruses cause disease in animals, plants and even other micro-organisms.

FACT FILE: Bacteria

Average size:	0.001 mm
Structure:	Bacteria are single-celled with a strong cell wall. Their genetic material is not in a nucleus.
Found:	Most bacteria live in water, soil and decaying matter.
Uses:	To make yoghurt, cheese and vinegar.
Diseases:	Typhoid, cholera, food poisoning.

2 How many times bigger is the average bacterium than the average virus?

Some fungi are micro-organisms, for example yeast and mould. Yeast is made of single cells that reproduce by budding off new cells. Yeast cells are larger than viruses.

Moulds are fine threads that grow on rotting food; they also give blue cheese its colour and flavour.

Fungi can be helpful; we use yeast to make bread, wine and beer and mould to make antibiotics. They can also be harmful; fungi cause athlete's foot and ringworm.

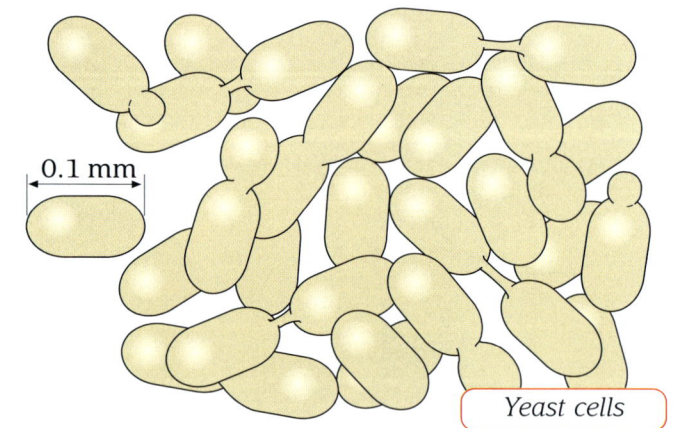

0.1 mm

Yeast cells

3 Which type of micro-organism is the smallest?

4 Which <u>two</u> types of micro-organism make food rot?

5 Use the headings of the fact files to make a table of information about viruses, bacteria and fungi.

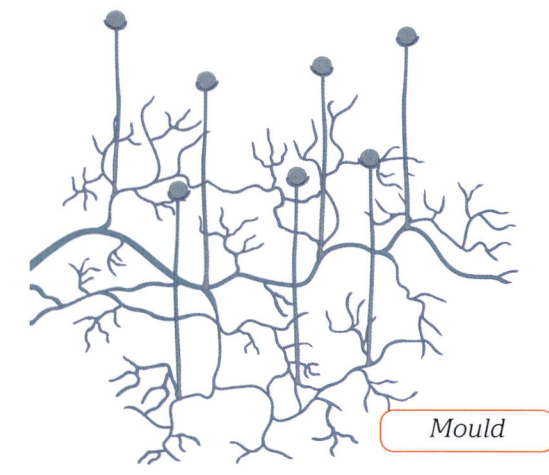

Mould

How to grow micro-organisms

Yeast is the most commonly grown micro-organism in the world. We use it to make beer, wine and bread. Yeast is a living thing, so it needs warmth and food to grow.

Just like all living things, yeast breaks down food to get energy; we call this process respiration. If it uses oxygen, we call it aerobic respiration. But yeast can also respire without oxygen. When it does this it makes alcohol. In both cases, it produces carbon dioxide.

6 Write down <u>three</u> things that both yeast and humans do.

7 The yeast cells in this vat respire aerobically. How can you tell this from the design of the vat?

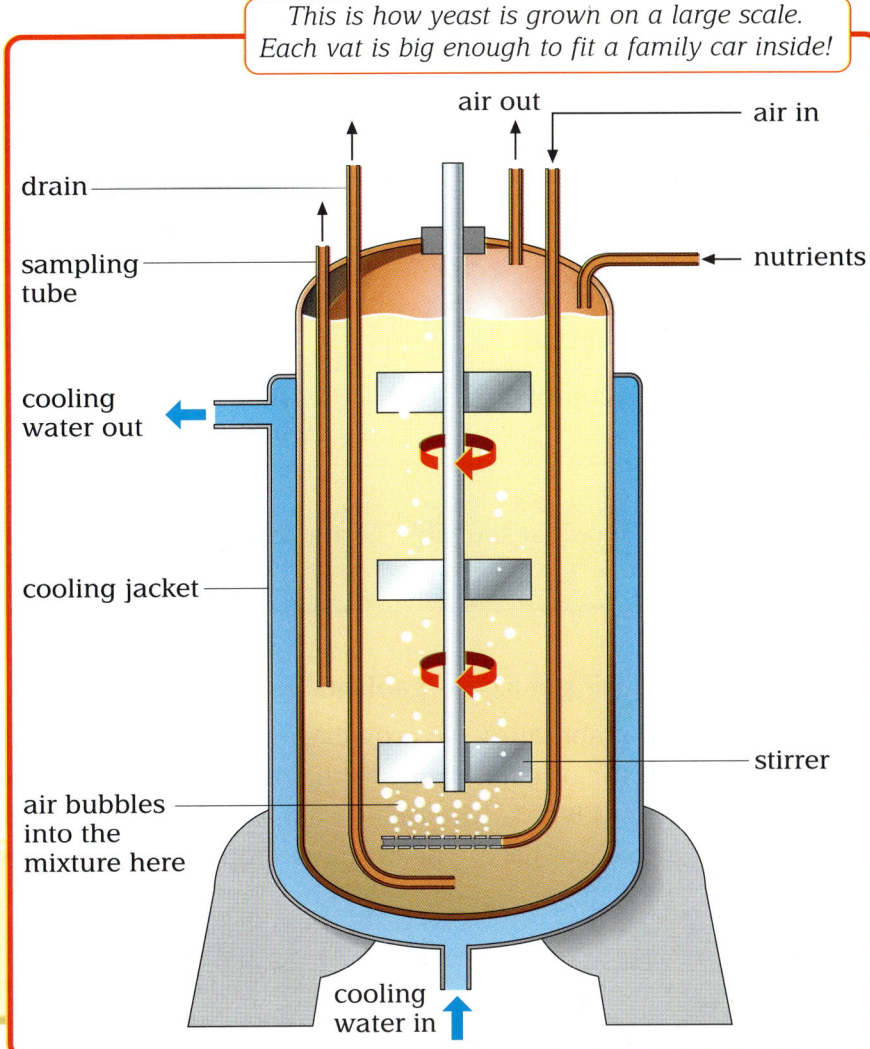

This is how yeast is grown on a large scale. Each vat is big enough to fit a family car inside!

air out — air in

drain

sampling tube

nutrients

cooling water out

cooling jacket

stirrer

air bubbles into the mixture here

cooling water in

Bread dough is made of yeast, flour, water and a little sugar and salt. Laura did an experiment to see if sugar helps dough rise. She measured the amount of dough in each measuring cylinder after 30 minutes.

8 How does the amount of sugar affect how high the dough rises?

9 What is the gas that makes dough rise?

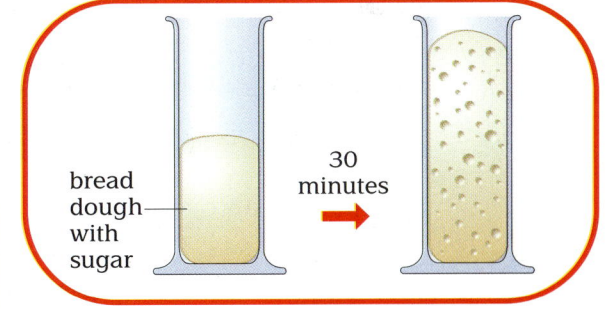

bread dough with sugar

30 minutes

10 When making bread, you leave the dough to rise for several hours. Then you bake it for 30 minutes at 200°C. What do you think happens to yeast during baking? (Remember: yeast is a living thing.)

Amount of sugar in the dough (g)	Volume of the dough after 30 minutes (cm³)
0	40
5	52
10	66
15	74
20	80

Yeast is just one type of fungus. We can also grow other fungi in large vats to make useful products.

Product made by fungi	Use
Penicillin	An antibiotic to treat some diseases
Citric acid	Added to make soft drinks taste tangy
Cortisone	To treat arthritis
Pectinase	Added to fruit juice to make it clear
Mycoprotein	A substitute for meat that is suitable for vegetarians (for example, Quorn)

 **11** Look at the table. Write down <u>two</u> medicines made by fungi.

Growing micro-organisms in a laboratory

In a laboratory we grow bacteria in Petri dishes – small plastic or glass dishes with lids. Food for the bacteria is mixed with a jelly called agar, which is made from seaweed. Each type of micro-organism needs its own particular balance of minerals and food to grow.

 **12** Bacteria are so small that you can only see them with a microscope. Why can you see bacteria growing on agar?

 **13** Why do you think the dishes used to grow bacteria are also called agar plates?

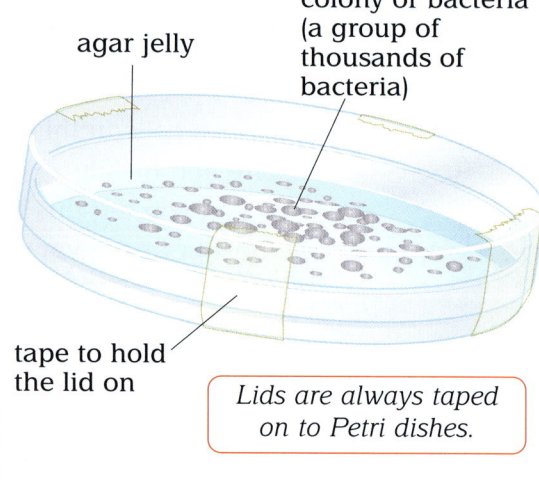

agar jelly

colony of bacteria (a group of thousands of bacteria)

tape to hold the lid on

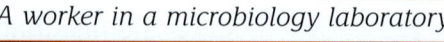
Lids are always taped on to Petri dishes.

We must clean everything we use to grow micro-organisms before it is used. Petri dishes and agar are heated to over 100 °C to sterilise them. It is important to keep all benches and equipment clean.

 **14** Look at the photograph. Write down <u>three</u> things the worker is wearing to prevent any unwanted micro-organisms from contaminating his work.

 **15** What do you think would happen if laboratory workers did not sterilise the equipment properly?

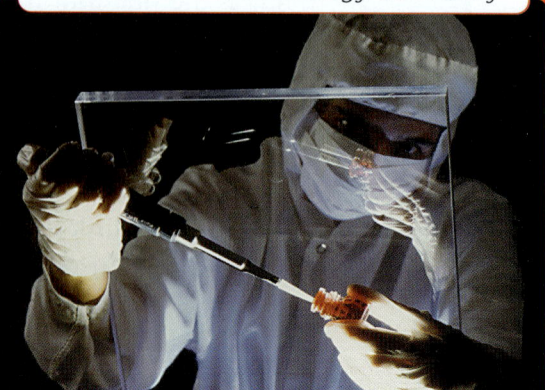
A worker in a microbiology laboratory

8C.2 Micro-organisms and disease

Illnesses caused by micro-organisms are called **infections**, or infectious diseases. They can be passed from one person to another. Some are spread in contaminated food and water.

Diseases can spread:

- by droplet, e.g. tuberculosis (TB) bacteria and chickenpox virus;

- by animals, e.g. malaria and yellow fever by mosquitoes, and rabies by mammals;

- in food, e.g. *Salmonella* bacteria from flies, dirty hands, or dirty knives and dishes;

- in contaminated water, e.g. typhoid bacteria.

1   How can a child at a birthday party give all the other children chickenpox?

2   Why is it important that you wash your hands before you prepare food?

3   How could you stop food poisoning being spread by flies?

4   Write down <u>one</u> way of making water safe to drink.

How human-to-human contact spreads diseases

Athlete's foot is a fungal disease spread by touch. Some diseases such as AIDS are spread when people have unprotected sex.
A pregnant woman can pass on a disease to her unborn child.
A baby can also catch a disease from his or her mother through breast milk.

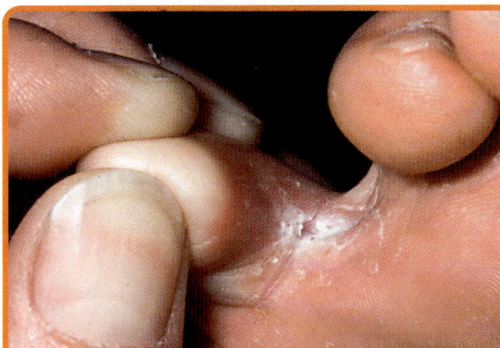

Athlete's foot

5   Write down <u>two</u> ways that a mother can pass on a disease to her baby.

How to stop an epidemic

An epidemic is an outbreak of a disease affecting a large number of people in a population.

In 1854 there was a terrible epidemic of a disease called cholera in London. In just a few weeks, thousands of people caught cholera in a small area of London called Soho. Over 600 people died. Cholera was a common disease in polluted city areas, so people thought that you caught cholera from bad air.

This is how quickly the disease spread in the first three days of the epidemic:

Date in 1854	Number of new cases of cholera	Number of deaths from cholera
31st August	56	3
1st September	143	70
2nd September	116	127

6 How many people died from cholera in the first three days of the epidemic?

Many more people would have died had it not been for a doctor called John Snow. He was convinced that cholera was caused by infected water rather than bad air. He heard about the deaths in Soho and went to investigate.

At that time few people had running water in their houses and mostly had to rely on public street pumps for all their water. John Snow suspected that people became infected when they drank the water from the Broad Street pump in Soho.

Key
- pump
- cholera death
- workhouse
- brewery

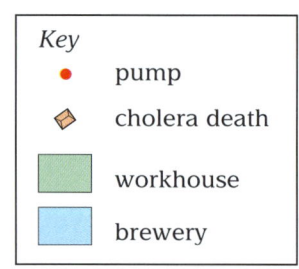

This was John Snow's evidence:

- Most people who died lived very near to the Broad Street pump.

- Only 5 out of 500 people died at the workhouse round the corner from the pump. The workhouse had its own well.

- No one in the local brewery died. All the workers drank beer instead of water.

- Two ladies who lived 8 km away died of cholera. They had a bottle of water brought to them from the Broad Street pump because they liked the taste.

By 7th September three-quarters of the people living in Soho had fled the area. Many of those who remained were ill and 28 more died that day. John Snow put his evidence to the Parish Board and they agreed to remove the handle of the pump the next day. People could no longer drink the water. The number of new cases began to fall.

7 Imagine you are the person who took the handle off the pump. A crowd of local people complain to you that now they will have to walk 10 minutes to get drinking water. What do you say to them?

A few months later John Snow found the cause of the epidemic.

- Water for the pump came from an underground well.

- Number 40 Broad Street had an underground cesspit for sewage.

- During August a baby at number 40 was ill with cholera and his mother washed his nappies in water that she then tipped into the cesspit.

- The cesspit wall was cracked and the sewage leaked out into the nearby well.

- This allowed the bacteria that cause cholera to reach the Broad Street pump.

8 John Snow could not see the bacteria that cause cholera. How could he be sure there were bacteria in the well of the Broad Street pump?

8C.3 Protecting ourselves against disease

Your body defends itself against micro-organisms in several ways.

1 Why can't micro-organisms normally get into your body through your skin?

2 In which part of your body are micro-organisms killed by acid?

3 Animals often lick their wounds. How does this help them to heal?

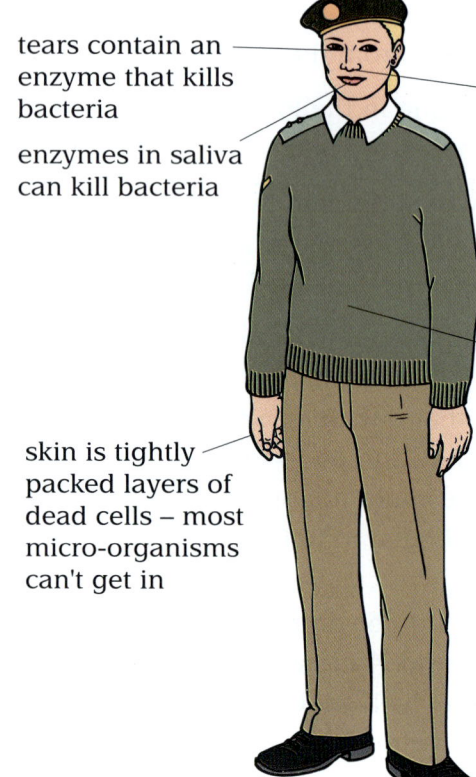

tears contain an enzyme that kills bacteria

enzymes in saliva can kill bacteria

hairs in your nostrils trap micro-organisms and mucus contains enzymes that can kill bacteria

most bacteria swallowed with food and drink are killed by acid in the stomach

skin is tightly packed layers of dead cells – most micro-organisms can't get in

But micro-organisms get past these defences!

Tuberculosis (TB) is a serious disease that destroys lung tissue. When someone has TB they have a bad cough and each time they cough they spray little droplets into the air. These droplets contain TB bacteria. If you are nearby, you can breathe them in. Sometimes bacteria get past the defences in your air passages and into your lungs.

4 Why are you less likely to catch TB if you breathe through your nose rather than through your mouth?

What happens when you catch a cold

Several different viruses cause colds. Most adults catch two or three colds a year; many children catch up to eight colds a year. When you have a cold and sneeze, you spray droplets of liquid into the air. Each droplet contains thousands of virus particles. When you first catch a cold, the virus multiplies very quickly; you start to feel ill, with a runny nose, sore throat and a cough. Then your body fights back against the invasion; cold viruses are destroyed and you start to feel better.

5 Why do you cover your nose and mouth when you sneeze?

6 Suggest <u>one</u> reason why children catch more colds than adults.

How your body destroys micro-organisms

Your blood contains red blood cells and white blood cells. There are two different types of white blood cells.

- One type of white blood cell engulfs (traps) micro-organisms and destroys them.

- Another type of white blood cell makes disease-fighting substances called antibodies. These can stop micro-organisms from causing disease.

Each antibody that you make is specific to fighting one type of micro-organism – an antibody won't work against any other type of micro-organism. Different micro-organisms need different antibodies. It takes time for your body to make these different antibodies, and you feel ill until you have made enough antibodies to destroy the micro-organisms.

Once you have had a disease, your white blood cells have learnt how to make the antibodies. They will be able to make the right ones much more quickly in future. If a second attack comes, your body can destroy the micro-organisms before they have time to make you ill. This means you are immune to the disease. You have **immunity**.

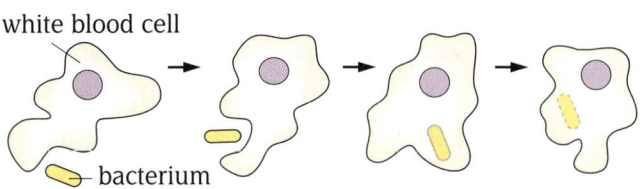

white blood cell

bacterium

The micro-organism is taken in to the white blood cell and destroyed.

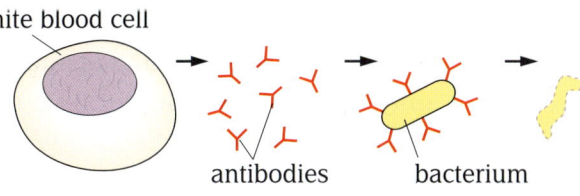

white blood cell

antibodies   bacterium

A white blood cell that produces antibodies.

7   Why don't you usually catch the same disease twice?

8   When you have had a cold you become immune to that particular virus. How is it that a few months later you can catch another cold?

9   Breast milk contains the mother's antibodies. How does this stop a breast-fed baby from catching some diseases?

Antibiotics

Antibiotics are substances made by one living thing that can kill another living thing. They were discovered by accident!

Mould is a type of fungus. For centuries, people knew that spreading mould on a wound or cut often helped it to heal. Scientists also noticed that mould could stop bacteria from growing, but they didn't realise how important this discovery was.

Mould often grows on rotten food. The mould on this orange is one species of Penicillium.

10 Would you put mouldy food on a cut to help it to heal? Explain your decision.

In 1928 some spores of mould landed by accident on a Petri dish of bacteria belonging to Alexander Fleming. He noticed that, where the mould grew, there were no bacteria. The mould had made a substance that stopped the bacteria growing. Since the mould was called *Penicillium*, Fleming named the substance penicillin.

 **11** What stopped bacteria from growing close to *Penicillium*?

In 1935, a team of Oxford scientists led by Howard Florey and Ernst Chain began to make and test penicillin. At first, they had only enough penicillin for tests on mice and a few patients. By 1942, during the Second World War, they could make large amounts. So penicillin was used to save sick and wounded soldiers.

without penicillin   with penicillin

12 Normally new drugs are tested and trialled for years before they are widely used. Why was penicillin used as soon as it could be made in large quantities?

13 Before penicillin was discovered, 1 in 3 people who caught pneumonia died. When penicillin was used, only 1 in 20 people died. If 300 people caught pneumonia, how many would probably die:

    a before penicillin?   **b** after penicillin?

14 Explain what the discovery of penicillin tells us about the way scientific knowledge can develop.

Penicillin was the first antibiotic discovered and its use has saved millions of lives. Since then, scientists have extracted other important antibiotics from different moulds and soil bacteria. These antibiotics can kill some of the bacteria that penicillin could not.

 **15** Mrs Sharples has flu (caused by a virus). She wants antibiotics to make her better. What would you tell her?

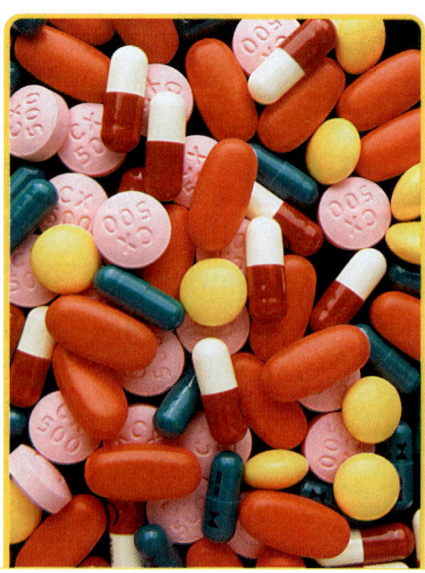

Different antibiotics treat different infections, but none of them has any effect on diseases caused by viruses.

Jabs

A jab is an injection; it contains a **vaccine** to make you immune to a particular disease. Your TB jab is just one of 11 injections you may have during your childhood. The **immunisation** for tuberculosis (TB) is called the BCG jab after two scientists who developed it: Calmette and Guérin.

A TB jab contains a weak version of TB bacteria.

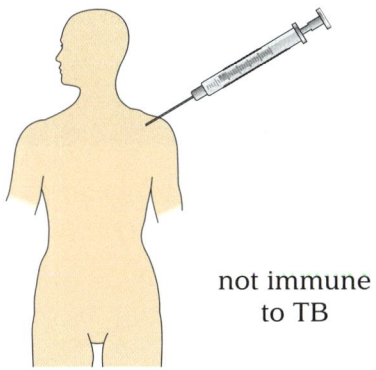

not immune to TB

16 Find out what vaccinations you have had, and when you had them.

How the TB jab works

The vaccine in a TB jab contains an extract of the bacteria that cause tuberculosis. The white blood cells in your body respond to the vaccine as if you've been infected with TB. They produce the correct antibodies to kill the bacteria that cause TB. Your arm may feel sore while this happens.

In future, your white blood cells will be able to make the right antibodies much more quickly. So if TB bacteria get into your body, you will make antibodies to destroy them and not become ill.

Before scientists developed the TB jab, the only way you could be immune to TB was by surviving the disease. A jab makes you immune without having the disease itself.

White blood cells make the right antibodies to kill TB bacteria.

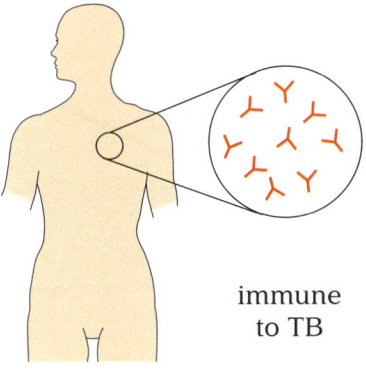

immune to TB

17 Why do your white blood cells make antibodies in response to the TB vaccine?

18 Draw a flowchart to show how the TB immunisation stops you catching TB.

19 Look at the graph. What year do you think TB jabs were first introduced as a routine immunisation for all children in England and Wales?

20 In the year 2000, there were still over 6000 cases of TB in England and Wales. Not everyone is immunised against TB. Write down <u>two</u> possible reasons why someone may not have had the TB jab.

Total annual number of cases of TB in England and Wales, 1940 to 2000. (From the Public Health Laboratory Service)

You should now understand these key words and ideas.

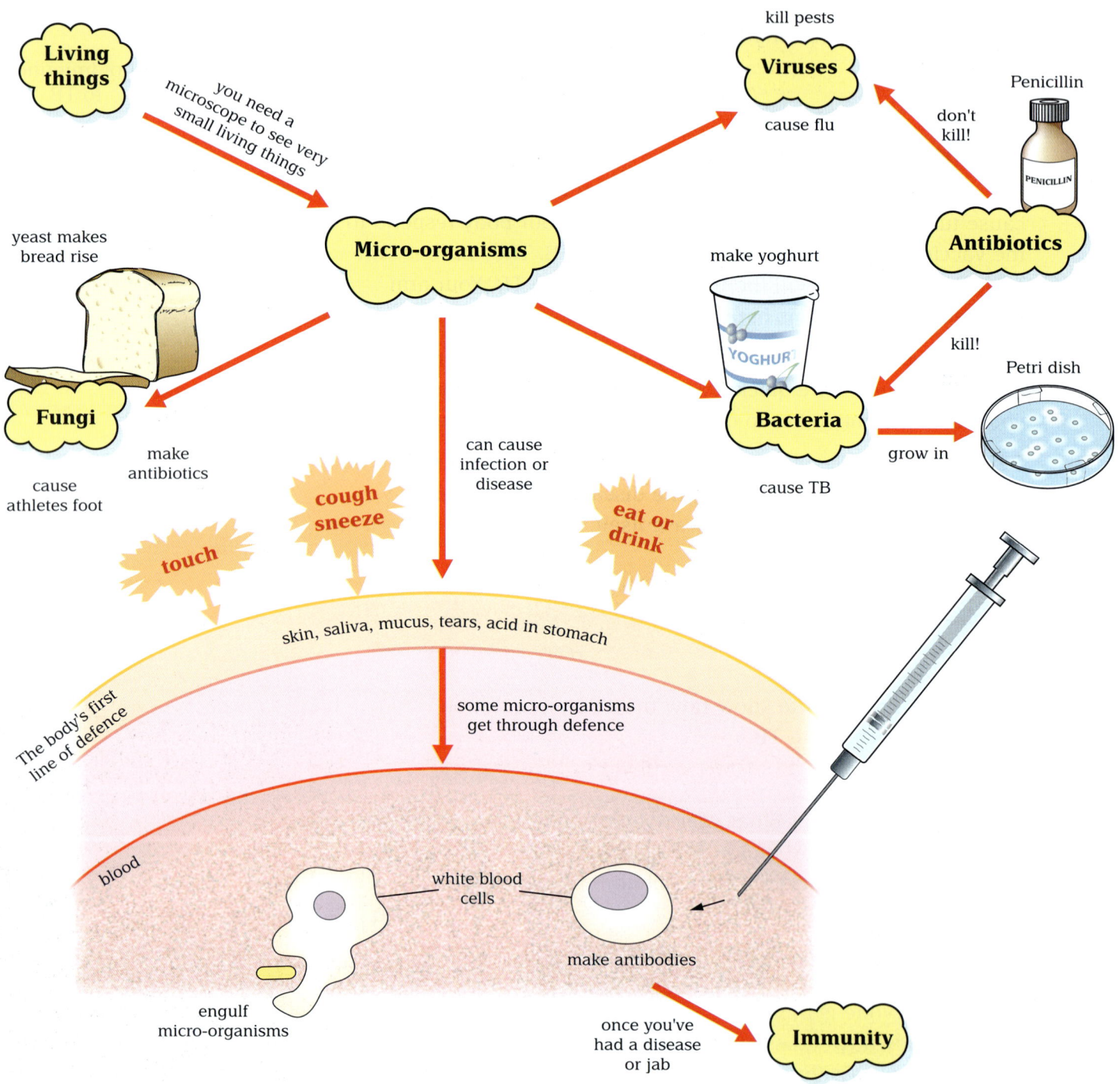

Living things

you need a microscope to see very small living things

Micro-organisms

Viruses
kill pests
cause flu

Penicillin

PENICILLIN

Antibiotics

don't kill!

kill!

yeast makes bread rise

Fungi

make antibiotics

cause athletes foot

make yoghurt

YOGHURT

Bacteria

cause TB

grow in

Petri dish

can cause infection or disease

touch

cough sneeze

eat or drink

skin, saliva, mucus, tears, acid in stomach

The body's first line of defence

some micro-organisms get through defence

blood

white blood cells

make antibodies

engulf micro-organisms

once you've had a disease or jab

Immunity

Ecological relationships

In this unit we shall extend our study of classification to include plants. We shall then look at how plants and animals in a community affect each other, and how their environment affects them.

KEY WORDS
habitat
environmental
  conditions
adapted
vertebrates
invertebrates
community
population
quadrat
food chain
producer
consumer
food web
herbivore
carnivore
pyramid of numbers

8D.1 Animals, plants and adaptations

You learned in Unit 7C that the place where a plant or animal lives is called its **habitat** and that different habitats have different **environmental conditions** such as temperature and amount of water.

The habitat of a plant or animal must provide all the things that it needs to live and reproduce. Different plants and animals have different needs. For example a gerbil can survive on less water than a mouse. This is because it has the features that help it to survive. We say that it is **adapted** to its environment.

Different plants and animals are adapted to live and reproduce in different habitats.

A gerbil is adapted to live in the desert.

1   What is the meaning of the word habitat?
2   Explain why organisms are adapted to their environments.

When you study a habitat you need to be able to identify the plants and animals that you find. It helps if you know which group they belong to. When we put plants and animals into groups we say that we <u>classify</u> them.

Classifying animals

In Unit 7D you learned how we classify animals.

- Animals with backbones are called **vertebrates**.

- Animals without backbones are called **invertebrates**.

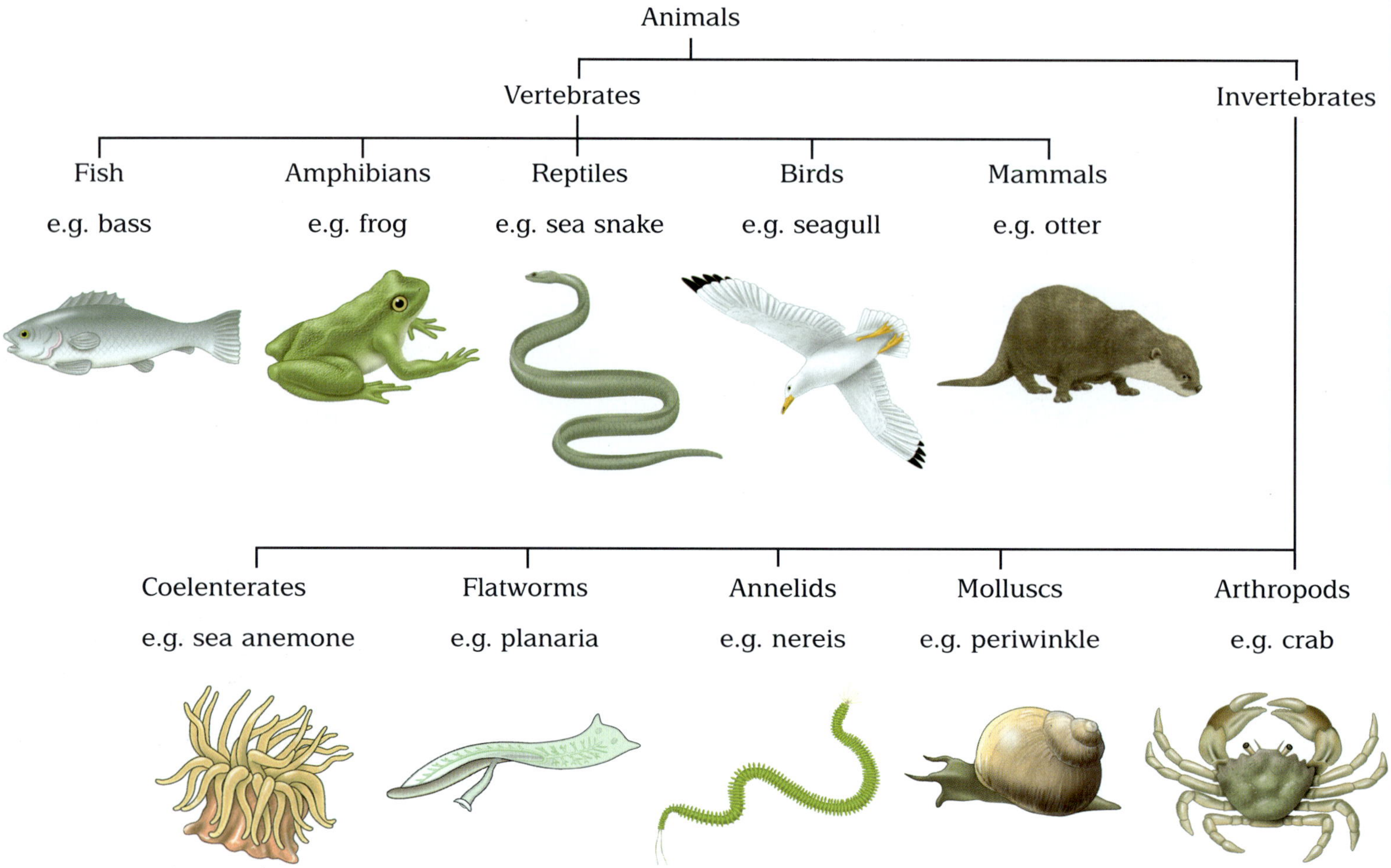

Animals

Vertebrates   Invertebrates

Fish   Amphibians   Reptiles   Birds   Mammals

e.g. bass   e.g. frog   e.g. sea snake   e.g. seagull   e.g. otter

Coelenterates   Flatworms   Annelids   Molluscs   Arthropods

e.g. sea anemone   e.g. planaria   e.g. nereis   e.g. periwinkle   e.g. crab

3 a Name the <u>two</u> main groups of animals.

   b Which of the two groups has an inside skeleton?

4 a Write down the <u>five</u> groups of vertebrates.

   b For each group, write down <u>one</u> feature that makes it different from the other groups.

5 Name some groups that invertebrates are divided into.

Now let's classify green plants

There are hundreds of thousand of different plants, so we divide them into smaller groups to help us to identify and to study them. There is more than one way of doing this.

Some plants have a special transport system for food and water called a vascular system. So we call these plants <u>vascular plants</u>.

Plants without a vascular system are called <u>non-vascular plants</u>.

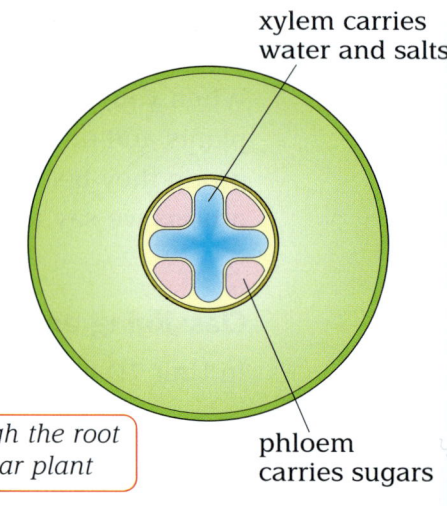

xylem carries water and salts

phloem carries sugars

A slice through the root of a vascular plant

Vascular and non-vascular plants are divided into smaller groups.

6 Name <u>two</u> types of vascular tissue found in vascular plants.

7 Why do we divide plants into groups?

```
                          Plants
          ┌──────────────────┴──────────────────┐
  Non-vascular plants                      Vascular plants
          │                   ┌───────────────┼───────────────┐
  Mosses and liverworts     Ferns          Conifers     Flowering plants
```

Ferns have strong roots, stems and leaves. They also have a waterproof layer to reduce water loss.

Flowering plants have a waterproof layer that reduces water loss, so they can live in dry, hot environments as well as in damp conditions.

Mosses and liverworts have thin leaves that do not have a waterproof layer. This makes them lose water easily. Mosses and liverworts do not have proper roots to absorb water so they are found mainly in damp places where water is readily available.

Conifers have leaves like needles. The needles have a waterproof layer to reduce water loss.

8 Explain why mosses and liverworts often live in a damp environment.

9 Why are vascular plants able to live in a wide range of habitats?

8D.2 Interactions in a habitat

In this topic you will be looking at some ways of finding out about habitats and the plants and animals that live in them.

Collecting data to answer questions about a habitat

Molly and her class did some fieldwork on a rocky shore. This is an interesting place to carry out work because you can find lots of plants and animals here. Animals are harder to see in many other habitats.

When the tide comes in it brings with it tiny plants and animals called plankton.

When the tide comes in, it brings with it a supply of food for the animals. The food includes a range of microscopic plants and animals floating in the water that together are called <u>plankton</u>. These are the food for many animals living on the shore.

The plants and animals found on the shore depend on each other. They are called a **community**.

1   Write down <u>one</u> advantage and <u>one</u> problem of doing fieldwork on a rocky shore.

It is easier to study the shore when the tide is out, but the seaweed makes it slippery.

Asking questions before the visit

In the lesson before the visit, Molly's teacher asked the class to think about what they'd like to find out about the rocky shore. Molly and her friend came up with these ideas.

What plants and animals live on the rocky shore?

Will we find the same plants and animals on all parts of the shore?

How can we find the numbers of the different plants and animals?

Will different areas of the shore have different environmental conditions?

2 Molly's friend David said, 'We can just count all the plants and animals that we see.' Write down why this is not a good idea.

Often it is not possible to count all the individuals in a **population** so we take a <u>sample</u>. Then we estimate the number of organisms that live in an area.

3 Write down <u>two</u> safety points that the class needs to think about before working on the rocky shore.

Collecting the information

Molly and her group decided to see if different plants and animals lived on different parts of the shore.

Molly's teacher gave her a **quadrat** to help her to do this. She threw a plastic card on the ground and placed the quadrat so the card was in the centre. Molly then wrote down the names of the different plants and animals that were in the quadrat.

She did this 10 times near the top of the shore. She then moved nearer the sea and used the quadrat another 10 times. When she completed this, she used the quadrat another 10 times in the middle of the shore.

Molly's teacher thought that this was a good idea and asked David's group to do the same experiment. The teacher said that they would compare the results when they got back to school.

4 Why was it a good idea for several groups to do the same experiment?

Finding out what lives on the shore

When Molly looked at her results she could see that different plants and animals lived in different areas of the shore.

Molly's teacher asked her to call the area nearest the sea the <u>lower shore</u>, and the area furthest from the sea the <u>upper shore</u>. The area between the two is called the <u>middle shore</u>.

The upper shore spends a lot of time not covered by water. It is exposed to different weather conditions.

The middle shore spends less time under water than the lower shore. It is not exposed to the weather for as long as the upper shore.

The lower shore spends a lot of time under the water.

Molly's teacher explained that the different areas of the shore are examples of different habitats. Different habitats support different living things.

5 Which of these areas is covered by the sea for the longest time?

Molly summarised her results in a table.

Area	Species found
Upper shore	Most of the rock is covered by black lichen. In rock crevices I found a few tiny periwinkles and barnacles.
Middle shore	I found lots of barnacles, limpets and mussels in this area of the shore. I also found some small pieces of seaweed in this area.
Lower shore	The seaweed was long and flexible. I could not remove it from the rock. I found crabs, starfish, limpets, fish and sea anemones here.

6 Look at the information in Molly's table. Write down which area of the shore has the widest variety of living organisms.

7 Molly's friend Patrick suggested that it would be a good idea to take some of the limpets back to the laboratory to look at in more detail. Why must they <u>not</u> do this?

Explaining the differences

When the class returned to school the teacher asked them to try to explain why there were different communities in different habitats. They thought that the environmental conditions were different in the different areas of the shore.

These are their ideas:

- **Upper shore** – This area can dry quickly because it spends a lot of the time not covered by the seawater. This means that there is less feeding time for the animals. It is often exposed to very hot or very cold weather conditions. Sometimes rain makes the water less salty.

- **Middle shore** – This area spends more time under water than the upper shore, but less time under water than the lower shore. The water brings with it a rich supply of food.

- **Lower shore** – This area spends most of the time under water. This means that there is less variation in temperature and not such a problem of drying.

Lichens are made of a green alga and a fungus. They often live on rocks and tree trunks. They can survive because they take a long time to dry out.

Many species of seaweed are long and flexible. They also have very strong holdfasts, which fix them to the rocks.

Limpet shells fit closely to the rock so that they don't dry out. They feed on tiny seaweeds on the rock when the tide is in.

Plants and animals on the shore have ways of making sure that the waves don't wash them away.

Mussels live attached to rocks. They filter plankton from the water when the tide is in.

Barnacles are cemented to the rock. When the tide is in they filter plankton from the water.

8 Explain why seaweeds have strong holdfasts.

9 Lichens take a long time to dry out. Why is this useful for an organism that lives on the upper shore?

Population size and environmental conditions

Molly's teacher agreed with their ideas. She said that the size of the population of an organism is affected by environmental conditions, such as amount of light, water and nutrients. The teacher also said that organisms will have more chance of survival where there is less variation in temperature.

Molly looked at the results of her quadrats for the population of barnacles.

Area	Number of barnacles
Upper shore	5
Middle shore	62
Lower shore	0

10 Which area of the shore contained the largest population of barnacles?

11 Molly said, 'More barnacles live on the middle shore than the upper shore because the barnacles on the middle shore have more time to feed from the water.'

Do you agree or disagree with Molly's conclusion? Explain your answer.

12 Molly made the conclusion just from looking at her own results. If she is a good scientist what should she do to make sure that the conclusion is correct?

13 Explain <u>one</u> other factor that makes it easier for barnacles to survive in the middle shore than the upper shore.

8D.3 How living things depend on each other

A **food chain** shows how energy is transferred from one organism to the next in a community.

Each food chain starts with a green plant, which is called a **producer**. An animal that feeds on green plants or other animals is called a **consumer**.

microscopic plants   mussel   starfish

A simple food chain

In most communities plants and animals belong to more than one food chain. A number of food chains joined together is called a **food web**. This gives a more complete picture of how an animal feeds.

The diagram shows part of a seashore food web.

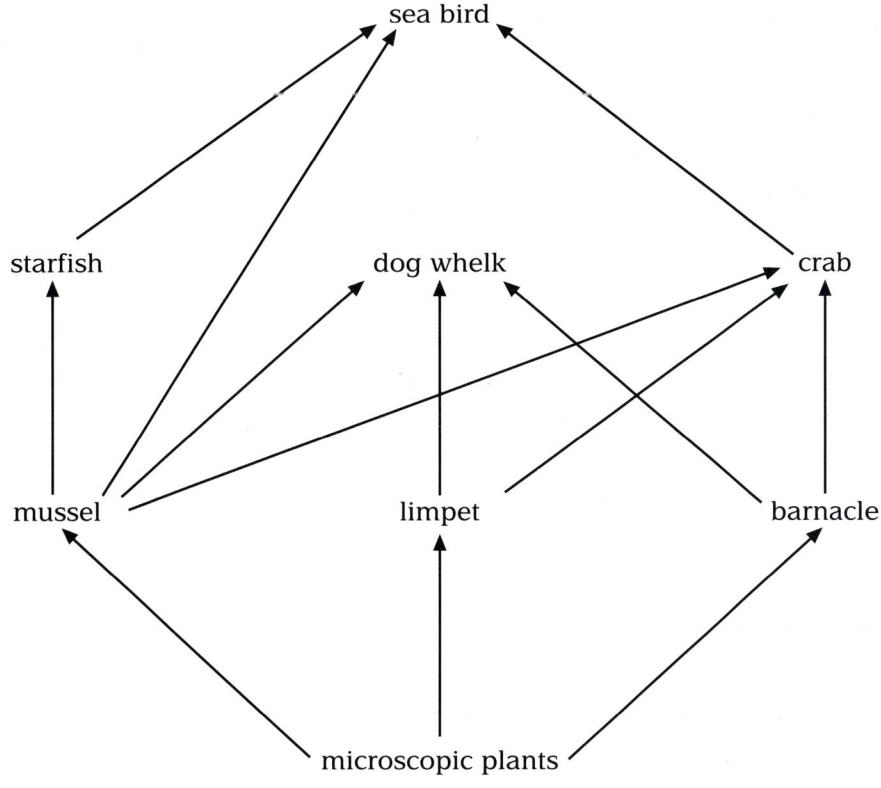

sea bird

crab

dog whelk

starfish

barnacle

limpet

mussel

1   From the food web, write down:

   a the producer;

   b <u>one</u> consumer.

2   Use the food web to find <u>two</u> things that crabs eat.

3   Write down <u>two</u> food chains in the food web that end with a sea bird.

An animal that only eats plants is called a **herbivore**. An animal that feeds on other animals is called a **carnivore**.

4   Name <u>one</u> herbivore in the food web.

5   Name <u>one</u> carnivore in the food web.

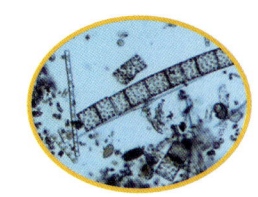

microscopic plants

Using food webs

We can use food webs to predict the effect of a rise or fall in the population size of a particular plant or animal in a community.

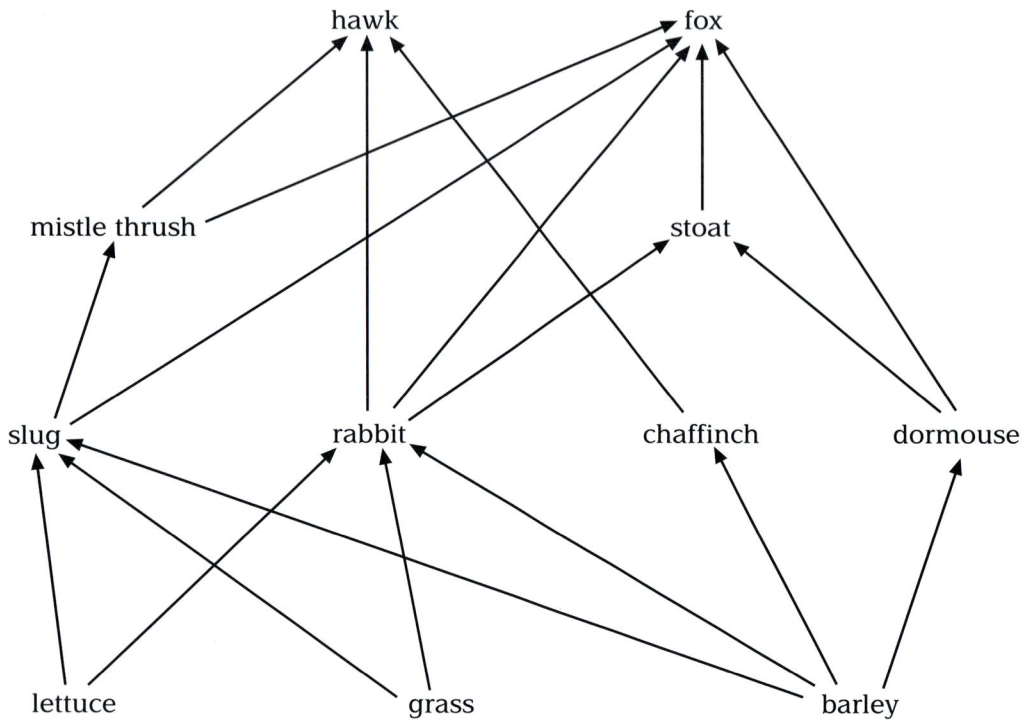

fox

hawk

stoat

mistle thrush

dormouse

chaffinch

If the population of one organism goes up or down it affects the rest of the food web.

If the rabbits are killed by a disease:

- the number of dormice may decrease – the stoats have fewer rabbits to eat, so they eat more dormice;

- the number of stoats may decrease because they have lost an important food source.

6 What will happen to the lettuce population if all the rabbits are killed?

7 What effect will the fall in rabbit population have on the slug population? Explain your answer.

lettuce

grass

barley

slug

rabbit

Pyramid of numbers

In a food chain, not all of the energy taken in by an organism passes to the next organism. Some is used for movement, growth and warmth. So there is less energy for the organisms at each stage.

Because of this, the number of animals gets lower as the food chain goes from stage to stage.

100 lettuces → 10 rabbits → 1 fox

We can show the change in population as we move along a food chain by a **pyramid of numbers**.

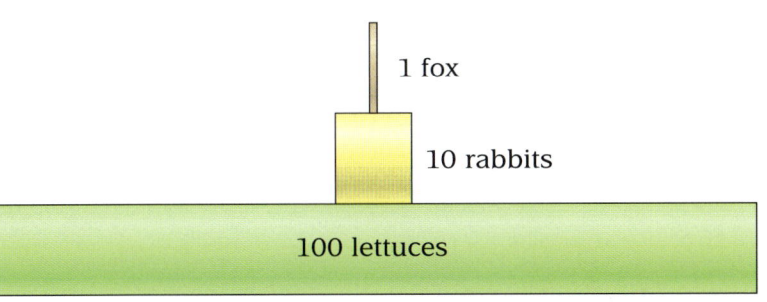

1 fox

10 rabbits

100 lettuces

8 Draw the shape of the pyramid of numbers for the following food chains.

a dandelions → rabbits → fox

b microscopic plants → insect larvae → perch → pike

A problem with pyramids of numbers is that they do not allow for the size of the organism at each level of the food chain.

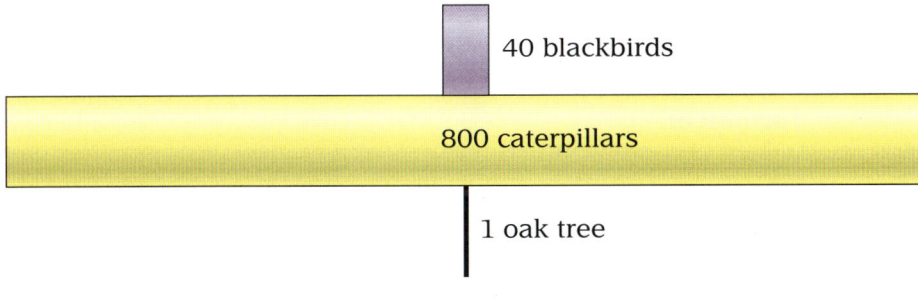

40 blackbirds

800 caterpillars

1 oak tree

An oak tree is very big compared to a caterpillar. There is only one oak tree, but it has thousands of leaves for caterpillars to feed on.

9 Draw a pyramid of numbers for each of the following food chains:

a 100 lettuces → 10 000 slugs → 100 thrushes → 1 hawk

b 1 rose bush → 10 000 greenfly → 1000 ladybirds

You should now have an understanding of these key ideas. You should also be able to spell and know the meaning of the key words. The key words are in **bold** on this page.

Animals with backbones are called **vertebrates**.

Animals without backbones are called **invertebrates**.

We classify plants and animals into smaller groups.

Plants are divided into two groups: those with a transport system (vascular) and those without a transport system (non-vascular).

The place where a plant or animal lives is called its **habitat**.

Plants and animals have features that suit them to where they live. We say they are **adapted** to their **environmental conditions**.

The plants and animals in a habitat interact.

A collection of species living in an area is called a **community**.

A group of organisms of the same species in an area is called the **population**.

To find the population size of an organism in an area we can use a **quadrat**.

Living things in a community depend on each other.

An organism that makes its own food is called a **producer**.

An animal that only eats plants is called a **herbivore**.

An animal that cannot make its own food, but gets it from other plants or animals is called a **consumer**.

An animal that feeds on other animals is called a **carnivore**.

A number of food chains joined together is called a **food web**.

Food chains show what animals eat.

A **pyramid of numbers** is a pyramid shaped diagram showing the numbers of organisms at each stage of a food chain.

Inheritance and selection

In this unit we shall be looking at how genetic information is passed on from generation to generation. We shall also look at how humans sometimes control this information to their advantage.

KEY WORDS
variation
characteristics
inherited
environmental variation
chromosomes
genes
fertilisation
selective breeding
asexual reproduction
clones

9A.1 What information is passed from parents?

In Unit 7D you found that living organisms vary. Even within the same species, animals and plants have differences. We say that they show **variation**.

There are lots of differences between people and cows.

Non-identical twins.

1 Write down <u>two</u> differences between the human and the cow.

Some differences are less obvious.

2 Write down <u>two</u> differences between the non-identical twins.

The things you described in your answers to questions 1 and 2 are called **characteristics**. These characteristics are passed from parents to offspring. We say they are **inherited**.

3 Write down <u>two</u> characteristics that the children in this family have inherited from their parents.

A family photograph

Are all characteristics inherited?

The young identical twins in the picture have inherited their characteristics from their parents.

The second picture shows adult identical twins. They are quite different from each other. The environment caused these differences. So this is called **environmental variation**.

Young identical twins

4 Write down <u>two</u> differences between the twins that are examples of environmental variation.

5 Look at the photograph of a member of four generations of one family. Write down:

   a <u>two</u> inherited characteristics;

   b <u>two</u> characteristics that you can see in the photograph that are affected by the environment.

Adult identical twins

9A.2 Why are we similar but not identical?

A complicated set of chemical instructions is needed to build your body. Your body cell nuclei contain these instructions. Each nucleus contains 23 pairs (that is, a total of 46) **chromosomes**. Small sections of these chromosomes are called **genes**. Each gene carries the instructions for a particular characteristic. So genes are coded instructions that make up your genetic material.

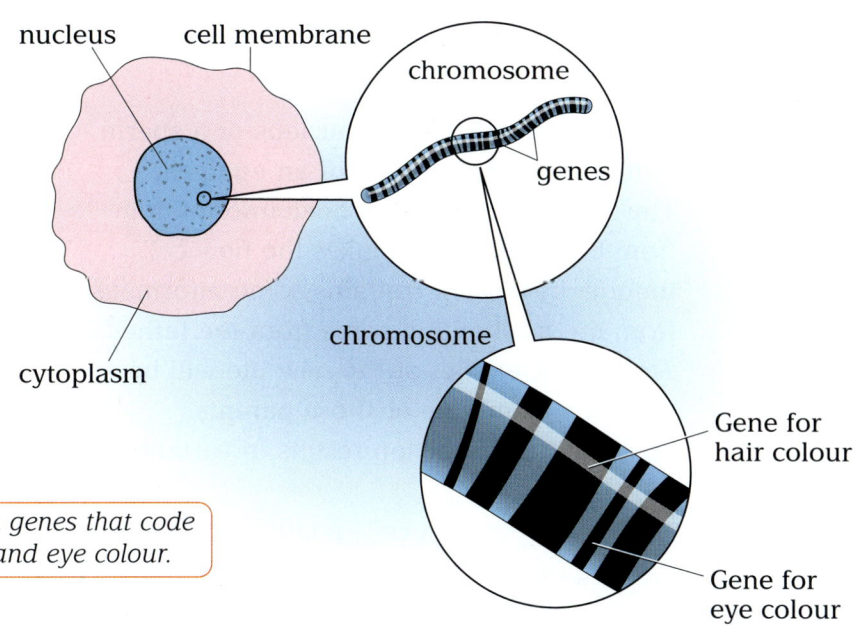

Chromosomes in your cell nuclei contain genes that code for characteristics such as hair colour and eye colour.

1 Which part of the cell contains the genetic information?

2 How many chromosomes are in a normal body cell?

In Unit 7B, you learned that the human sex cells are sperm from a man and egg cells from a woman. Sperm and egg cell nuclei each contain 23 chromosomes. The diagram shows how they are made.

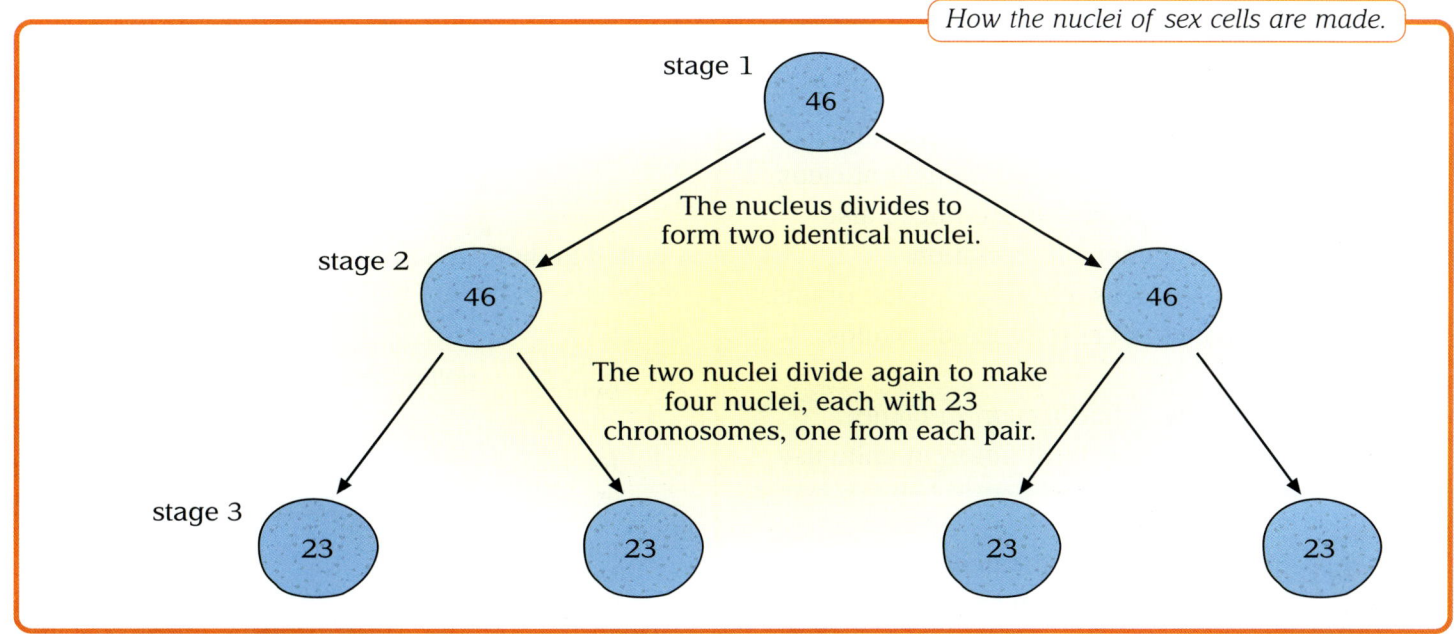

How the nuclei of sex cells are made.

stage 1

46

The nucleus divides to form two identical nuclei.

stage 2

46   46

The two nuclei divide again to make four nuclei, each with 23 chromosomes, one from each pair.

stage 3

23   23   23   23

3 What happens to the number of chromosomes in each nucleus between stage 2 and stage 3?

Passing on the instructions

For a new life to begin, a nucleus from a sperm must join with a nucleus from an egg cell. This is called **fertilisation**.

The diagram shows the nucleus of a sperm joining with the nucleus of an egg cell. The new cell receives genetic information from both cells. This makes the new cell unique, because it contains some information from the mother and some from the father. The characteristics of the new life will be a selection from both of those parents. So sexual reproduction results in variation.

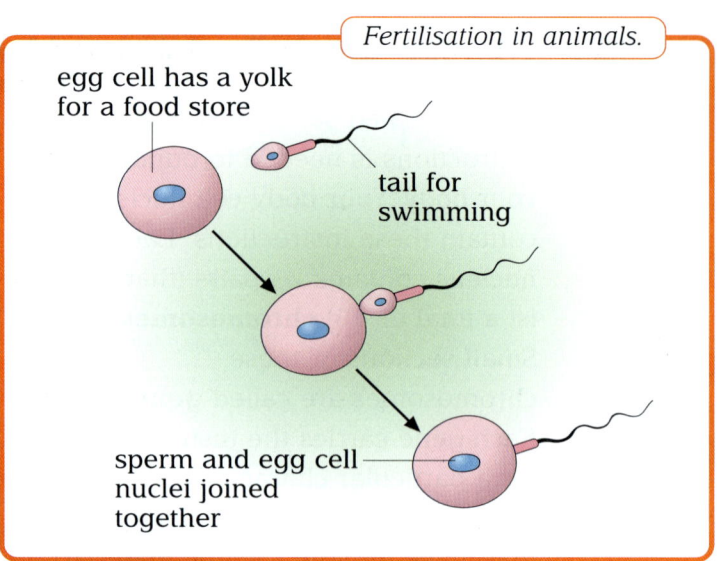

Fertilisation in animals.

egg cell has a yolk for a food store

tail for swimming

sperm and egg cell nuclei joined together

4   How are sperm cells adapted to reach egg cells?

5   How are egg cells different from many other cells in the body?

6   Why is a child not identical to either its father or its mother?

7   Use the information from the diagram to explain why a sperm cell and an egg cell each contain 23 chromosomes, but the cell after fertilisation contains 23 pairs of chromosomes.

Fertilisation in plants

Sexual reproduction in plants also involves a male and a female nucleus joining together. These nuclei also contain genetic information. Male sex cells are inside pollen grains. Female sex cells are inside ovules.

8   How is fertilisation in plants similar to fertilisation in animals?

9   Explain why the new plant that grows from each embryo is unique.

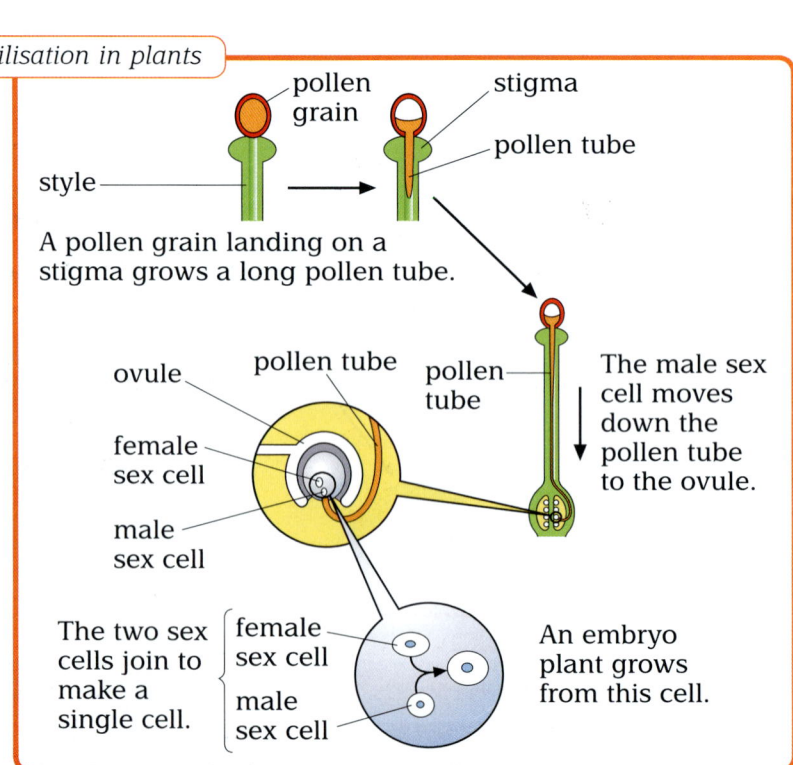

Fertilisation in plants

pollen grain

stigma

style

pollen tube

A pollen grain landing on a stigma grows a long pollen tube.

pollen tube

pollen tube

The male sex cell moves down the pollen tube to the ovule.

ovule

female sex cell

male sex cell

The two sex cells join to make a single cell.

female sex cell

male sex cell

An embryo plant grows from this cell.

9A.3 Differences between offspring

Different species of plants and animals look different.
Even members of the same species look different in many ways.
We say that they vary.

 **1** Look at the picture. Write down <u>two</u> ways in which the tomatoes are different from each other.

The yellow tomatoes come from seeds of yellow tomatoes. Tomato colour is passed from generation to generation. It is inherited.

 **2** What type of seed produces red tomatoes?

 **3** Write down <u>one</u> characteristic not shown in the picture that may be passed from generation to generation in tomatoes.

 **4** Explain why tomato A is bigger than tomato B on August 4th, but they are the same size on August 12th.

Sometimes tomatoes with identical inherited characteristics are different. The environment caused these differences.

 **5** Write down <u>two</u> environmental conditions that can affect how well a plant grows.

Patrick's experiment

I grew some plants using seeds from one plant. I had some problems. There were so many plants that I had to keep some next to the window and some on a shelf. Sometimes I forgot to water them. After 6 weeks I measured the heights of the plants.

 **6** Draw a bar chart of Patrick's results.

 **7** The differences between Patrick's plants could have been caused by inheritance, by the environment or a mixture of both. What do you think? Explain your answer.

8 Imagine that you are Patrick's teacher. Write him a note explaining how to make his experiment a fair test.

Different varieties of tomatoes.

On August 4th, tomato A is bigger than tomato B. On August 12th, they are both fully grown and are the same size. To grow, plants need sunlight, water, carbon dioxide and minerals.

A August 4th   **B** August 12th

Height of plant (cm)	Number of plants
31–40	6
41–50	10
51–60	15
61–70	12
71–80	8

Patrick's results

9A.4 The right breed for the right job

Even though they look different, the animals in the picture belong to the same species. Breeders have selected dogs with certain characteristics and allowed them to breed. Some examples of characteristics they have selected are size, colour and thickness of coat.

 1 Look at the picture. Write down <u>two</u> ways in which the dogs are:

    a alike;

    b different.

 2 **a** Which of these dogs do hunters and poachers use to bring animals out of their burrows?

    b Write down <u>two</u> characteristics of the dog that make it suitable for this job.

Selecting individuals with the most suitable characteristics and breeding from them is called **selective breeding**. There is evidence that humans domesticated a few wolves in Asia tens of thousands of years ago. Over the millennia, they developed all the different varieties of dogs from just these few wolves by selective breeding.

How selective breeding works

When animals breed naturally, they choose their own mates. Genes for lots of different characteristics are mixed over and over again. It's a bit like shuffling cards and dealing them out. You never know which characteristics will appear in each hand of cards.

In selective breeding, humans decide which animals will mate. Humans choose animals with the characteristics that they want. Think of it like choosing your cards instead of relying on chance.

What breeders do.

Choose, from the animals that they have, male and female animals with the characteristics that they want.

↓

Breed from these animals.

↓

Select the offspring with the required characteristics and breed from them.

↓

Repeat for several generations.

 3 When animals breed, a sperm cell from the male fertilises an egg cell in the female. What part of a cell contains the genes that control an animal's characteristics?

Farmer Mansfield wants to breed goats with longer, softer coats.

A B C

Some of Farmer Mansfield's female goats.

4 Look at the picture of the female goats. Which two goats will Farmer Mansfield let the male mate with?

5 How will the farmer decide which of the baby goats to keep and which to sell?

6 What is the next step in the breeding programme? Explain your answer.

7 Why do breeders make sure that both the male and female animals have the required characteristics before they allow them to breed?

8 Explain why breeders try to control the environmental conditions for the breeding animals.

Why humans produce new breeds

Selective breeding benefits humans in many ways. For example, Farmer Mansfield expects to be able to get more money for the hair from his goats if it is softer and longer.

9 Look at the pictures. Choose <u>two</u> examples and explain why the characteristics are useful for consumers.

10 What characteristics do you think that farmers try to develop in:

  a apples;

  b sheep?

Breeders select:

beef cattle to get the best taste, appearance and texture for their beef;

cows that produce more milk;

dogs for a variety of uses, such as guard dogs, guide dogs, sheepdogs and cute pets;

hens that lay more eggs.

9A.5 How new varieties of plant are produced

Plant breeders are producing new varieties of plants all the time. The different varieties of tomatoes shown on page 107 and the beans on this page were all produced by selective breeding.

Farmer Kirkby's bean plants varied.

1 Look at the pictures of Farmer Kirkby's plants. Write down:

a the useful characteristics of the tall plant;

b the useful characteristics of the small plant.

This plant is tall and has a strong stem but produces only a small amount of fruit. It can survive in strong winds and cold weather.

This plant is small but produces very big fruits. Strong winds and cold weather damage it.

Farmer Kirkby wanted tall, strong plants that yield lots of fruit. She produced them by selective breeding. She chose the plants that were most like the ones that she wanted and transferred pollen from one plant to the other. After several generations, she had bred offspring with the characteristics that she wanted.

Look at the diagram.

2 Farmer Kirkby did not get the type of plant that she wanted straight away. What other combinations of characteristics did her first set of plants have?

3 Which of this first set of plants did Farmer Kirkby breed from, and why?

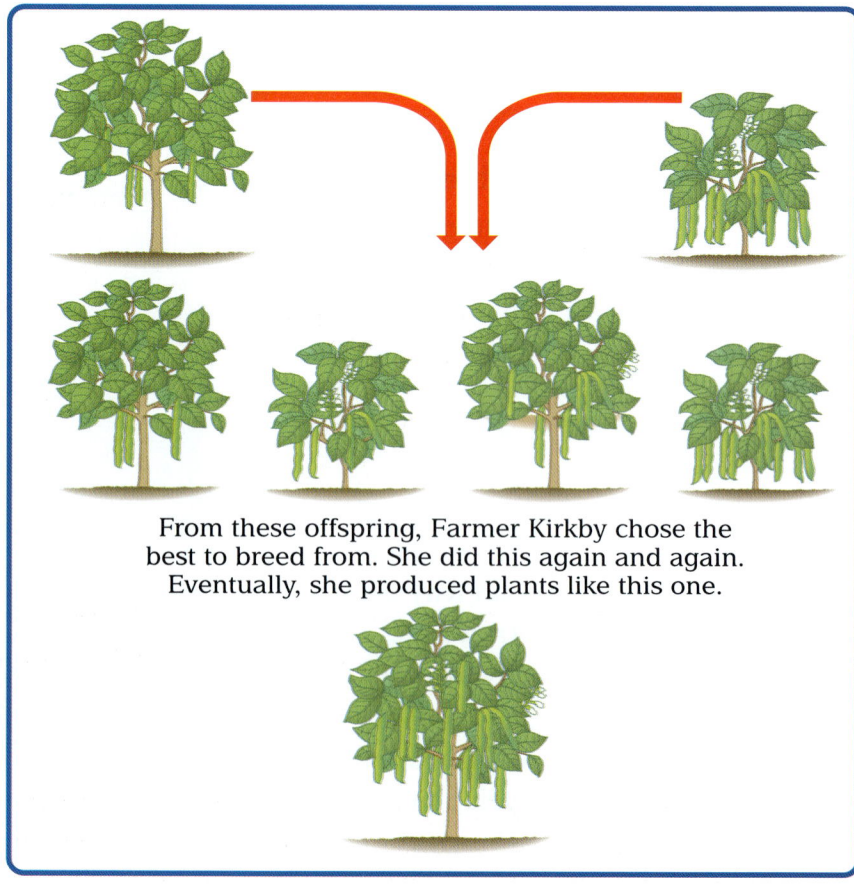

From these offspring, Farmer Kirkby chose the best to breed from. She did this again and again. Eventually, she produced plants like this one.

Fertilising the plant

On page 106, you saw how pollen on a stigma grows a long pollen tube. Then the male sex cell goes down the tube to the ovule and joins with the female sex cell.

> *The two nuclei join together. We call this fertilisation.*

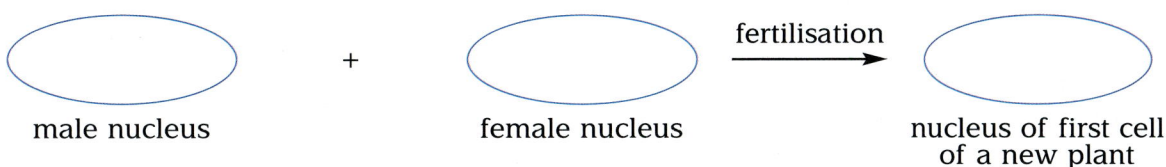

male nucleus + female nucleus →(fertilisation)→ nucleus of first cell of a new plant

Plant breeders have to make sure that flowers are pollinated only with pollen from the plants that they have selected. It is important that plants are not pollinated by accident.

The diagram shows what plant breeders do.

① Remove the anthers before they burst and release their pollen.

② Cover the flower with a pollen-proof bag.

Wait for the stigma to mature.

③ Use a paintbrush to transfer pollen from the chosen plant to the mature stigma.

4 Explain why plant breeders have to make sure that flowers are pollinated only with pollen from the plant that they have selected.

5 Explain why plant breeders use a paintbrush to transfer pollen from the chosen plant to a mature stigma.

9A.6 What is a clone?

Asexual reproduction is a type of reproduction in which only one parent is involved. The offspring have exactly the same genes as the parent. We say they are genetically identical. They are called **clones**.

1 What is a clone?

2 Write down <u>one</u> difference between asexual reproduction and sexual reproduction.

3 Describe the difference in the amount of variation resulting from sexual and asexual reproduction. Explain your answer.

Taking cuttings

Taking cuttings is a quick and cheap way of producing lots of new plants.

These new plants have exactly the same genes as the parent plant and as each other. So they are clones.

4 Which part of the rhubarb plant can you use to make cuttings?

5 Explain why taking cuttings is useful for a farmer who makes a living by growing rhubarb.

6 How soon would you expect the farmer to be able to harvest rhubarb from the new plants? Explain your answer.

7 A farmer grows each new rhubarb plant in the same conditions. Explain why all the plants will be identical.

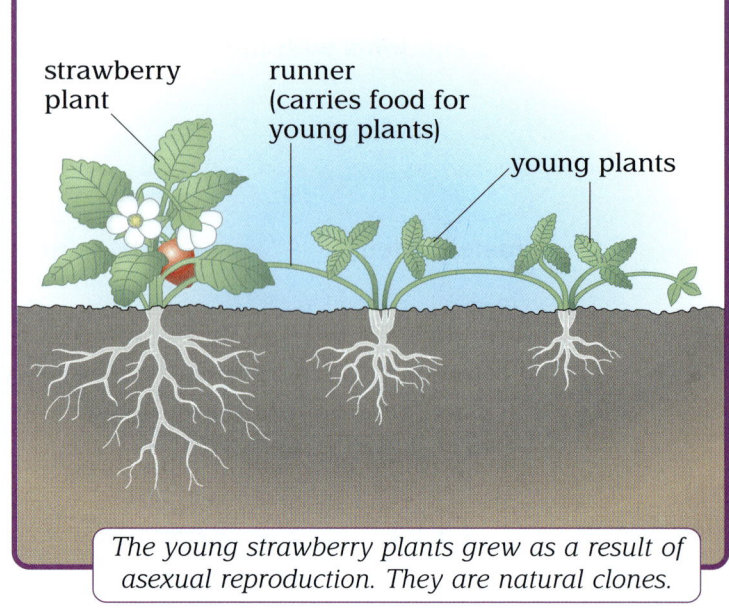

strawberry plant

runner (carries food for young plants)

young plants

The young strawberry plants grew as a result of asexual reproduction. They are natural clones.

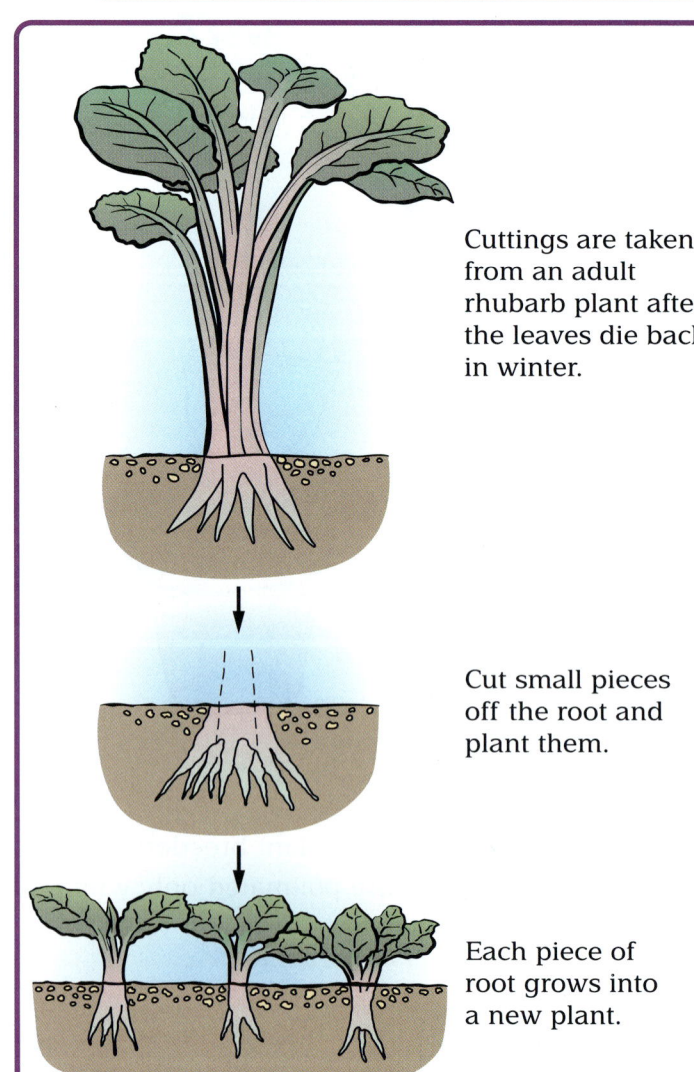

Cuttings are taken from an adult rhubarb plant after the leaves die back in winter.

Cut small pieces off the root and plant them.

Each piece of root grows into a new plant.

Producing plants by grafting

Grafting is a method of reproducing trees that gardeners use. The cut stems of two plants are taped so that the tissues grow together.

 **8** Look at the diagram of plant grafting. Why are the two surfaces taped together?

Fruit trees grown from seed vary. If you plant an apple pip, it will be several years before the tree is big enough to produce apples. You will have no idea what the apples will be like. Grafted fruit trees are clones, so their characteristics are exactly the same as those of the tree from which the graft was taken.

 **9** Explain the advantages of growing clones of apple trees.

Animal clones

Some tiny animals reproduce asexually and form clones. But sexual reproduction is normal in larger animals.

Cut a twig from the plant you want to reproduce from.

Join the twig to the stem of a rooted tree. The rooted part of the tree is called the <u>stock</u>.

rooted stock

tape

Tape the surfaces together. The cut heals to make a new plant.

Plant grafting

Scientists are finding out how to clone farm animals. Dolly the sheep was produced by cloning.

 **10** Lots of people are against cloning animals such as sheep. Find out some of the reasons for this.

You should now understand these key words and key ideas.

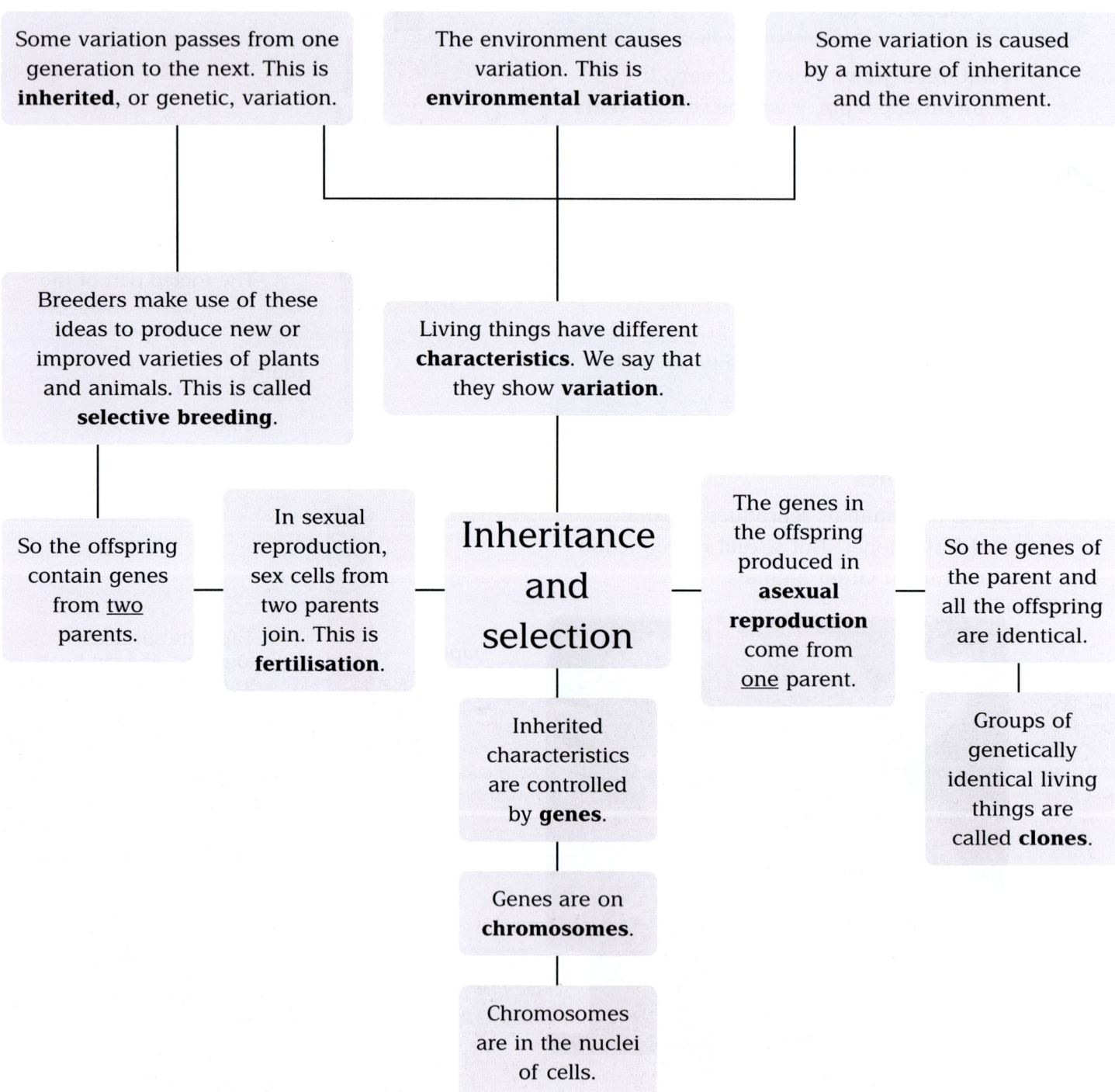

Some variation passes from one generation to the next. This is **inherited**, or genetic, variation.

The environment causes variation. This is **environmental variation**.

Some variation is caused by a mixture of inheritance and the environment.

Breeders make use of these ideas to produce new or improved varieties of plants and animals. This is called **selective breeding**.

Living things have different **characteristics**. We say that they show **variation**.

So the offspring contain genes from <u>two</u> parents.

In sexual reproduction, sex cells from two parents join. This is **fertilisation**.

Inheritance and selection

The genes in the offspring produced in **asexual reproduction** come from <u>one</u> parent.

So the genes of the parent and all the offspring are identical.

Inherited characteristics are controlled by **genes**.

Groups of genetically identical living things are called **clones**.

Genes are on **chromosomes**.

Chromosomes are in the nuclei of cells.

Fitness and health

In this unit we shall be exploring what it means to be fit and healthy, and how different parts of your body work together to keep you fit. We shall also investigate the important things that you can do to improve your health.

9B.1 Ideas about fitness

We often hear statements such as 'She's super-fit!', 'I really need to get fit', 'I've never been fitter!'. But we need to think about what it means to be fit.

1 Look at the photographs. Discuss the following questions in a small group before you write down your answers. Give reasons for your answers.

   a For each person, decide whether or not you think they are fit.

   b Which person shown is probably the most unfit?

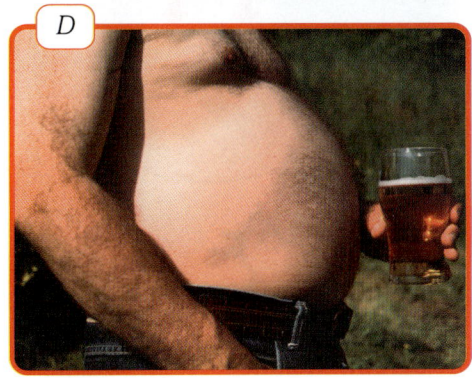

Fitness means different things to different people. Just because they're disabled or old doesn't mean that a person is unfit.
The fat young man in the photograph is probably very unfit for his age. If you are fit, your body uses energy in an efficient way during exercise. Usually, the fitter you are, the more exercise you can do without getting tired.

2 In a small group, try to agree on a list of different kinds of fitness. Write it down.

Energy gets you going

The cells in your body require supplies of glucose and oxygen to release the energy they need.

Your skeleton and muscles work together to move your body.

Your cells use oxygen to release the energy stored in the glucose molecules. This is **respiration** and it takes place in every cell in your body.

Your circulatory system, including your heart and blood vessels, transports digested food and oxygen to your cells, including your muscle cells.

Your **breathing** system moves oxygen into your blood, and removes carbon dioxide from your blood.

Your digestive system breaks food down into simple molecules, such as glucose. These can then enter the bloodstream.

Different systems in your body work together to keep you fit.

3 Why do all your cells need glucose and oxygen? Explain this as fully as you can.

4 Look at the diagram. Write down <u>three</u> systems in your body that help to get glucose and oxygen to your cells.

5 Choose <u>one</u> of the three systems and explain briefly how your fitness is affected when that system is not working properly.

6 Write a word equation for respiration.
Use the information in the diagram to help you.

Respiration takes place in every cell in your body.

glucose (fuel)   oxygen to react with glucose

energy

carbon dioxide   water

9B.2 Breathing in action

You have learned that every cell in your body takes in oxygen for respiration and releases carbon dioxide. The air containing these gases goes into and out of your lungs when you breathe.

Your chest works a bit like a pair of bellows, drawing the air in and then forcing it out.

Place one hand on the middle of your upper chest. Place your other hand on your side, just above your waist. Take a few deep breaths.

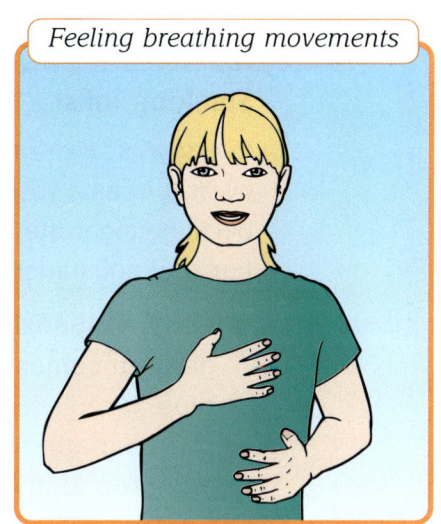
Feeling breathing movements

1   Describe the movements that you feel, first as you inhale (breathe in), and then as you exhale (breathe out).

Breathing in

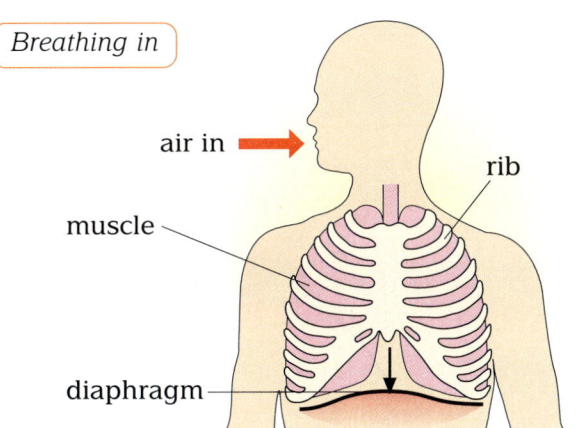

air in

rib

muscle

diaphragm

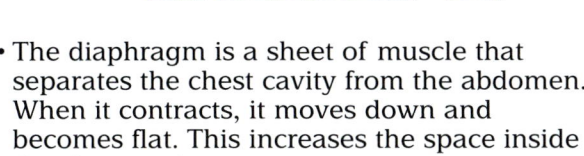

Breathing out

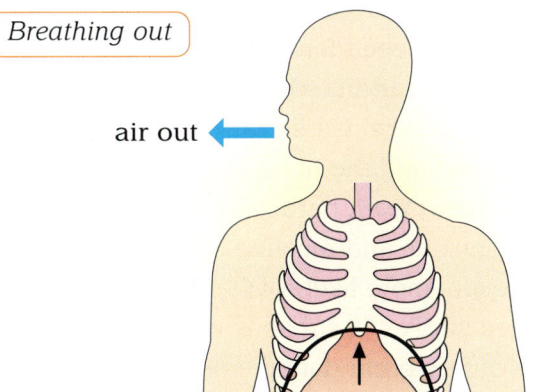

air out

- The diaphragm is a sheet of muscle that separates the chest cavity from the abdomen. When it contracts, it moves down and becomes flat. This increases the space inside the chest cavity.

- The muscles between the ribs contract, causing the ribcage to move out and up. This increases the volume of the chest cavity.

- The increase in chest volume causes air to be drawn into the lungs.

- The diaphragm relaxes. It moves up and becomes dome-shaped, decreasing the volume of the chest cavity.

- The muscles between the ribs relax, and the ribs move down and in. This decreases the size of the chest cavity.

- Air is forced out of the lungs.

2   Name <u>four</u> parts of your body that are involved in breathing.

3   Explain what makes air go into your lungs.

4   Which requires more effort, breathing in or breathing out? Explain why.

5   What happens to your breathing rate when you:

   a exercise;

   b go to sleep?

9B.3 The dangers of smoking

Smoking kills!

Every year, more than 100 000 people die in Britain as a result of smoking. This is because cigarette smoke contains many harmful substances.

- Carbon monoxide is the same poisonous gas that comes out of a car's exhaust pipe. It replaces oxygen in your blood so important organs such as your heart and brain don't get enough oxygen.

- Nicotine is an addictive drug that makes your body want more of it. When people's bodies become dependent on a drug, we say that they are **addicted**. Nicotine is as addictive as cocaine. It also raises the blood pressure and the heart rate, and makes the heart work harder. So the carbon monoxide and nicotine together make smokers more likely to have heart attacks and strokes. A stroke is when a clot of blood causes brain damage or death.

- Tar is a mixture of chemicals that cause **cancer** of the mouth, throat and lungs, as well as other lung conditions.

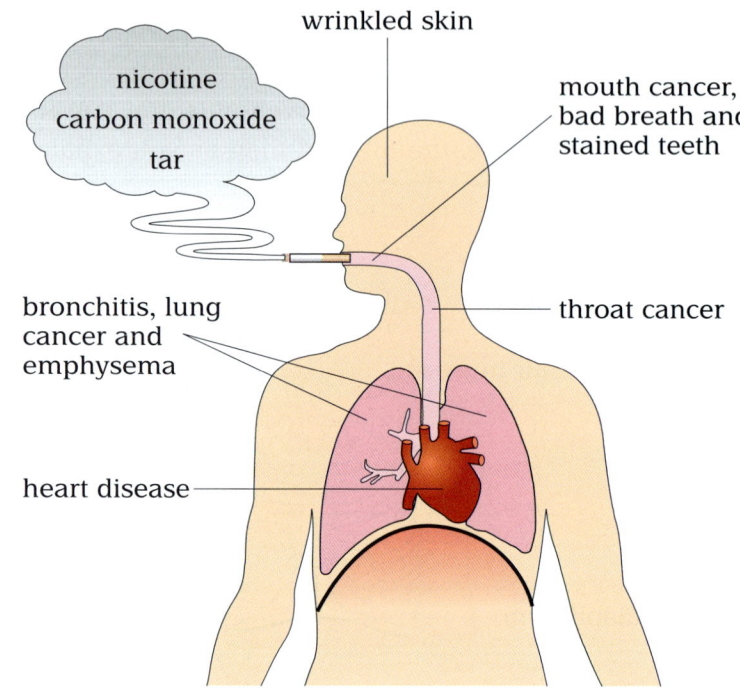

The effects of smoking are not 'cool' or exciting.

nicotine
carbon monoxide
tar

wrinkled skin

mouth cancer, bad breath and stained teeth

throat cancer

bronchitis, lung cancer and emphysema

heart disease

1   Draw a table to show the dangerous substances in cigarette smoke. In one column name the substances, and in the other column list the parts of the body that are most affected by them.

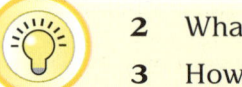

2   What does the graph show?

3   How many people (per 10 000) who don't smoke die of lung cancer?

4   How many people (per 10 000) who smoke 20 cigarettes a day die of lung cancer?

Remember, this doesn't mean that if you smoke you will get lung cancer, or that if you don't smoke you can't get lung cancer. It means that your risk of getting lung cancer increases as the number of cigarettes you smoke increases.

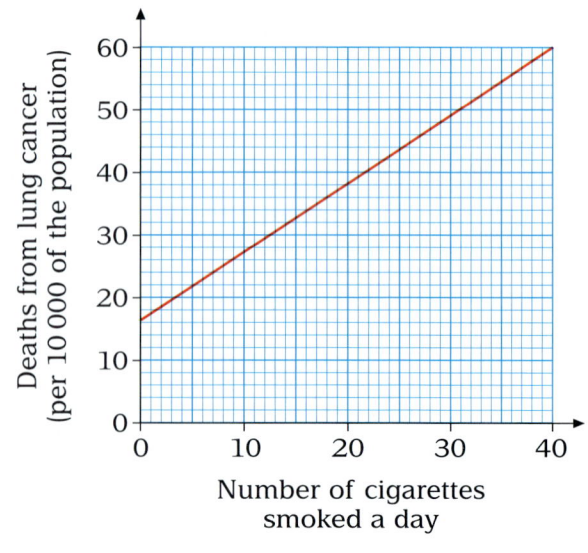

The number of deaths related to smoking in England and Wales.

How smoking damages the lungs

In the photograph you can see some lung damage caused by smoking.

In a healthy person, the cilia and mucus in the air pipes work together to keep harmful particles out of the lungs. But the poisonous substances in cigarette smoke destroy the cilia.

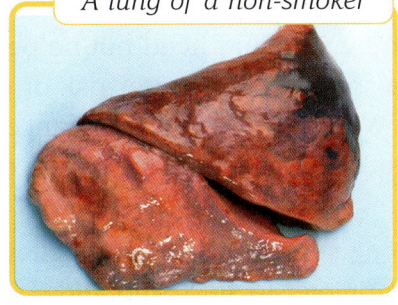

A lung of a non-smoker

A lung of a smoker

Instead of getting swept out of the lungs, the mucus and particles trickle down into them. Smokers cough to try and get rid of the mucus, but often bacteria remain and cause an infection called **bronchitis**.

Constant coughing can break the walls of the air sacs. This reduces the surface area of the lungs, so the person struggles to get enough oxygen. We say that he or she is short of breath. This illness is called **emphysema**.

70 per cent of the tar in cigarette smoke stays in the lungs. It forms a black coating inside the tiny tubes and air sacs. Tar can make the normal cells lining the air tubes change into cancer cells. These cells divide more than normal cells, and they form a lump called a tumour. Lung cancer is difficult to cure.

Harmful particles get trapped in mucus that lines the air pipes.

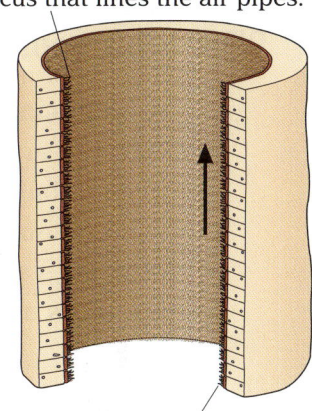

Tiny hairs called cilia move the mucus upwards and into the throat. Then you swallow it!

5 How does the breathing system work to stop harmful substances in air getting into the lungs?

6 Explain why smokers often cough when they wake up in the morning.

7 Find out more about either bronchitis or emphysema. In your research, include the symptoms of the illness and how it is treated.

8 Discuss the following questions and then write down your views.

a Should smoking be banned completely?

b Should the National Health Service (NHS) pay for a heart operation needed by a smoker?

The lining of the air pipes is designed to keep harmful substances in the air, such as dust, bacteria and viruses, away from the lungs.

- Cigarette smoke contains more than 4000 chemicals.
- The longer you smoke, the greater your risk of developing different cancers.
- Women who smoke during pregnancy increase their chance of miscarriage and of having very small babies.
- Smoking can cause eye and ear problems, tooth decay and weakening of bones, called osteoporosis.
- Smoking costs the NHS about £1.7 billion a year.

Carbon particles, arsenic, ammonia, acetone, hydrogen cyanide

The good news

The damage caused by smoking need not be permanent. If a heavy smoker stops smoking, his or her risk of getting lung cancer slowly falls. Within 10 years, that chance is the same as for a person who doesn't smoke. So, it's never too late to STOP!

9 Write down in <u>one</u> sentence what you believe is the most important reason never to start smoking.

9B.4 Why your diet is important

A balancing act

To be fit and healthy, it is important to eat a balanced diet. This is one that contains the right amounts of proteins, carbohydrates, fats, **vitamins** and **minerals**, fibre and water.

For centuries, scientists have been gathering evidence about how what we eat affects our health. For example, in the early 1900s a famous English scientist, Sir Frederick Gowland Hopkins, fed rats on a diet of pure carbohydrates, fats, proteins and minerals. He thought that these were all the things needed for good health. Within weeks, all the rats were dead. Another group of rats that had the same diet, but with a little milk added, all survived. Something in milk, needed in tiny amounts, kept the rats healthy. We now call these things vitamins.

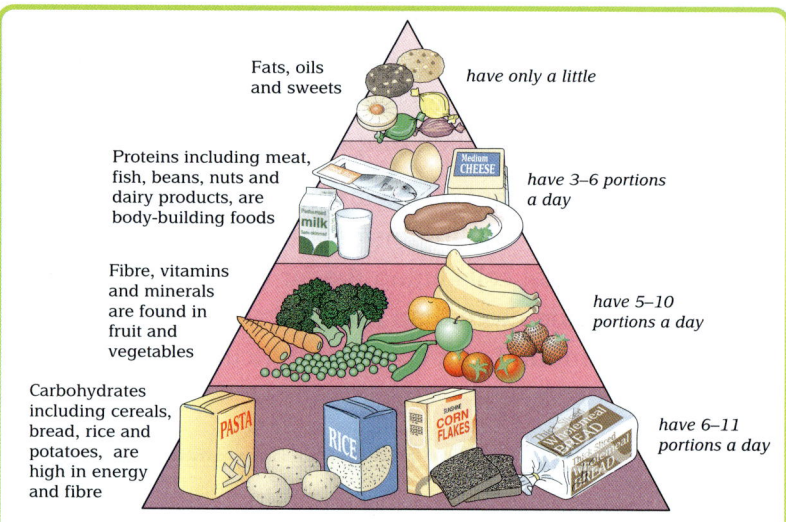

A pyramid is an easy way of showing how much food to eat from the different groups.

1 Draw a table to summarise the main food groups and examples of foods that contain them.

2 Explain why it is better to get most of your energy from carbohydrates such as cereals, potatoes and pasta, rather than from fats, oils and sweets.

3 Plan a healthy, balanced picnic meal. It should taste good too! Use the pyramid to help you.

4 Explain how the evidence gathered by Sir Frederick Gowland Hopkins affects your life.

Feast or famine

Malnutrition means 'bad eating'. A malnourished person eats too much or too little of a particular food. In Britain, most malnourished people either eat the wrong foods or they eat too much food. If you take in more food energy than your body uses, the extra is stored as fat. You can become overweight or obese. To reduce your weight, you can either eat less or exercise more. You use up more energy when you exercise.

In some countries, many people die of starvation. Others suffer from kwashiorkor, which is malnutrition caused by a lack of protein. Many people worldwide have other diseases caused by a shortage of just one thing in their diet. We call these deficiency diseases.

A deficient diet can lead to many diseases or problems.

Nutrient	Sources	Symptoms of deficiency
Iron	Red meat Eggs Cereals	Anaemia: people look pale and feel weak because the blood does not carry enough oxygen
Calcium	Dairy products Dark green vegetables Sardines (bones)	Poor growth of bones and rotting teeth
Vitamin C	Citrus fruit Fresh vegetables	Scurvy: gums crack and wounds don't heal; bleeding under the skin
Vitamin D	Eggs Dairy products Fish oil Made by your skin in sunlight	Rickets: softening and bending of the bones
Protein	Meat Fish Eggs Dairy products Pulses (peas, beans, lentils)	Kwashiorkor: poor growth, swelling due to water collecting in tissues

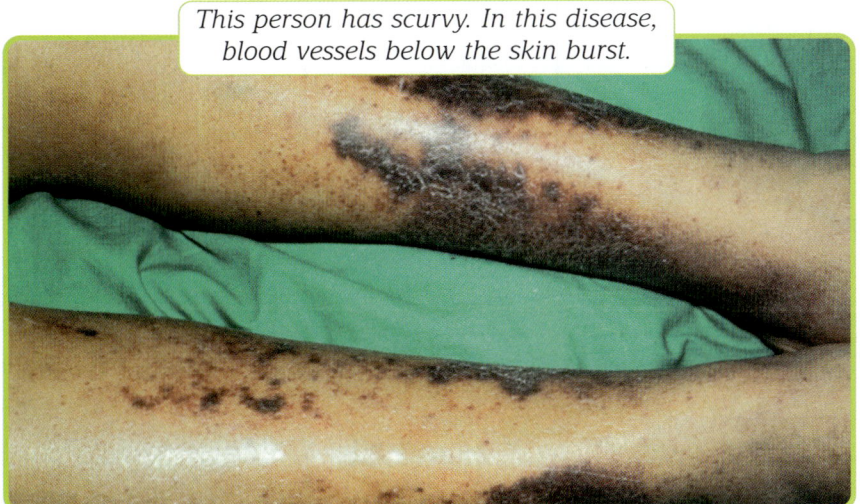

This person has scurvy. In this disease, blood vessels below the skin burst.

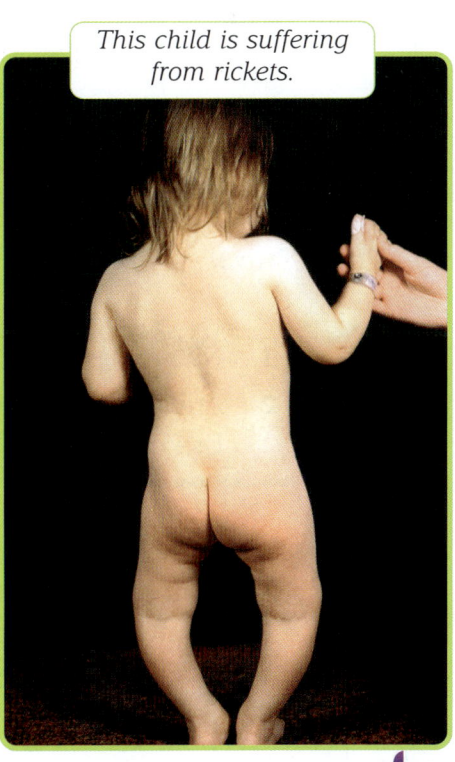

This child is suffering from rickets.

5 Explain what you need to add to your diet if:

a your teeth often need filling and your bones break easily;

b you are suffering from kwashiorkor.

9B.5 The use and abuse of drugs

A **drug** is any substance that changes the way your body or mind works. So alcohol, aspirin, cocaine, Ecstasy, antibiotics, nicotine, paracetamol and caffeine are all drugs. Changes to the body or mind can be helpful or harmful. Some drugs improve your mood, feelings or behaviour; others make them worse. Some drugs heal, and others damage organs in your body. Even drugs that heal can have bad effects, such as headaches and nausea. We call these side effects.

There are many different ways of grouping drugs. The diagram shows one way.

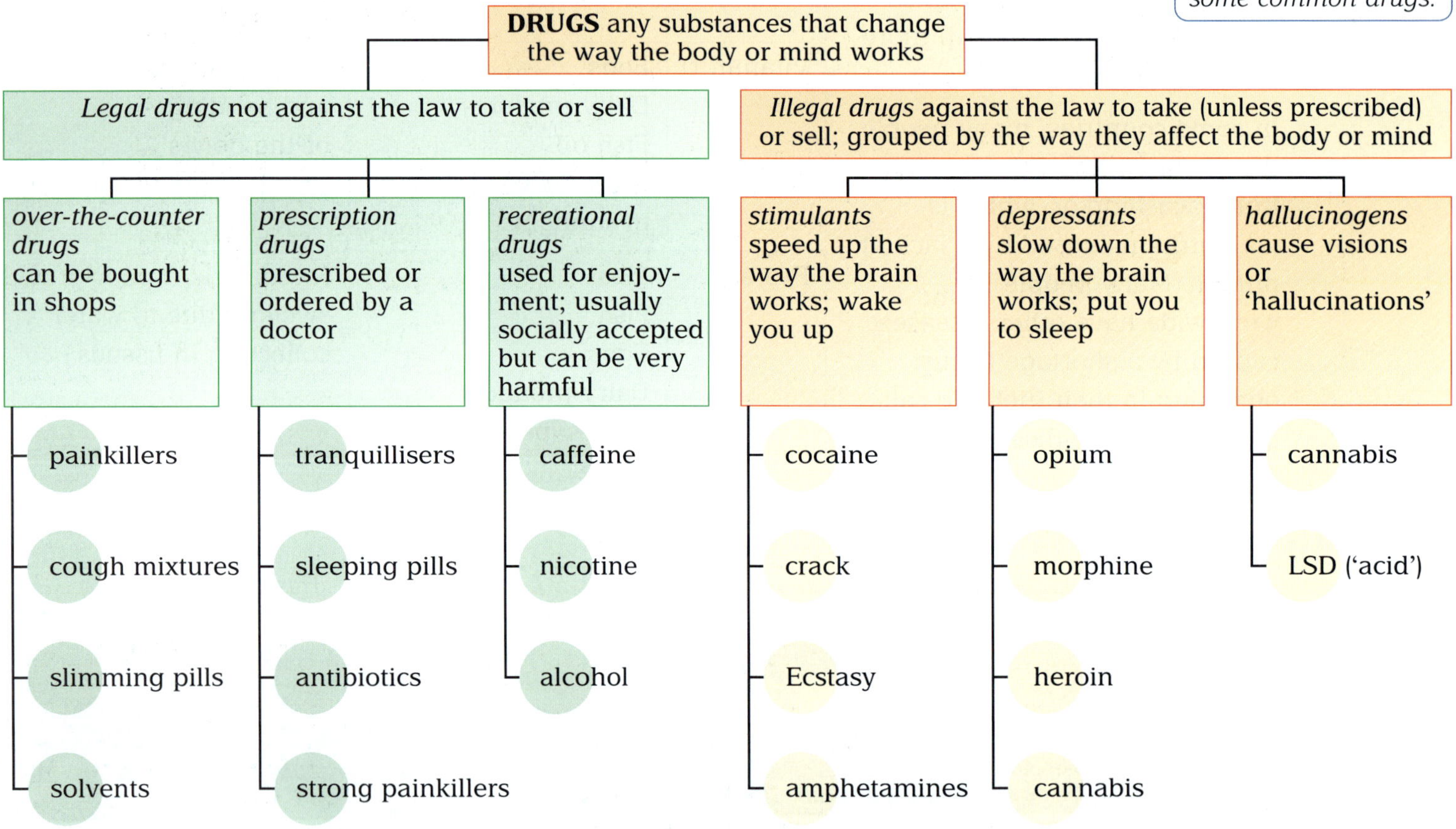

Classification of some common drugs.

```
                    DRUGS any substances that change
                    the way the body or mind works

    Legal drugs not against the law to take or sell        Illegal drugs against the law to take (unless prescribed)
                                                            or sell; grouped by the way they affect the body or mind

  over-the-counter    prescription     recreational      stimulants        depressants       hallucinogens
  drugs               drugs            drugs             speed up the      slow down the     cause visions
  can be bought       prescribed or    used for enjoy-   way the brain     way the brain     or
  in shops            ordered by a     ment; usually     works; wake       works; put you    'hallucinations'
                      doctor           socially accepted you up            to sleep
                                       but can be very
                                       harmful

  painkillers         tranquillisers   caffeine          cocaine           opium             cannabis

  cough mixtures      sleeping pills   nicotine          crack             morphine          LSD ('acid')

  slimming pills      antibiotics      alcohol           Ecstasy           heroin

  solvents            strong painkillers                 amphetamines      cannabis
```

1   Name <u>three</u> groups of legal drugs.

2   Are any legal drugs harmful or dangerous?
Use examples to explain your answer.

3   Write down <u>one</u> example of a drug that falls into more than one group. Explain your answer.

4   Many drugs have side effects.
Use an example to explain what this means.

The danger of drugs

<u>All</u> drugs can be dangerous if they are not used in the correct way. When you use a legal drug, you should follow the instructions very carefully. If you don't, or if you use a drug prescribed for someone else, then you are misusing or abusing the drug. Abuse of legal and illegal drugs is extremely dangerous. Some reasons why are shown in the photographs.

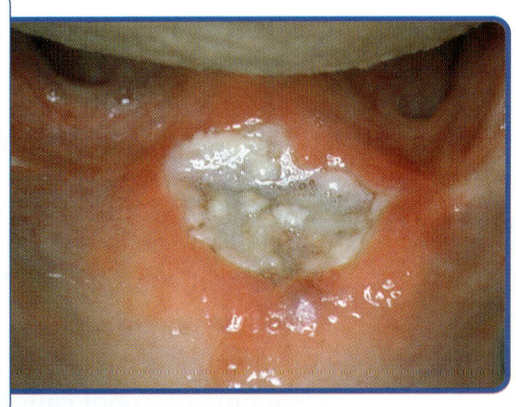

Drugs can damage cells, often in the brain, heart, liver or kidneys. Overdose of drugs causes thousands of deaths every year. This person has mouth cancer from smoking tobacco and cannabis.

Drugs such as alcohol slow reactions, causing accidents on the road, at work or in the home. One of the drivers had been drinking alcohol.

*Many drugs are addictive. This means that if you take the drug for some time, you become dependent on the drug and need it to function. If addicts stop taking drugs, they feel ill, anxious and may shake or vomit. These are called **withdrawal symptoms**.*

 **5** What do we call drugs that can be taken only with a doctor's permission?

 **6** Name <u>two</u> legal drugs that are addictive.

7 Besides the three dangers of drugs mentioned, in what other harmful ways can drugs affect a person's life?

The effect of alcohol on your body

Alcohol is a drug because it changes the way your body works. It is also a poison. When you drink alcohol, it is absorbed into your bloodstream within a few minutes. It is carried to all parts of your body and begins to affect every cell.

A function of your liver is to protect your body from the harmful effects of alcohol. As the blood passes through the liver, it breaks down the alcohol into less harmful substances. It takes about one hour for a healthy liver to get rid of one unit of alcohol from the body. If the liver receives alcohol at a faster rate than this, its own cells become damaged. Drinking heavily over a long period of time can scar the liver. This is called cirrhosis and can cause death.

Children shouldn't drink alcohol. If adults choose to drink, then they should do so sensibly. Health advisers suggest an upper limit for adults of 14 units a week for women and 21 units a week for men.

Alcohol slows down the way the brain works and affects your behaviour. It can reduce your will power and control, which often leads to violence, accidents and unwanted pregnancies. It can make you sleepy and clumsy and can slur your speech. Sometimes alcohol causes loss of memory and even permanent brain damage. It also increases your blood pressure and pulse rate. Over a long period, alcohol damages the heart and increases your risk of a heart attack.

Alcohol can irritate the lining of the stomach and eventually cause stomach ulcers. Alcohol also increases the flow of blood to the skin. This makes the drinker look flushed and feel warm. In fact, the body will lose heat quickly in this situation.

When a pregnant woman drinks, alcohol passes to the baby through the placenta. Drinking too much can slow down the baby's development and even cause brain damage.

One way of comparing the amount of alcohol in different drinks is by using 'units' of alcohol as a measurement. A unit is 10 ml of pure alcohol. As a rough guide:

1 unit = half a pint of beer

= one tot (25 ml) of spirit, such as whisky, brandy, gin or vodka

= a small glass (125 ml) of wine

= 150 ml of 'alco pop'

How much is too much?

8 List <u>four</u> organs in the body that can be damaged by alcohol.

9 Read again through the section on the effects of alcohol on the body. Summarise the main points by annotating a diagram of the human body. The first annotation has been done for you.

Some parts of the body affected by alcohol

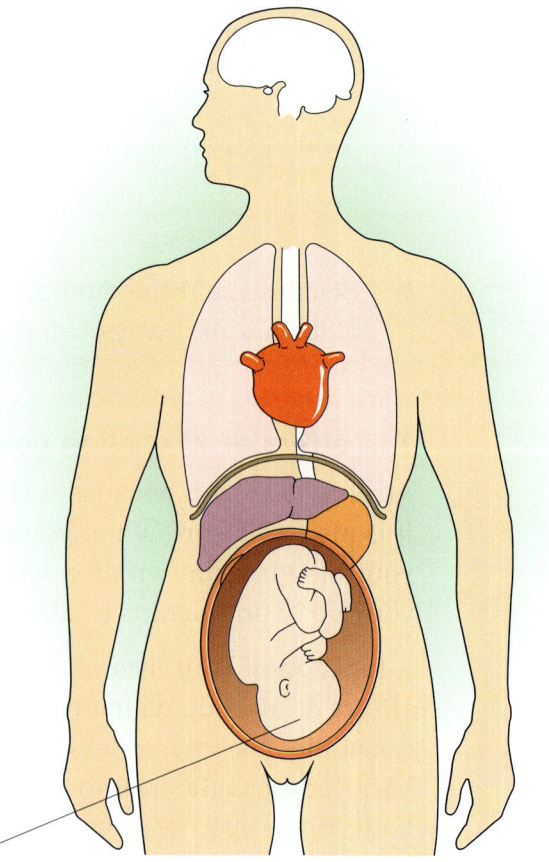

Alcohol can cause brain damage and stunt the growth of a developing fetus.

Some frightening facts

Alcohol is legal, socially acceptable and used regularly by most people in Britain. But before you decide to drink, remember the following.

- Twice as many people are addicted to alcohol as to all other drugs put together.

- Violent crime and violence in the home are often linked to alcohol.

- More than 1000 young people are admitted to hospital each year with alcohol poisoning.

- About half of adult pedestrians killed in road accidents have been drinking too much. One result is shown in the poster.

- If you drink heavily in the evening, you can still be over the legal drink-drive limit the next morning.

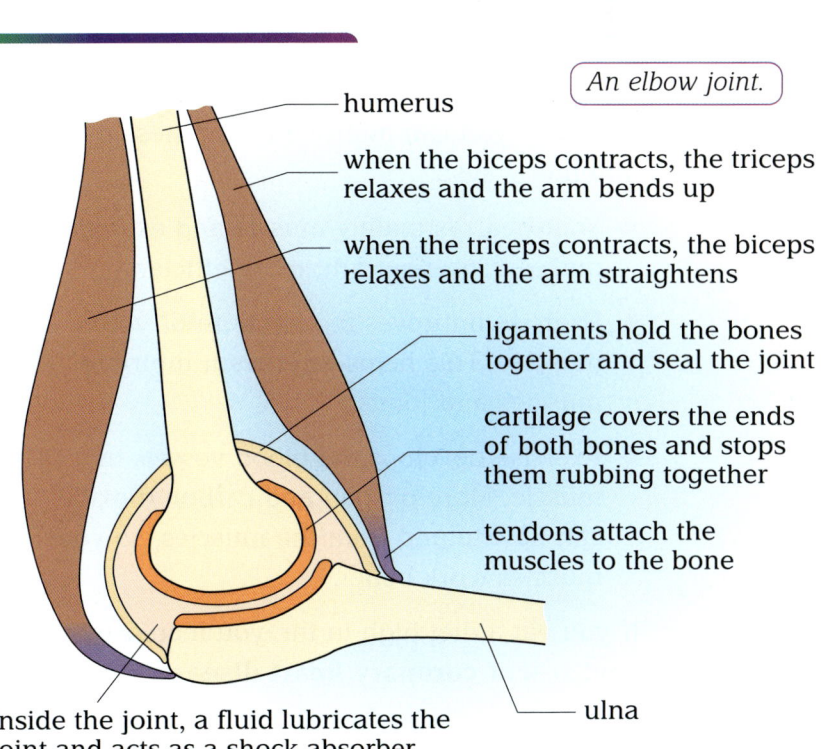

Think before you drink!

Look her in the eye. Then say a quick drink never hurt anybody.

DRINKING AND DRIVING WRECKS LIVES.

 **10** Use examples to explain the difference between the 'use' and 'abuse' of alcohol and other drugs.

11 Discuss and write down your views on the question 'Should alcohol be banned or more controlled, given the number of people harmed by the abuse of alcohol?'.

9B.6 Fit for life

Joints in action

The place where two bones connect is called a joint. Muscles are fixed to your bones on both sides of a joint. The muscles pull on the bones to make you move.

 **1** What is a joint?

 **2** Write a paragraph to explain how a joint works. Use the diagram to help you.

An elbow joint.

humerus

when the biceps contracts, the triceps relaxes and the arm bends up

when the triceps contracts, the biceps relaxes and the arm straightens

ligaments hold the bones together and seal the joint

cartilage covers the ends of both bones and stops them rubbing together

tendons attach the muscles to the bone

inside the joint, a fluid lubricates the joint and acts as a shock absorber

ulna

You have learned how important exercise is for keeping you fit and healthy. However, too much exercise, or the wrong kind of exercise or movement, can damage the joints and muscles.

If you twist your foot inwards suddenly, you can overstretch or tear the ligaments. A <u>sprain</u> like this causes your ankle to swell.

If you do sudden vigorous exercise, you might injure a muscle. This is called a <u>strain</u> or 'pulled muscle'. Overdoing exercise can also cause muscles to contract so powerfully that they hurt. This is called <u>cramp</u>. A 'stitch' is a type of cramp in the abdominal muscles, caused by very hard exercise.

You can reduce the chance of getting a sports injury by warming up before exercise.

 **3**   Explain the difference between a sprain and a strain.

 **4**   List some of the common causes of sports injuries.

 **5**   Find out about <u>one</u> of the following conditions: tennis elbow, water on the knee, dislocated hip, arthritis, slipped disc or any sports injury.

Eating and exercising for your heart

In this unit, you have looked at the effects of diet, drugs and exercise on health and fitness.

Being fit and healthy is about making the right choices. If you choose to exercise regularly, you can improve your fitness in different ways.

- Your heart is mainly muscle and exercise makes it stronger and more efficient.

- Exercise improves the strength of your muscles. This helps to prevent injury to muscles and joints.

- Exercise develops the blood vessels in muscle. More oxygen and carbon dioxide can flow to and from the muscles, so your muscles work better.

If you eat a diet high in fat, you increase your risk of **coronary heart disease**.

Coronary heart disease begins when the blood vessels in the heart become narrow because of a build-up of fatty material. This fatty material is made from cholesterol, which the body makes from fat in food.

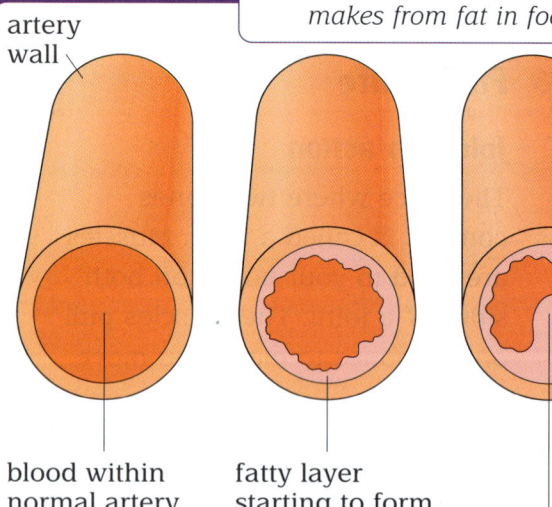

artery wall

blood within normal artery

fatty layer starting to form

fatty layer, which stops the blood flowing freely. The heart muscle becomes short of oxygen, and this causes angina, which is very painful. A heart attack happens when the narrowed arteries become blocked by a blood clot.

To lower your chance of heart disease, you need to:

- eat at least five portions of fruit and vegetables a day;

- eat less fat;

- keep your weight normal, so your heart doesn't need to overwork;

- not eat too much salt, because salt raises your blood pressure.

 **6** Explain the cause of angina.

 **7** You are a doctor, and you are with a patient who has heart problems. List <u>five</u> questions you would ask your patient, to find out if they need to make some lifestyle changes.

Are we healthier than our great-grandparents were?

Science is about finding answers to questions. The question in the heading is a broad and general question. Scientists first break down a general question into a few smaller questions that are easier to investigate. They then plan a suitable investigation and collect the evidence. Evidence is information that can be used to make a decision or to answer a question. Lastly, they use the answers to the smaller questions to help them answer the general question.

Scientists develop new vaccine.

People spend more time in cars than ever before.

In this unit, we have looked at many questions related to fitness and health. One final one is 'Are we healthier than our great-grandparents were?' Your first response might be 'Yes, of course we are.' But we need to investigate this general question in a scientific way – finding evidence to back up our answer. First, we need to think about differences between our lifestyles and those of our great-grandparents that might have an effect on health – different diets, for example.

 **8** Write down at least <u>three</u> things affecting health that were different in your great-grandparents' time. The photographs and newspaper articles will help you.

9 Write down <u>one</u> question you could investigate in a scientific way that would help you to decide whether or not we are healthier than our great-grandparents were.

9B

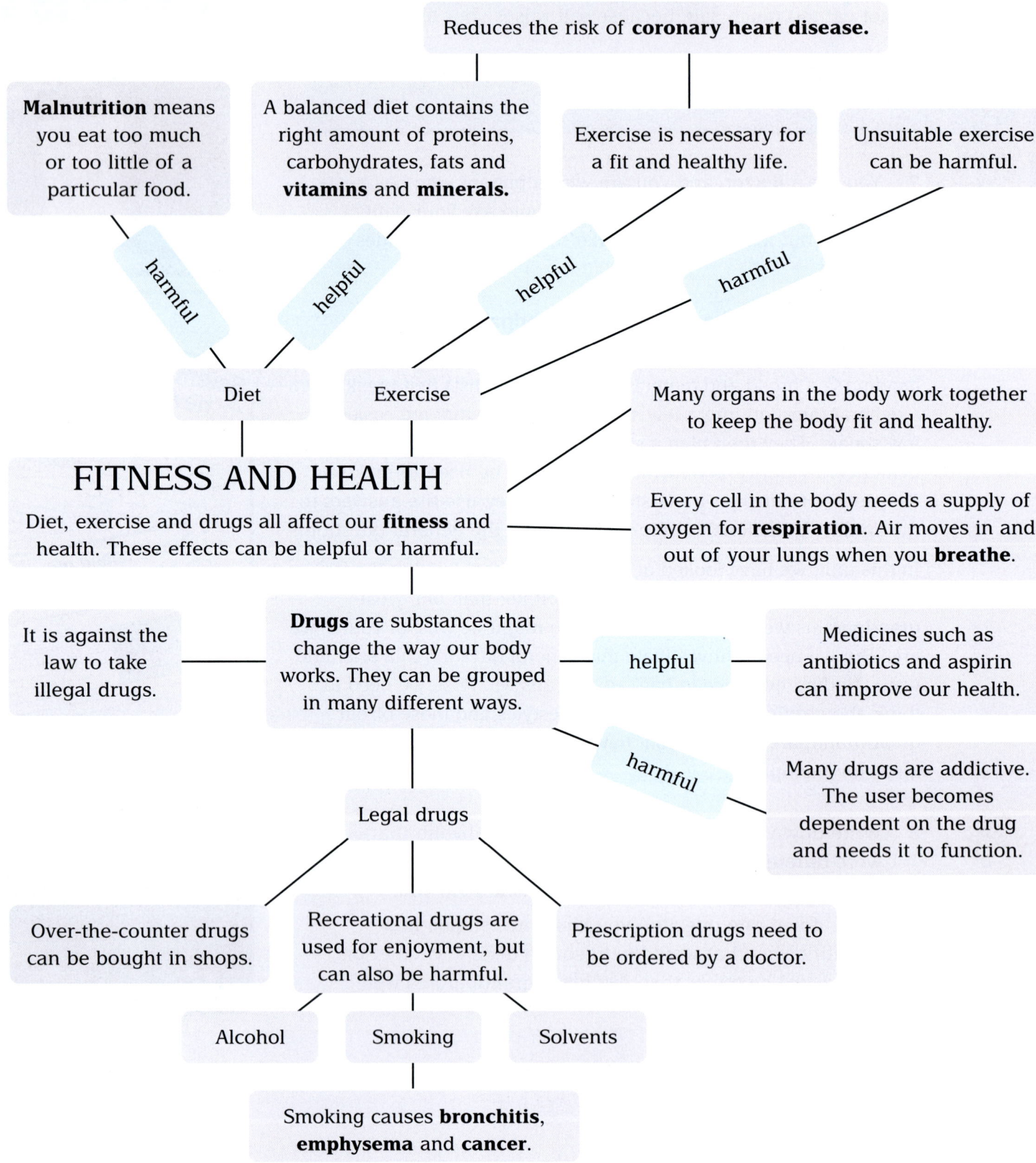

Reduces the risk of **coronary heart disease.**

Malnutrition means you eat too much or too little of a particular food.

A balanced diet contains the right amount of proteins, carbohydrates, fats and **vitamins** and **minerals.**

Exercise is necessary for a fit and healthy life.

Unsuitable exercise can be harmful.

harmful

helpful

helpful

harmful

Diet

Exercise

Many organs in the body work together to keep the body fit and healthy.

FITNESS AND HEALTH

Diet, exercise and drugs all affect our **fitness** and health. These effects can be helpful or harmful.

Every cell in the body needs a supply of oxygen for **respiration**. Air moves in and out of your lungs when you **breathe**.

It is against the law to take illegal drugs.

Drugs are substances that change the way our body works. They can be grouped in many different ways.

helpful

Medicines such as antibiotics and aspirin can improve our health.

harmful

Many drugs are addictive. The user becomes dependent on the drug and needs it to function.

Legal drugs

Over-the-counter drugs can be bought in shops.

Recreational drugs are used for enjoyment, but can also be harmful.

Prescription drugs need to be ordered by a doctor.

Alcohol

Smoking

Solvents

Smoking causes **bronchitis, emphysema** and **cancer.**

Plants and photosynthesis

In this unit we shall be learning about how the leaves of green plants are adapted to make food from carbon dioxide and water using light energy. We shall consider the importance of this food to humans and other animals.

KEY WORDS

photosynthesis
glucose
biomass
chloroplasts
starch
chlorophyll
root hairs
respiration
minerals
nitrates
energy
conservation

9C.1 How do plants grow?

Only green plants make food. We and other animals eat the food that plants make, or eat other animals that have fed on plants.

The leaves of plants are like little food factories.
The raw materials that they use to make food are:

● carbon dioxide, taken from the air through pores in the leaves;

● water, absorbed from the soil by the roots.

The energy for the process of making food is light. The word 'photo' means light, and the word 'synthesis' means making, so we call the process **photosynthesis**.

1   Use the information in the diagram to write a word equation.

The first substance that plants make is **glucose** (a type of sugar). Then they change the glucose into other substances. These are the materials that plants are made of. We call the mass of all these materials the **biomass** of the plant.

2   The word 'biomass' is made up of the words 'bio' and 'mass'. Use a dictionary to find out what these two words mean.

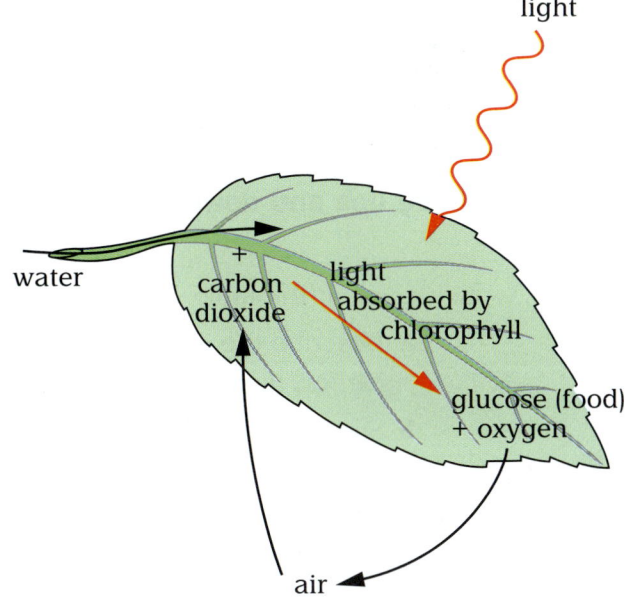

light

water

+ carbon dioxide

light absorbed by chlorophyll

glucose (food) + oxygen

air

What happens in a leaf

A bit of history

In the 17th century, a Dutch scientist called Jan Baptista van Helmont believed that the biomass of a plant came from just water. He planted a willow tree weighing only 1 kg in a big pot containing 90 kg of dry soil. He covered the soil with a piece of tin with lots of holes in it so that only rainwater went through it. Five years later, the tree weighed 100 kg.

 **3** Van Helmont realised that plants need water to make food and to grow. Write down <u>two</u> other things that a plant needs to make its food.

 4 a Suggest why van Helmont thought that water is enough for plants to grow.

b What is the evidence that a plant's food does not come from the soil?

5 Eleanor told her science teacher, Mr Holmes, that she wasn't convinced by van Helmont's experiment. She still believed that plants take their food from the soil. Write a few sentences to explain to Eleanor how Mr Holmes' experiment provides evidence that a plant's food does not come from the soil.

Daily ups and downs

 6 Look at the table.

a Describe the changes in the amount of carbon dioxide over 24 hours.

b Suggest an explanation for these changes.

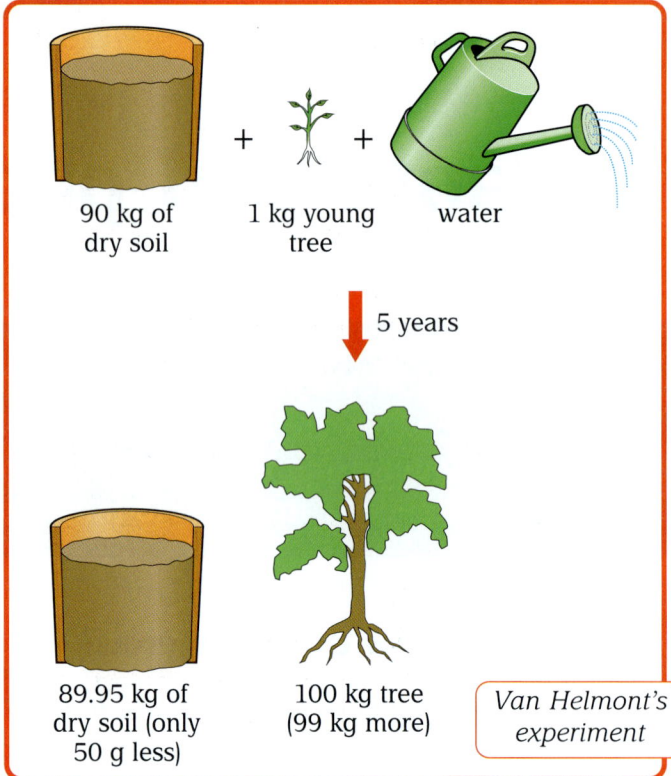

90 kg of dry soil + 1 kg young tree + water

5 years

89.95 kg of dry soil (only 50 g less) | 100 kg tree (99 kg more)

Van Helmont's experiment

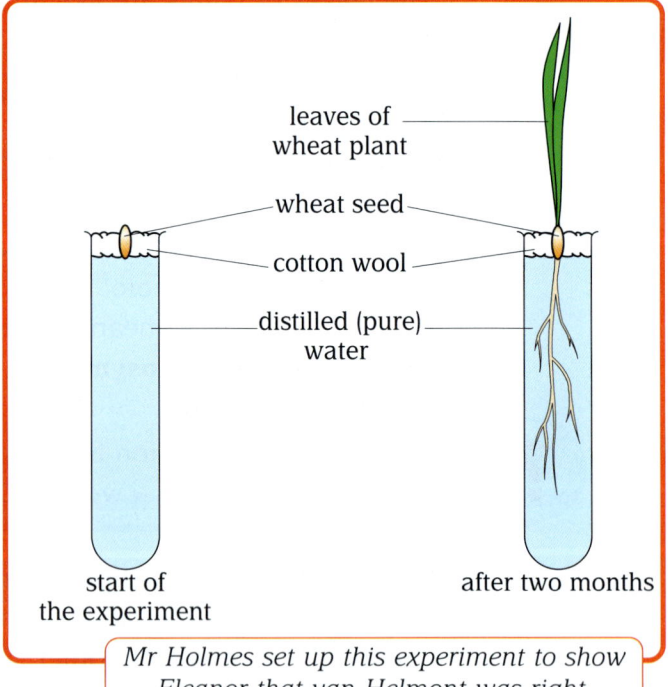

leaves of wheat plant
wheat seed
cotton wool
distilled (pure) water

start of the experiment | after two months

Mr Holmes set up this experiment to show Eleanor that van Helmont was right.

Time	2 am	5 am	8 am	11 am	2 pm	5 pm	8 pm	11 pm
CO_2 concentration (parts per million) amongst leaves	425	352	300	285	280	287	335	380

9C.2 Leaves and photosynthesis

Taking a closer look at a leaf

In a plant, the leaf is the special organ in which most photosynthesis takes place.

The diagram shows the cells in which most photosynthesis happens. These are called palisade cells.

1 Describe the shape of the palisade cells.

2 Suggest how the shape of the palisade cells helps the leaf in photosynthesis.

3 Why are most chloroplasts found near the top of the palisade cells?

Evidence for photosynthesis in the leaf

Once the concentration of glucose in a leaf cell rises above normal, any extra glucose made is changed into **starch**. Plants store their food as starch because it is insoluble. So, when leaves have been photosynthesising, they will have starch inside them.

4 Look at the diagram. What can you conclude from this experiment?

The need for chlorophyll

Chlorophyll is the green substance in leaves that absorbs light. Without chlorophyll, a leaf cannot trap and use the light it needs to make food. Plants that are kept in the dark cannot make food. They end up weak and spindly.

Starch turns blue/black when iodine solution is added to it.

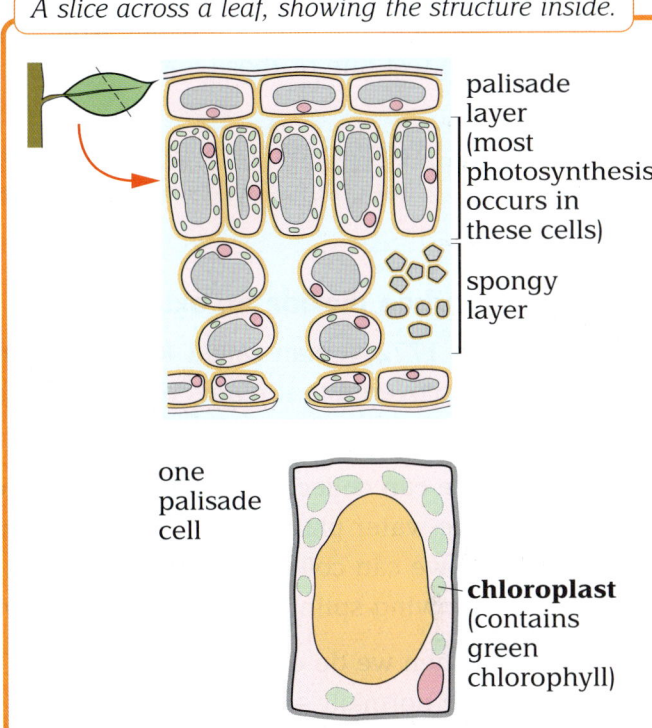

A slice across a leaf, showing the structure inside.

palisade layer (most photosynthesis occurs in these cells)

spongy layer

one palisade cell

chloroplast (contains green chlorophyll)

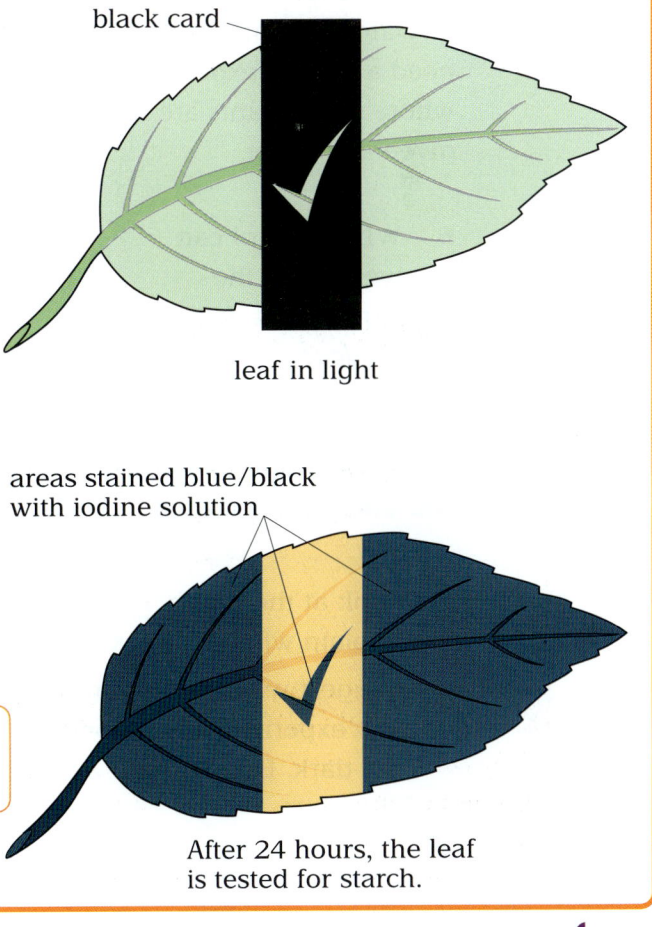

black card

leaf in light

areas stained blue/black with iodine solution

After 24 hours, the leaf is tested for starch.

Some leaves have green parts (containing chlorophyll) and white parts (not containing chlorophyll). We call them variegated leaves. Look at the diagram to see what happens when we test one of these leaves for starch.

 **5** What evidence is there from the experiment that chlorophyll is needed to make starch?

leaf before the test

leaf after testing with iodine solution

Carbon dioxide in, oxygen out

In 1772, a man called Joseph Priestley discovered that plants produce a gas that animals need. We now know that this gas is oxygen.

We can collect the bubbles of gas produced by the water plant *Elodea* and test them for oxygen. If we can collect enough gas, it will relight a glowing splint, so we know it is oxygen.

When we do experiments, we normally set up controls. For example, when we look at the effect of water on plants, we need a control experiment where some plants are not given any water.

 **6** What control can we use for the experiment with *Elodea*?

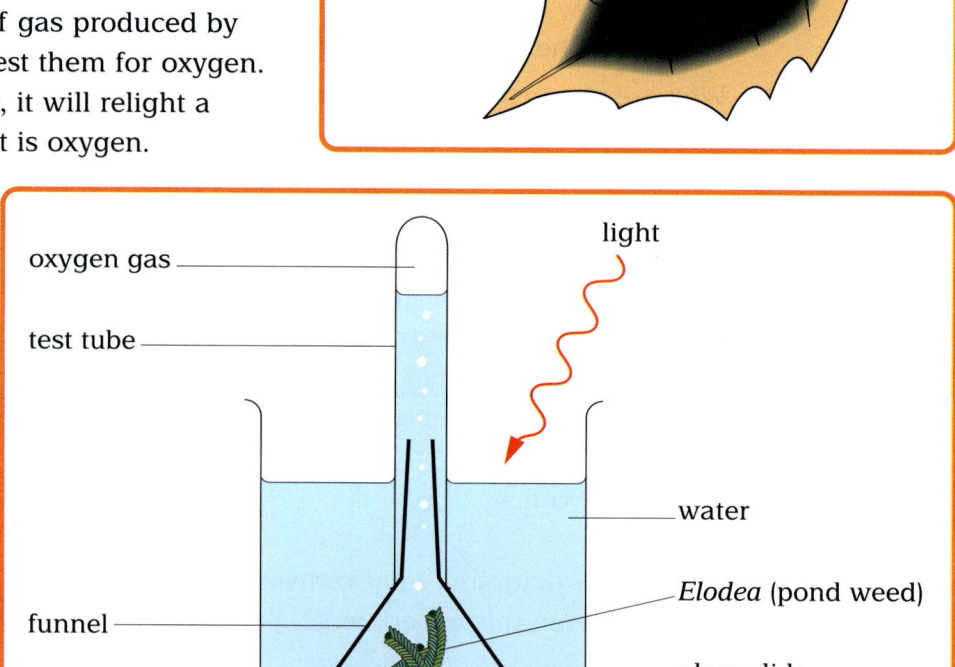

oxygen gas

test tube

light

water

Elodea (pond weed)

funnel

glass slide

How does light intensity affect the amount of oxygen produced?

 **7** Look at the graph. Explain what it shows.

8 Suggest what would happen if this experiment was done in the dark. Explain your answer.

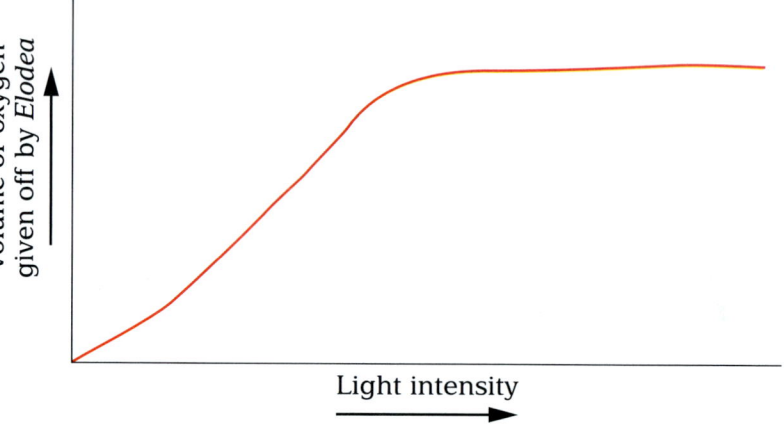

Volume of oxygen given off by *Elodea*

Light intensity

9C.3 What happens to the glucose made in leaves?

Plants use glucose for many things.

● Making starch: plants join together lots of small glucose molecules to make long starch molecules. Starch is stored in roots, stems, leaves, fruits and seeds.

● Releasing energy in respiration: plants need this energy for their life processes.

● Making new materials such as proteins, oils and cellulose.

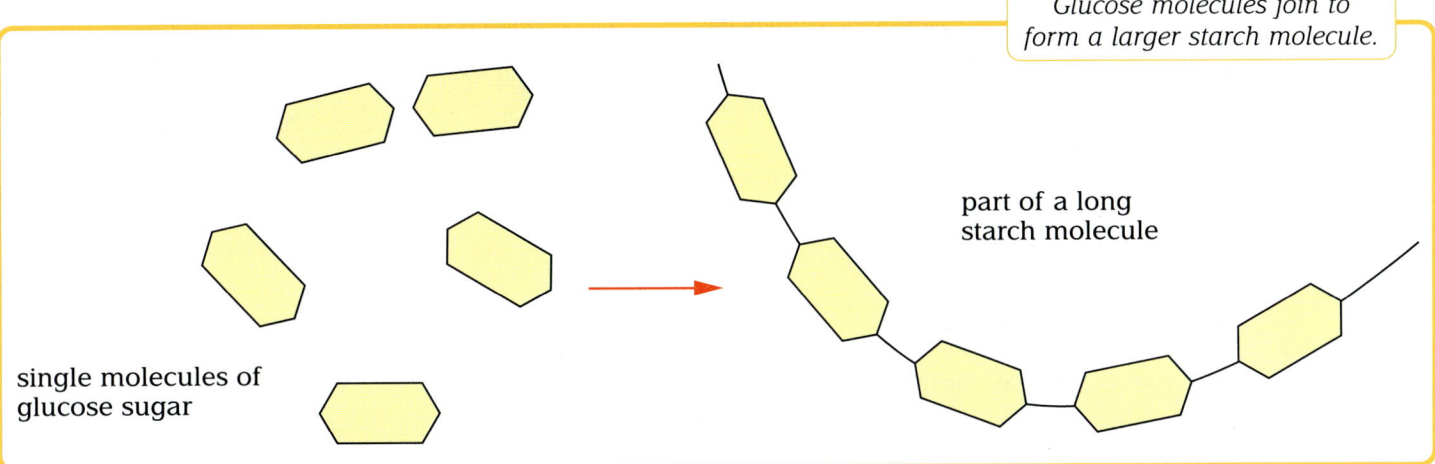

Glucose molecules join to form a larger starch molecule.

single molecules of glucose sugar

part of a long starch molecule

So, some of the glucose is used to release energy, while the rest increases the biomass of the plant.

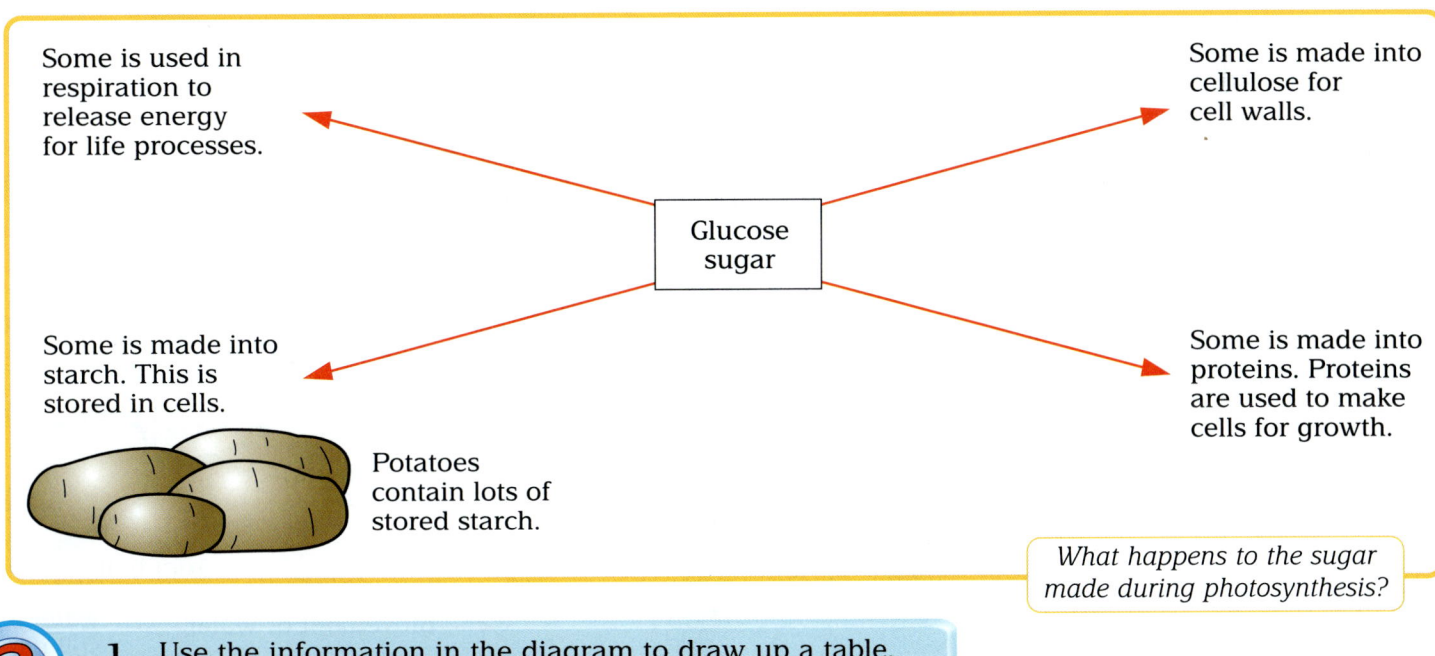

Some is used in respiration to release energy for life processes.

Some is made into cellulose for cell walls.

Glucose sugar

Some is made into starch. This is stored in cells.

Potatoes contain lots of stored starch.

Some is made into proteins. Proteins are used to make cells for growth.

What happens to the sugar made during photosynthesis?

? 1 Use the information in the diagram to draw up a table. Use the following headings for your table:

● **Substance made from glucose**

● **How the substance is used in the plant**

9C.4 Roots, water and minerals

Plant roots are important for anchorage and because they take up water from the soil. You learnt about root hairs in Unit 7A.

1   Describe the route that water takes in a plant from the soil to the leaves.

2   What do the leaves use the water for?

3   Look at the diagram. Write down <u>two</u> things that give roots a larger surface area for absorbing water.

4   How does the shape of the root hair cells help the plant take up water?

Root hair cells, like other living cells, need oxygen for **respiration**. The oxygen is needed to release energy from food for the cell's life processes.

5   Where do root cells get their oxygen for respiration?

Many plants cannot survive in flooded or waterlogged soil. Water does not have as much oxygen dissolved in it as there is oxygen in air.

Antonis is a farmer in a small village called Livadia on the south coast of Cyprus. Livadia is in a valley between the coast and the hills. For many years, when Antonis was a young man, his crops were ruined when the valley flooded. Nowadays, man-made rivers take any flood water away from the valley and into the sea.

6   Why did the flooding kill Antonis' crops?

7   Write down <u>two</u> things that roots take from the soil.

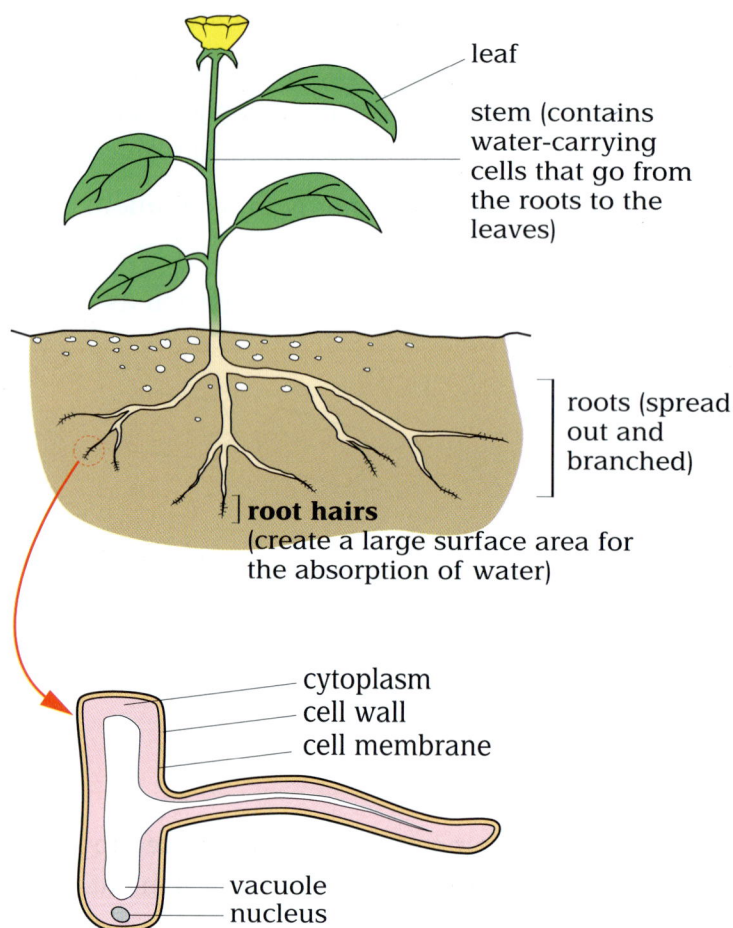

leaf

stem (contains water-carrying cells that go from the roots to the leaves)

roots (spread out and branched)

root hairs (create a large surface area for the absorption of water)

cytoplasm
cell wall
cell membrane

vacuole
nucleus

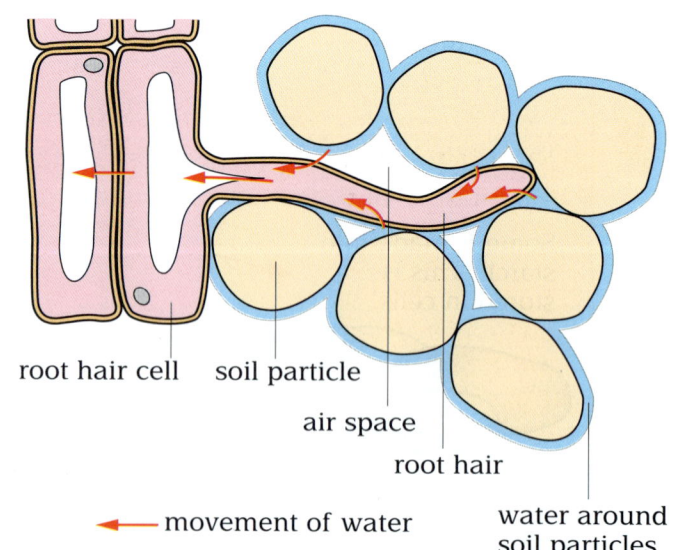

root hair cell   soil particle

air space

root hair

← movement of water

water around soil particles

A root hair cell in the soil

How plants use water

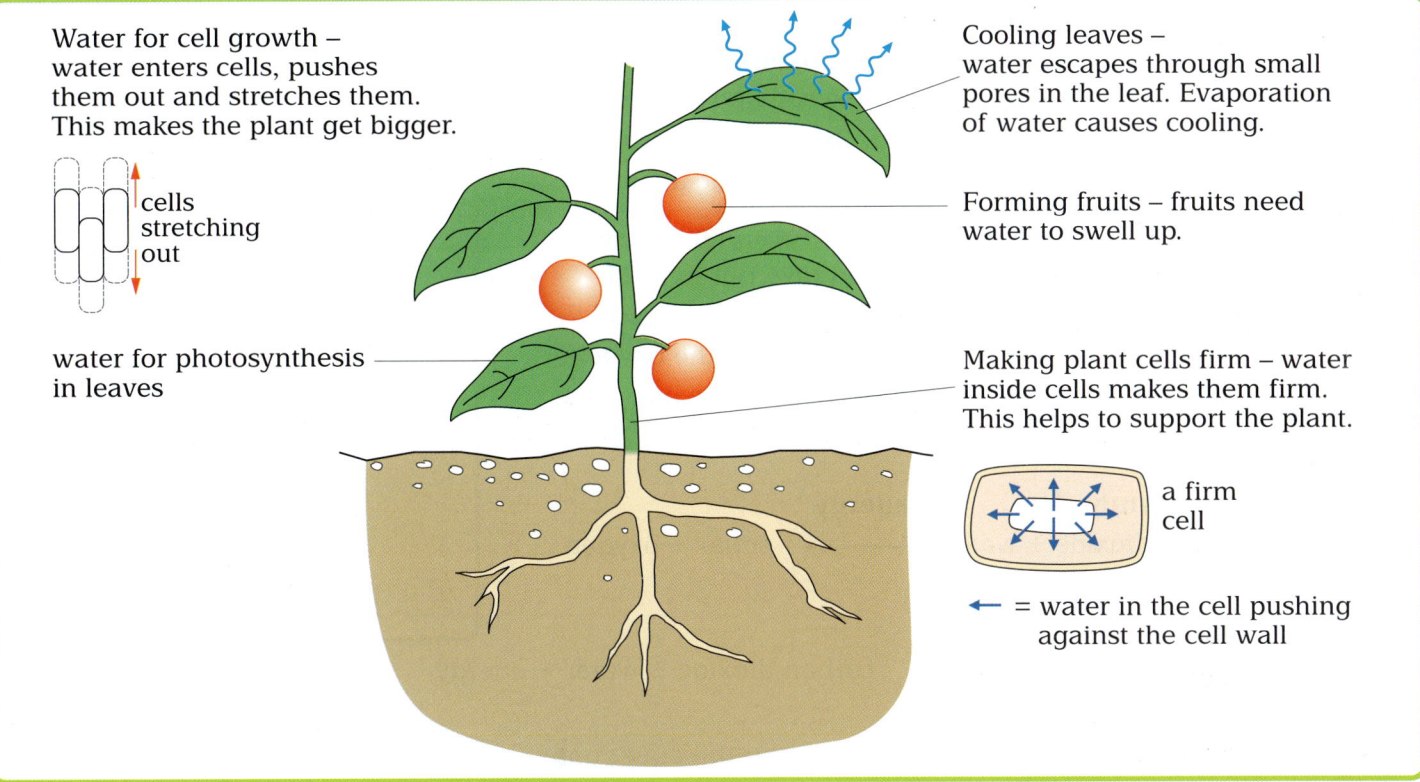

Water for cell growth – water enters cells, pushes them out and stretches them. This makes the plant get bigger.

cells stretching out

water for photosynthesis in leaves

Cooling leaves – water escapes through small pores in the leaf. Evaporation of water causes cooling.

Forming fruits – fruits need water to swell up.

Making plant cells firm – water inside cells makes them firm. This helps to support the plant.

a firm cell

← = water in the cell pushing against the cell wall

8 Use the information in the diagram to draw a table. Use the following headings in your table:

- **Use of water**
- **How does it happen?**

The use of minerals in plants

The water in soil has **minerals**, such as **nitrates**, dissolved in it. Plants need nitrates to make proteins. They need proteins to make and repair cells.

Look at the pictures of plants growing in solutions of minerals.

9 The experiment was set up to find out the effects of a lack of nitrate. Why was bottle A needed?

10 Explain why you need to set up 10 plants like this in each solution, not just the one of each shown.

11 Describe and explain the effects of a lack of nitrate on the plant.

12 Find out how farmers get extra minerals into the soil for their crops.

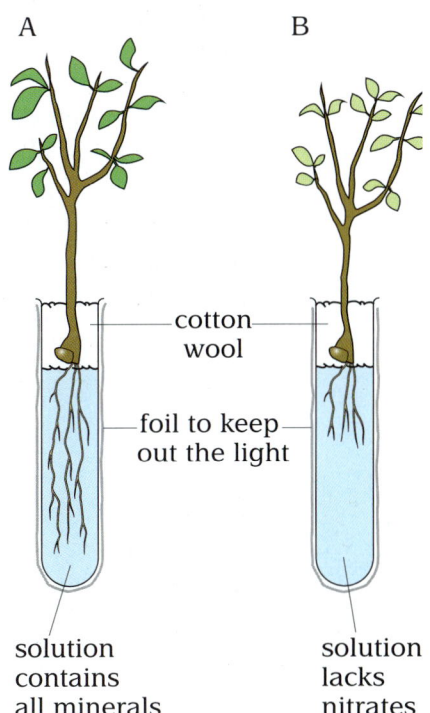

A   B

cotton wool

foil to keep out the light

solution contains all minerals

solution lacks nitrates

Millions of years ago, there was no oxygen in the Earth's atmosphere. Then green plants began to add oxygen. Now, the amounts of oxygen and carbon dioxide remain more or less balanced. Oxygen makes up about 21% of the atmosphere and carbon dioxide about 0.03%.

When they photosynthesise, all green plants take in carbon dioxide from the air and give out oxygen. Because of their large numbers, plants in tropical rainforests and oceans produce most of the oxygen. They also remove carbon dioxide from the air.

Look at the equations.

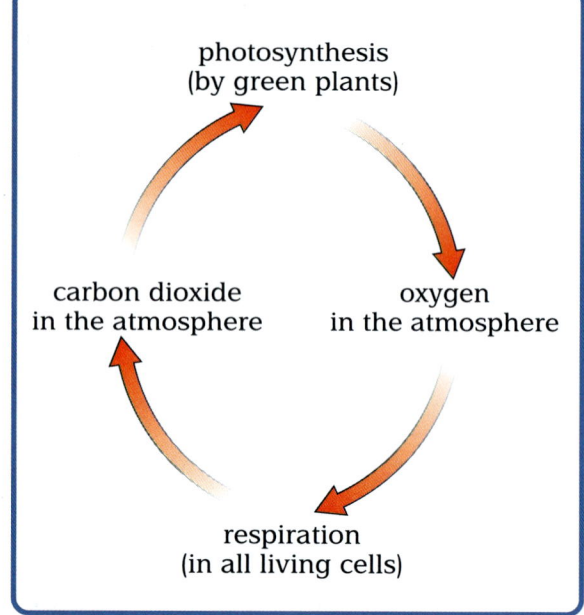

Photosynthesis: **energy**
carbon dioxide + water $\longrightarrow$ sugar + oxygen

Respiration:
sugar + oxygen $\longrightarrow$ carbon dioxide + water + energy

 **1** Make a list of differences between the equations.

Altering the balance

As more forests are cut down, less carbon dioxide is removed from the atmosphere by plants. Also, the burning and rotting of wood increases the amount of carbon dioxide in the atmosphere.

 **2** How much did the amount of carbon dioxide in the atmosphere increase between 1960 and 1990?

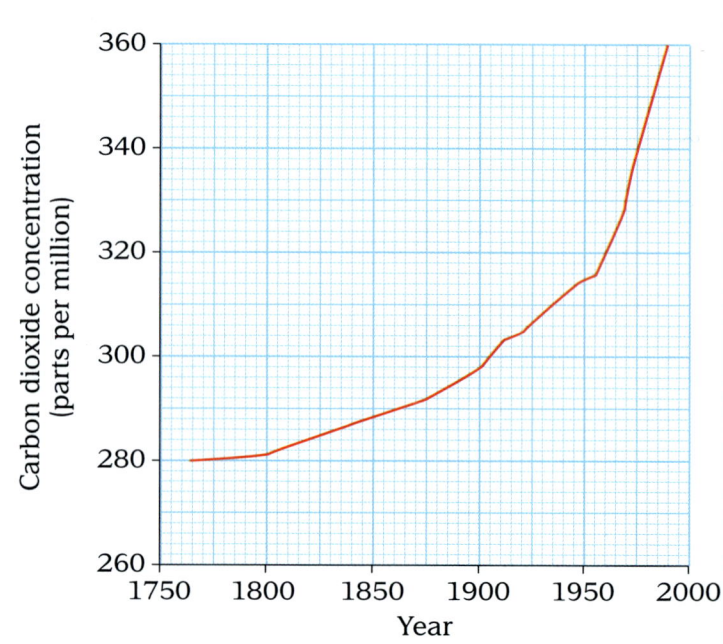

Carbon dioxide is one of a number of gases called greenhouse gases. Greenhouse gases stop heat escaping into space. Many scientists believe that this trapped heat is causing the planet to warm up. This is called global warming.

3 Find out the name of <u>one</u> other greenhouse gas.

Over millions of years, the temperature of our planet has often changed. Also, pollution that causes acid rain has a cooling effect on the planet.

4 Why has it been so difficult to say whether humans are causing global warming?

5 What types of evidence are scientists using to work out a link between global warming and what humans are doing?

Conservation is the protection of the environment. Conserving the forests of the world has many advantages.

- It helps to maintain the balance of gases in the atmosphere. This protects us from climate change.

- Forests provide timber, fruits, nuts, medicines and rubber.

- Forests provide a home for many living things.

6 Find out:

    a the name of a place in the world where people are cutting down forests;

    b why they are cutting the trees down there;

    c what the effects on their environment are.

You should now understand these key words and key ideas.

- Plants make food in their leaves by **photosynthesis**.

- The raw materials for photosynthesis are carbon dioxide and water.

- The light **energy** needed for photosynthesis is trapped by **chlorophyll**.

- Chlorophyll is found in **chloroplasts** in green parts of leaves.

- A plant's **biomass** is the matter that it is made of.

- **Glucose** from photosynthesis is used to make **starch**, to release energy during **respiration** and to make new materials.

- Roots are branched and have **root hairs** to increase their surface area. They need oxygen to respire.

- Plants use their roots to take up water and **minerals** such as nitrates.

- Plants need **nitrates** to make proteins for making and repairing cells.

- A plant uses water to cool its leaves, to swell up fruits, to make its cells firm and to stretch its cells for growth.

- Most photosynthesis happens in the cells near the top of the leaf.

- Plants produce oxygen in photosynthesis.

- About 21% of the air today is oxygen and about 0.03% is carbon dioxide.

- Plants in oceans and forests help to maintain the balance of oxygen and carbon dioxide in the atmosphere.

- Respiration, rotting and burning release carbon dioxide.

Plants for food

In this unit we shall be learning more about where our food comes from and some of the things that affect how much food we produce.

9D.1 Where does our food come from?

You learned in Unit 8A that your food supplies you with:

- energy for all your life processes;

- materials for growth and repair.

Only green plants <u>make</u> food. That is why we call them <u>producers</u>. Animals eat or consume food. So they are called <u>consumers</u>.

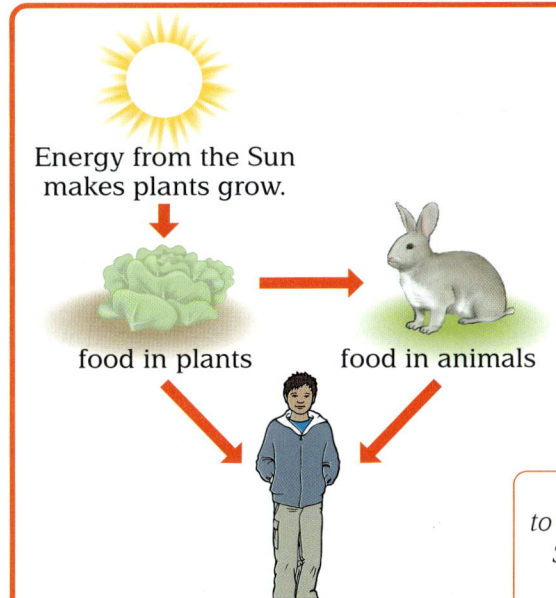

Energy from the Sun makes plants grow.

food in plants   food in animals

KEY WORDS
carnivore
herbivore
nutrients
fertilisers
yield
compete
weedkiller
pests
pesticide
herbicide
fungicide
insecticide
bioaccumulation
biodegradable
sustainable
  development

Plants use sunlight energy to make food in photosynthesis. So, the source of the <u>energy</u> in the food is the Sun.

1   Write down <u>two</u> examples of food from:
a green plants;   **b** animals.

2   If it were not for the Sun and green plants, you'd have no food. Explain why.

3   Are you feeding as a primary consumer or a secondary consumer when you feed on:

a green plants;

b herbivores?

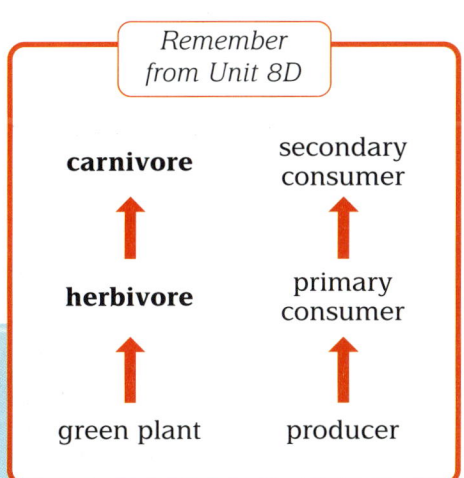

Remember from Unit 8D

carnivore   secondary consumer

herbivore   primary consumer

green plant   producer

Plants make glucose first; then they change some of it into other foods. Look at the diagram.

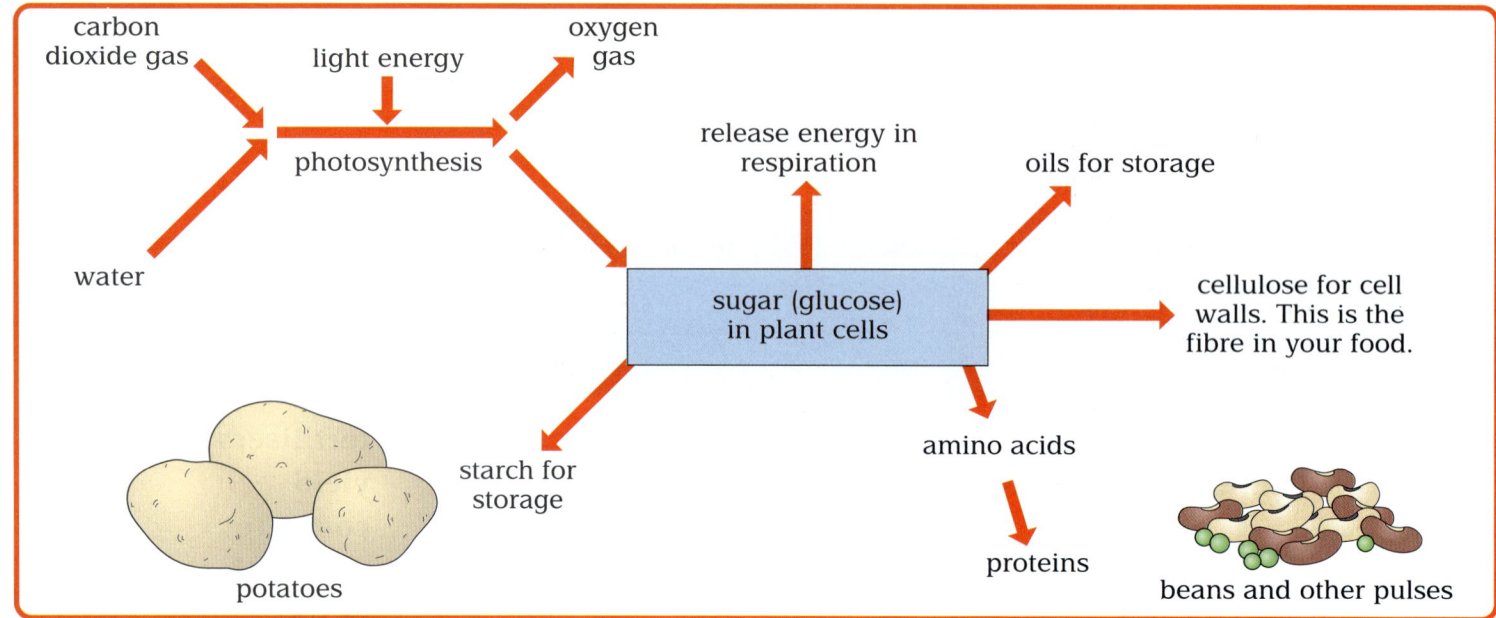

- carbon dioxide gas
- light energy
- oxygen gas
- photosynthesis
- water
- release energy in respiration
- oils for storage
- sugar (glucose) in plant cells
- cellulose for cell walls. This is the fibre in your food.
- starch for storage
- amino acids
- proteins
- potatoes
- beans and other pulses

4 Plant cells use sugars in respiration.
Why do plant cells respire?

5 Why do plants make proteins?

A lot of our food is processed. Sometimes it is hard to tell which animals and plants it came from.

6 Look at the ingredients in the chicken pie.
Which ingredients come from:

a green plants?   **b** animals?

Ingredients

chicken	margarine
onion	herbs
flour	pepper
lard	salt

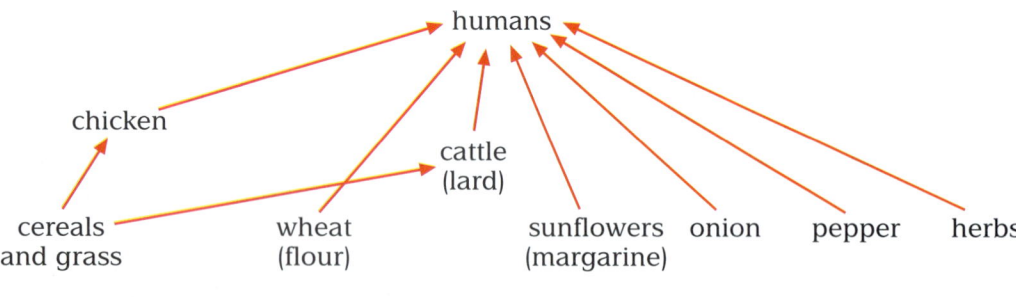

humans

chicken

cattle (lard)

cereals and grass

wheat (flour)

sunflowers (margarine)

onion

pepper

herbs

This food web shows where the ingredients in the chicken pie came from.

7 Draw a food web, like the one for the chicken pie, for your favourite meal.

Most of us don't grow or catch and kill our own food. Farmers in the UK and around the world grow the food we eat. As you saw in Unit 8A, people in different parts of the world often eat different things.

We eat different parts of different plants

Sometimes we can eat one part of a plant but not another.

In the food web for the chicken pie:

- flour, pepper and cooking oil come from seeds;

- onions are bulbs;

- herbs are usually leaves.

Some parts of plants are nicer to eat than others. Some contain more **nutrients** than others. Nutrients are materials, such as starches, oils and proteins, that <u>our</u> cells use. Like us, plants release energy from carbohydrates and fats in respiration. They store food so that they can survive the winter and grow new leaves in the spring. So we eat the food that plants make and store for their own benefit, not ours.

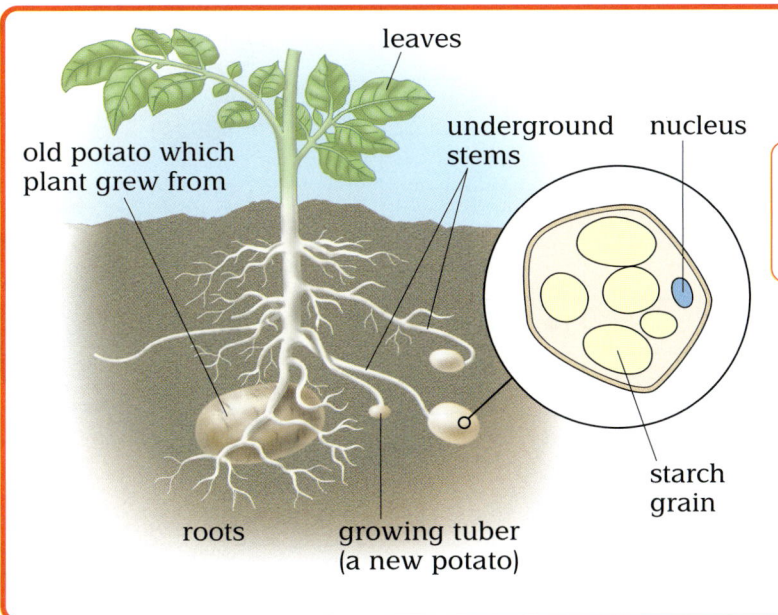

leaves

old potato which plant grew from

underground stems

nucleus

roots

growing tuber (a new potato)

starch grain

We eat potatoes, but the green parts of a potato plant are poisonous.

You can enjoy eating the apples, but not the bark or the leaves of an apple tree.

Look at the pictures.

8 Write down <u>two</u> reasons why we don't eat some parts of plants.

9 Write down:

a <u>one</u> important nutrient that we get from potatoes;

b <u>two</u> nutrients that we get from seeds.

10 Why do seeds contain proteins and an energy source?

11 The fleshy part of fruit, such as plums, contains sugars. The plum tree doesn't use these sugars in respiration. Animals eat and use them. Explain how the tree benefits from the sugars in plums.

	root	stem	leaves	leaf stalk	flower	fruit or seed
beans						●
broccoli					●	
cabbage			●			
carrot	●					
celery				●		
rice						●
sugar cane		●				
tomato						●
wheat						●

12 The table shows some parts of plants that we eat. Draw a similar table for the following foods.

apple   coconut   grape   lettuce   maize   pea
mango   onion   potato   radish   soya bean

Fruits and seeds contain proteins for growth and carbohydrate or fats for energy. When humans and other animals carry away and eat the soft, sugary parts of fruits, they are helping to spread the seeds that are inside the fruits.

9D.2 How do fertilisers affect plant growth?

The equation shows the raw materials and the products of photosynthesis.

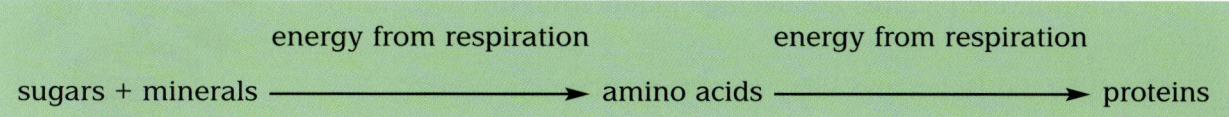

energy from sunlight

carbon dioxide + water ⟶ sugars + oxygen

To make proteins, plants use sugars and minerals such as nitrates too.

energy from respiration   energy from respiration

sugars + minerals ⟶ amino acids ⟶ proteins

Plants also need small amounts of minerals to make chlorophyll and other chemicals. So minerals are <u>plant nutrients</u> and plants take them into their roots from the soil.

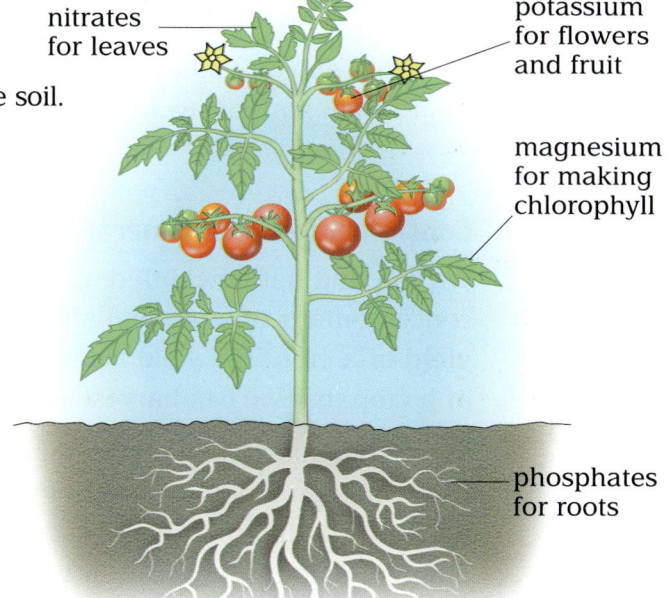

nitrates for leaves

potassium for flowers and fruit

magnesium for making chlorophyll

phosphates for roots

1   Write down <u>two</u> reasons why plants need minerals.

2   Write down the minerals that plants need for healthy growth of:

   a leaves;   **b** roots.

When farmers and gardeners harvest plants, they take away the minerals stored in them. So to make sure that the next crop gets enough minerals, they add **fertilisers** to the soil.

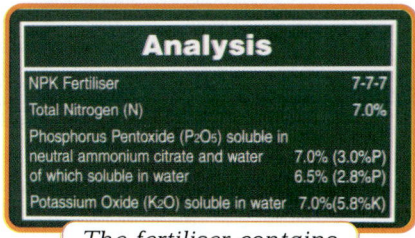

Analysis

NPK Fertiliser	7-7-7
Total Nitrogen (N)	7.0%
Phosphorus Pentoxide (P₂O₅) soluble in neutral ammonium citrate and water	7.0% (3.0%P)
of which soluble in water	6.5% (2.8%P)
Potassium Oxide (K₂O) soluble in water	7.0% (5.8%K)

The fertiliser contains the minerals that plants use most.

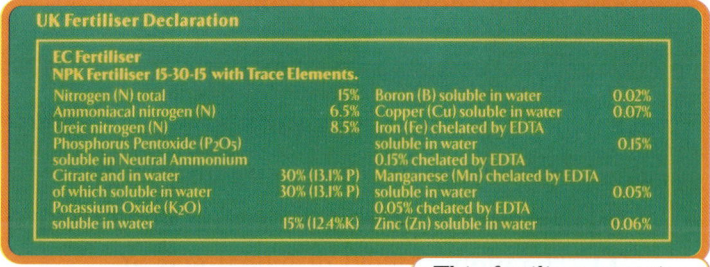

UK Fertiliser Declaration

EC Fertiliser
NPK Fertiliser 15-30-15 with Trace Elements.

Nitrogen (N) total	15%	Boron (B) soluble in water	0.02%
Ammoniacal nitrogen (N)	6.5%	Copper (Cu) soluble in water	0.07%
Ureic nitrogen (N)	8.5%	Iron (Fe) chelated by EDTA	
Phosphorus Pentoxide (P₂O₅)		soluble in water	0.15%
soluble in Neutral Ammonium		0.15% chelated by EDTA	
Citrate and in water	30% (13.1% P)	Manganese (Mn) chelated by EDTA	
of which soluble in water	30% (13.1% P)	soluble in water	0.05%
Potassium Oxide (K₂O)		0.05% chelated by EDTA	
soluble in water	15% (12.4%K)	Zinc (Zn) soluble in water	0.06%

This fertiliser contains extra minerals.

3   **a** Write down <u>three</u> minerals that both fertilisers supply.

   b Write down <u>three</u> extra minerals in the second fertiliser.

4   Write down <u>two</u> things that you think farmers and gardeners take into account when they choose a fertiliser.

Lack of a mineral

We can investigate the lack of a particular mineral by putting small plants in water or clean sand that contains no minerals. Then we can add different minerals to find out what effects they have on plant growth.

Helen and Vijay grew 20 cuttings in sand. They gave 10 plants a fertiliser containing all the minerals that plants need. For a second group of 10 plants, they left out just one mineral. Plants A and B in the pictures are average plants from the two groups.

Plant A had all the minerals it needed.

5   Why did Helen and Vijay grow their plants in sand?

6   Explain why they used 20 plants, rather than just two.

7   Suggest <u>two</u> other ways to make Helen and Vijay's test fair.

8   What do you think plants use magnesium for?
    Explain your answer.

Plant B lacked magnesium.

Concentration of a mineral

We can find out how different concentrations of a mineral affect the **yield** of a crop. The yield is the amount of a crop that we can harvest.

Some students at an agricultural college used different amounts of nitrate fertiliser on wheat in different fields. They mixed different amounts of fertiliser with the same amount of water for each hectare. The graph shows their results.

Spreading fertiliser on a wheat crop.

9   Why do you think the students dissolved the different amounts of fertiliser in the same amount of water?

10 Describe what the students found out.

11 The highest yield of wheat was at 300 kg of fertiliser per hectare. But the students decided that using 200 kg per hectare was more sensible. Suggest a reason for this.

When you investigate fertilisers yourself, remember some of the ideas in this topic.

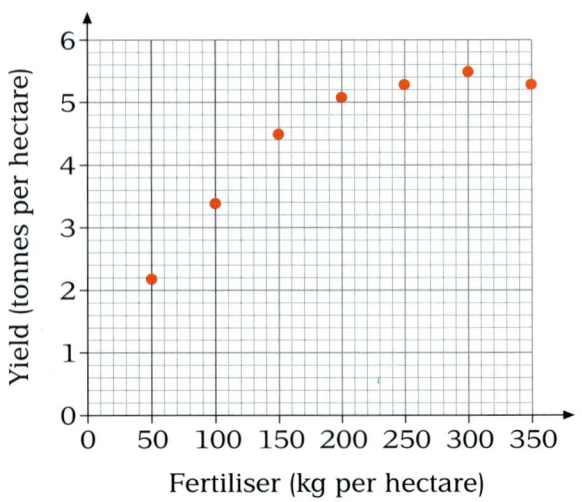

9D.3 Plants out of place

What is a weed?

A weed is a fast-growing plant that is growing where it is not wanted.

Couch grass in a flower border

Daisies in a lawn

1   In which photograph is the grass the weed?

2   In which photograph are the flowers the weed?

How do weeds affect crop production?

3   What do the roots of weeds and crops compete for?

4   What do the leaves of weeds and crops compete for?

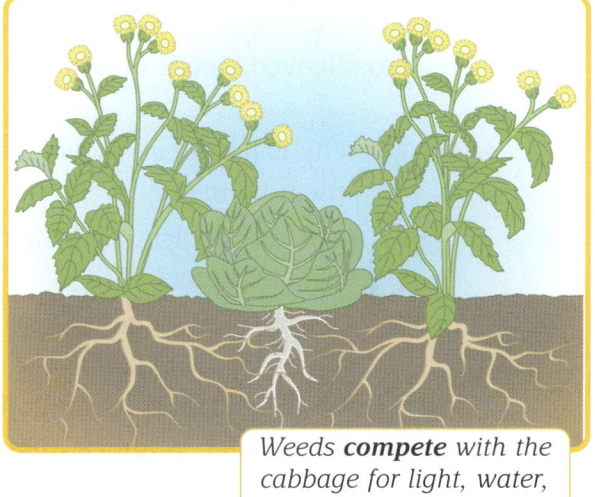

Weeds **compete** with the cabbage for light, water, minerals and space.

How do we control weeds?

Weeds can be removed by hand if crops are grown in rows that are far enough apart. This takes a lot of time and effort.

Farm workers weeding a field of strawberries.

A **weedkiller** is a chemical that kills weeds. You have to choose a weedkiller that doesn't kill your crop plants as well as the weeds. Look at the table.

Weedkiller	Action	Type of plant that it kills
Glyphosate	Plants wilt, leaves turn brown, then the plant dies.	All plants – leaves and roots
2,4-D	Causes unequal growth of leaf stalks and leaves. Leaves cup and twist as they grow, then the plant dies.	Broadleaved plants such as dandelion, plantain, daisy, clover and many crop plants
Diquat	Leaves turn yellow, then black.	Most plants, but not those with deep roots.

5   Which type of weedkiller would you use to get rid of couch grass? Couch grass has underground stems and deep roots that are very hard to kill.

6   Which weedkiller would you choose for getting rid of daisies in a lawn?

Farmers use selective weedkiller to kill broadleaved weeds in their wheat fields.

7   Why is it difficult to weed a field of wheat by hand?

8   Look at the pictures. Which field do farmers prefer?

9   Conservationists are people who want to preserve wild plants and animals. Which field do conservationists prefer?

10 Some weeds produce seeds that wild birds feed on. What will happen to the population of birds if farmers use weedkiller?

11 In a field of crops, nettles are weeds. But they are food for several animals. Find out what animals feed on nettles.

9D.4 Pests

These animals are **pests** because they eat farmers' crops, but they are also important food for other animals.

Some common pests of crop plants.

greenfly   slug   snail   mouse   cabbage white butterfly

Mrs Gilbert has a field of cabbages. Last year, her crop was badly damaged by slugs. This year, she has decided to use a **pesticide** to kill the slugs. She has chosen to use slug pellets – a pesticide that it is claimed kills only slugs and snails and is safe for other wildlife.

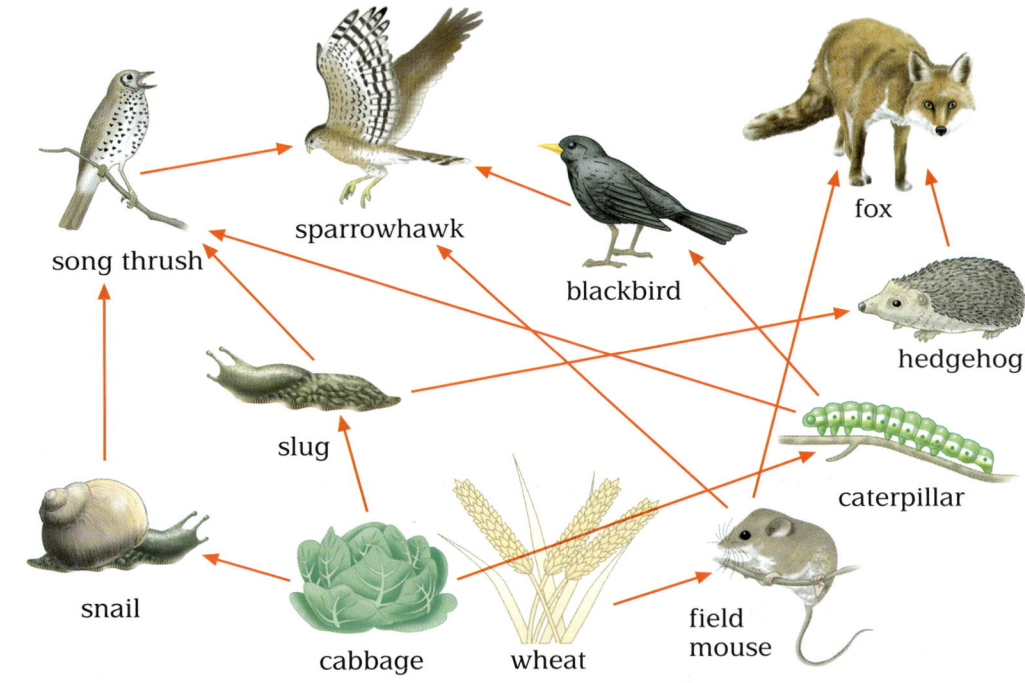

song thrush   sparrowhawk   blackbird   fox   hedgehog   caterpillar   slug   snail   cabbage   wheat   field mouse

A food web in Mrs Gilbert's cabbage field.

1 Caterpillars are usually treated as pests by humans, but name <u>two</u> animals which find caterpillars useful.

2 Look at the food web and describe how you think using slug pellets will affect the population of:

a snails;   **b** song thrushes;   **c** sparrowhawks.

3 If slugs and snails are killed, the cabbage white caterpillar population will change. Explain why the caterpillar population might go:

a up;   **b** down.

4 How can you explain to Mrs Gilbert that, even if the claim that slug pellets kill only snails and slugs is true, other wildlife will still be affected?

5 Find out if slug pellets really are safe for other wildlife.

What are pesticides?

Pests can damage up to 40% of a crop. Farmers use pesticides so that they can produce:

- more food and make more profit;
- undamaged food, which will sell for a good price.

Pesticides kill other wildlife as well as pests.

Type of pesticide	What it kills
Herbicide	Plants
Fungicide	Fungi
Insecticide	Insects

6 Farmers don't spray their crops with insecticide when the crops are flowering. Why do you think this is?

7 What do you think '-cide' means at the end of a word?

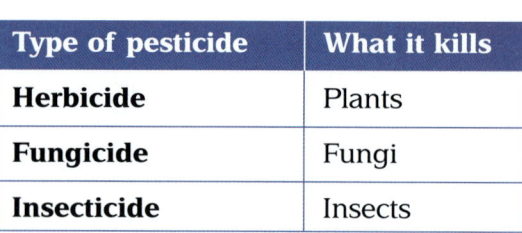

Not all insects are pests of crop plants. Useful insects, such as bees, pollinate flowers.

8 Make up a name for a pesticide that kills <u>rodents</u> such as rats and mice.

Persistent pesticides

Some pesticides aren't broken down easily in the body or in the environment. We call these persistent pesticides. DDT is an example of a persistent pesticide that is now banned in Europe and many other parts of the world.

1 DDT is sprayed onto fields at a safe dose for wildlife. Some is washed into streams and is absorbed by tiny water plants and animals.

4 A heron eats hundreds of fish, so it could accumulate a toxic amount of DDT – enough to kill it.

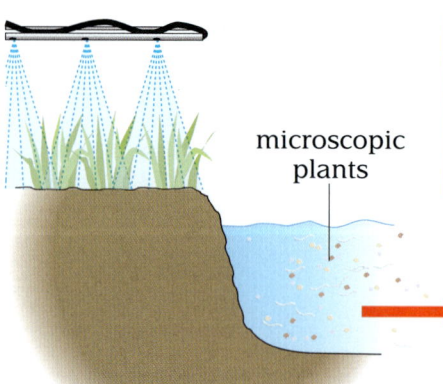

microscopic plants

2 Small fish eat the tiny plants and animals and the DDT is stored in their bodies.

3 Even more builds up in larger fish. We call this **bioaccumulation**.

9 Look at the diagram. How did DDT kill herons when it was sprayed on crops in a dilute 'safe' amount?

10 Why do you think it was 10 years before scientists realised there was a problem with DDT?

Non-persistent pesticides

Pyrethroids are non-persistent pesticides; they break down into simpler substances in living cells and in the environment. We say that they are **biodegradable**.

11 Why do farmers now use non-persistent pesticides? Explain as fully as you can.

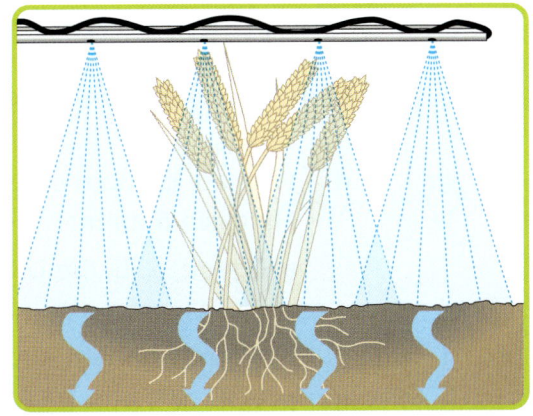

Pyrethroid is sprayed onto fields at a safe dose for wildlife. It breaks down quickly into harmless chemicals once it reaches the soil and is no longer toxic.

9D.5 Producing more food

How the environment affects plant growth

The diagram summarises what you should know about the effects of the environment on plants.

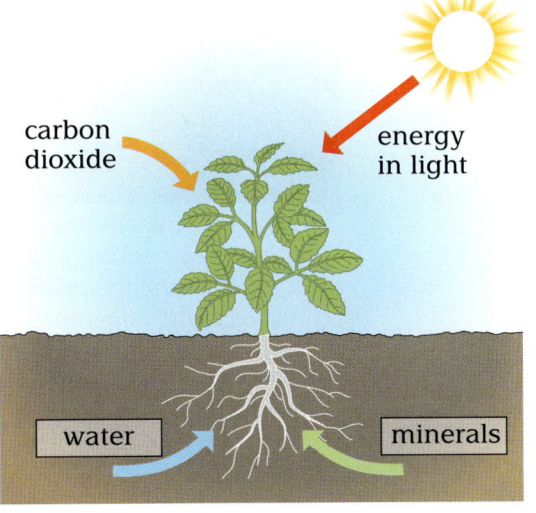

carbon dioxide

energy in light

water

minerals

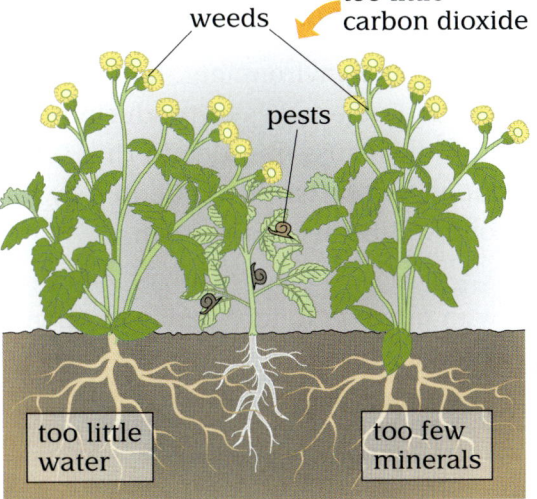

weeds

too little carbon dioxide

pests

too little water

too few minerals

1 Write down <u>five</u> environmental conditions that affect plant growth.

2 **a** Write down <u>two</u> forms of energy that plants need for growth.

  b Where does this energy usually come from?

Improving the environment for plants

Farmers and gardeners control some environmental conditions for their plants. They can buy fertilisers or grow plants in heated greenhouses, but it is too expensive to control everything.

3 Look at the diagram again. Write a list of substances that farmers might need to add to make their crops grow faster.

Some environments provide better conditions for plants than others, and the better the conditions, the higher the yield of a crop. So farmers in different places supply different things.

4   Why are outdoor crops larger and faster growing in Malaysia than in:

a Egypt;   **b** the UK?

5   Tomato growers in the UK heat their greenhouses. Write down <u>one</u> benefit and <u>one</u> disadvantage of doing this.

6   In the UK, crops such as wheat and beans grow faster in higher temperatures. Why don't we provide higher temperatures for them?

7   Find out some benefits and some disadvantages of growing crops in greenhouses.

Can we produce more food?

As well as controlling the environment, farmers and scientists use selective breeding and other ways of producing plants that give better crops. You came across this idea in Unit 9A. But scientists think that the population of Earth will double by the year 2050. So even more food will be needed by then.

8   Compared with growing fodder barley in open fields, explain why fodder units:

a produce fodder more quickly;

b use much less water.

One problem is that in other places good land is being destroyed by overuse. What we need are ways of continuing to produce more food without damaging the Earth. This will let development continue, so we call it **sustainable development**.

9   Write down <u>two</u> reasons why we need scientists to carry on researching crops and crop production.

In Malaysia, the climate is wet, hot and sunny. Farmers use manure as a fertiliser and need to control pests, weeds and diseases.

Egypt is dry, hot and sunny. Salim uses manure to provide plant nutrients, takes out weeds and sometimes uses pesticides. He pumps water into channels in his fields daily. We call this <u>irrigation</u>.

Some farmers use fodder units to grow barley 'grass' from seed. It takes 2 or 3 litres of water to produce each kilogram of fodder. Solar oanels provide heat and light.

In commercial greenhouses in the UK, growers control pests and diseases and the amounts of water and fertilisers. Opening and closing of windows is automatic.

You should now understand these key words and key ideas.

carnivore
herbivore
nutrients
fertilisers
yield
compete
weedkiller
pests
pesticide
herbicide
fungicide
insecticide
bioaccumulation
biodegradable
sustainable
  development

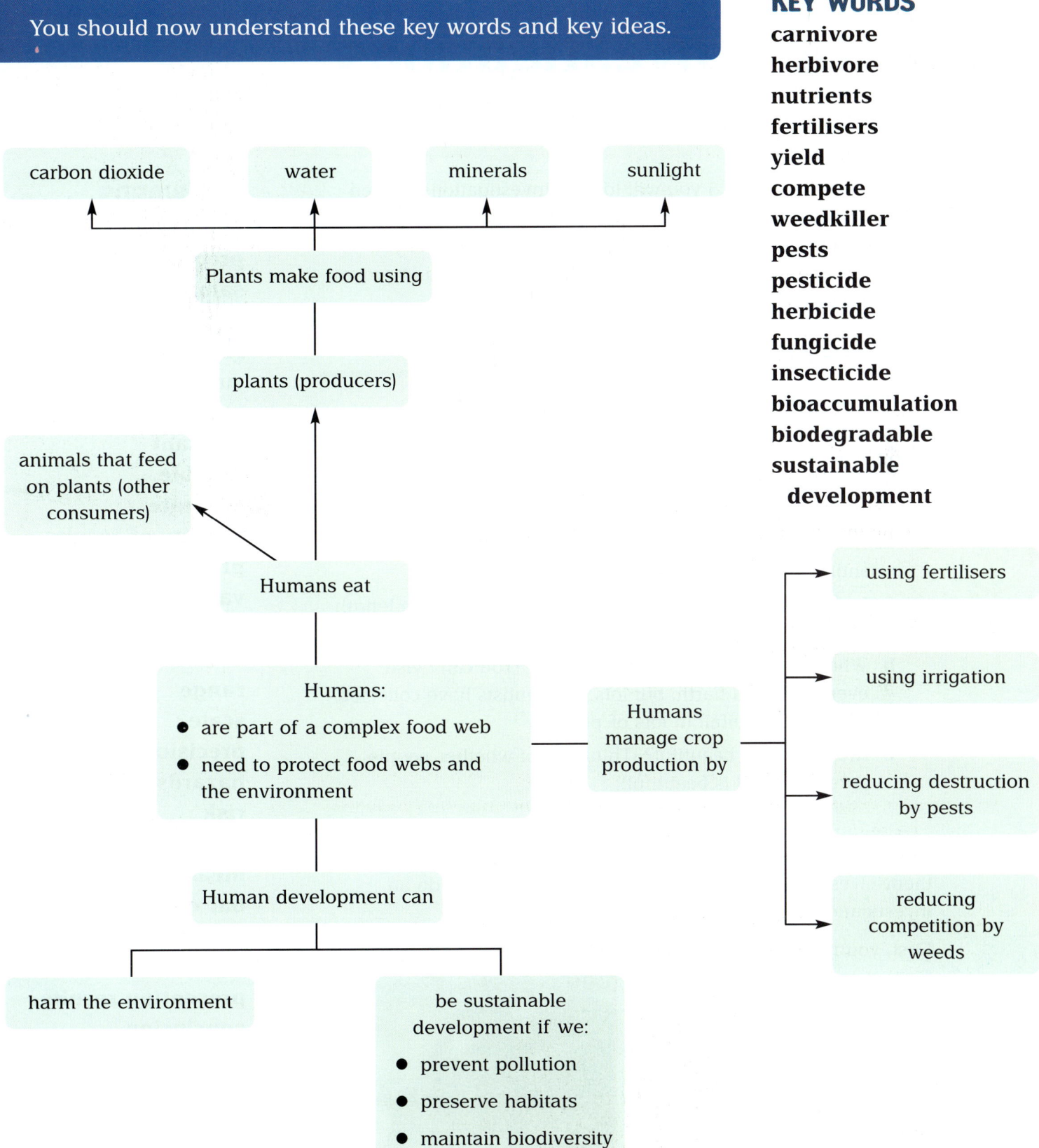

carbon dioxide   water   minerals   sunlight

Plants make food using

plants (producers)

animals that feed on plants (other consumers)

Humans eat

Humans:
- are part of a complex food web
- need to protect food webs and the environment

Humans manage crop production by

- using fertilisers
- using irrigation
- reducing destruction by pests
- reducing competition by weeds

Human development can

harm the environment

be sustainable development if we:
- prevent pollution
- preserve habitats
- maintain biodiversity

Scientific investigations

Throughout Key Stage 3 you will look at investigations carried out by scientists, past and present, and carry out your own investigations. This chapter will remind you of the skills you learnt at Key Stage 2 and will help you to practise and improve them. It will also introduce new skills.

Planning investigations

Finding suitable questions for investigations

When you do an investigation, you have a question to answer. Then you plan an investigation that you hope will give you the answer. But you can't answer all questions by doing a scientific investigation.

1   Look at parts **a** to **c**. Can you answer them by doing a scientific investigation? Explain your answers.

   a Is there a link between the height of a cat and the length of its whiskers?

   b Where is the rainiest place on Earth? (You can't visit everywhere on Earth, but lots of scientists have collected data about rainfall in lots of places.)

   c Are waterfalls beautiful? (Think about whether people agree on what is beautiful!)

Now think about the question of why elephants throw water over themselves. You can't answer it directly, but you can do an investigation using a model.

First, you need to think of <u>ideas</u> that might explain why elephants throw water over themselves. We call these ideas **hypotheses**.

Elephants often spray water over themselves like this.

KEY WORDS

hypotheses
prediction
sample size
sampling
random
surveys
secondary data
relevant
reliable
accurate
validity of results
preliminary tests
variable
vary
control
range
scale
precision
hazards
risk
risk assessment
mean
bar chart
line graph
data collection
presenting results
conclusion
evidence
evaluation
anomalous results
opinions
biased

The idea that elephants do this to cool themselves is one that you can test. You probably haven't got an elephant, so you have to use a model! A plastic bottle full of hot water makes a suitable model. You can use a thermometer or a temperature probe and a datalogger to show any temperature changes.

File Edit Object Type Tools View Help

The elephants are:
* just having a wash;
* trying to cool themselves;
* getting rid of parasites;
* chasing away flies;
* just playing.

2 Draw your idea of what the model elephant apparatus looks like.

3 Remember that you are trying to find out if water makes the elephants cooler.

   a Describe how to model throwing the water over the elephant.

   b What measurements will you need to write down?

Next, you need to say what you think your results will be. This is called making a **prediction**. You need to use the science that you know to give reasons for your prediction. Kirsty has made a prediction:

I think that when we pour cold water over the plastic bottle, the temperature of the water inside will fall.

4 Do you think that Kirsty's prediction is correct? Explain your answer as fully as you can. Remember that an explanation using scientific ideas will get you the best marks.

Choosing the best strategy for an investigation

Often there are several possible ways of doing an investigation. However, one method may be better than the others. For example, one way may be easier, safer or produce more useful data than all the other methods.

You are likely to have done investigations involving fair testing in which you learnt about the importance of controlling variables. However, some variables are easier to control than others. Physical factors such as light and temperature are fairly easy to control.

Living things are a particular problem because they themselves vary. So when you investigate living things, you use 10 or 20 or more, not just one. We call this using a sample. You have to think about a suitable **sample size**. In *Spectrum Biology* Unit 8D you learn how to estimate the numbers of different living things by **sampling** using quadrats.

*By taking a sample of 20 **random** quadrats, these pupils are allowing for the fact that conditions are not the same in all parts of the beach.*

5 Explain why the sample needs to be random.

You can also use sampling to do **surveys** of data about people, including people's opinions. These often involve questionnaires.

Information collected by other people is useful in some investigations. We call the information **secondary data**. Examples are the data in leaflets produced by companies, consumer reports, libraries and the Internet. You need to be careful as some of this information may be biased.

You can find out information from secondary sources such as this.

6 List some secondary sources of information about factors affecting the pH of soil.

Collecting appropriate data

To answer your question, the data that you collect must be relevant, reliable and accurate. So you need to:

- choose a suitable design of your investigation to ensure that your evidence is **relevant**. That is why scientists often do trial runs. Relevant evidence is evidence that will help you to answer your question;

- record sufficient observations or readings to ensure that your evidence is **reliable**;

- choose suitable measuring instruments and take accurate and precise readings to ensure that your evidence is **accurate**.

The **validity of results** depends on the accuracy and precision of the <u>measuring instruments</u> that you choose and <u>how well you use them</u>.

Using preliminary work such as trial runs

Scientists often do trial runs of experiments to find out whether their approach will work or not.

Mrs Tasker asked her class to find out which of three varieties of apples gave the most juice by finding out how much of each apple is water. She set her class some preliminary work using books to research a method. No one found that actual experiment, but Bryan found one about the amount of water in soil. Using the same idea, he suggested an experiment:

- Find the mass of an apple.
- Heat it to get rid of all the water.
- Find its mass again. The loss in mass will be equal to the mass of water that was in the apple.

Anna found out that you needed to repeat this several times until two masses were the same. It is called heating to constant mass and you do it so you can be sure that all the water has gone. Lee thought that chopping the apple might make drying faster. Mrs Tasker was pleased with the ideas so far – but she pointed out that they hadn't described how to heat the apple.

She suggested that they needed to do some **preliminary tests**. They needed to try out their ideas to find out which one worked best.

7 What <u>two</u> kinds of preliminary work did the class do before they planned their investigation?

Size of apple pieces	Heat over Bunsen flame		Dry on an open shelf at 20°C		Heat in an oven at 100°C		Heat in an oven at 300°C	
	cut into 1/8ths	chopped up small	cut into 1/8ths	chopped up small	cut into 1/8ths	chopped up small	cut into 1/8ths	chopped up small
Mass at start (g)	140.8	136.4	142.3	143.5	138.6	136.7	133.6	139.1
Mass after 40 mins (g)	12.7	10.1	137.6	135.2	103.5	100.8	10.9	10.1
Mass after 1 day (g)	not done	not done	69.1	67.7	17.3	16.2	9.4	8.4
Mass after 7 days (g)	not done	not done	28.5	28.9	17.3	16.2	not done	not done
Loss in mass (g)	128.1	126.3	113.8	114.6	121.3	120.5	124.2	130.7
% loss in mass	91	92.5	80	80	87.5	88	93	94
Observations	black (burnt)	black (burnt)	brown and mouldy	brown and mouldy	brown	brown	black (burnt)	black (burnt)

Results of preliminary tests.

8 The pupils rejected heating over a Bunsen and in an oven at 300°C because the apple lost more than just water.

  a What evidence is there that more than just water was lost?

  b Suggest what else was lost.

9 Suggest <u>two</u> problems of drying the apple at 20°C.

10 These tests didn't show whether chopping up the apple made a difference to the time taken to dry the apple. What extra tests can the class do to find out the answer?

11 In the final plan for their investigation, why did the pupils:

  a chop up the apples;

  b find the mass of the apples on a digital balance;

  c heat in an oven at 100°C;

  d heat to constant mass?

12 Write a list of other ideas that the pupils probably used to make their investigation safe and their results valid.

Controlling variables

In an experiment, lots of things affect the results.
We call these **variables**.

To find out the effect of temperature on dissolving salt, you **vary** the temperature but keep the other things the same. We say that you **control** them. This is to make your test fair.

It makes it easier to spot a pattern in your results if you use a wide **range** for your variable. For example, your results may be too similar to be sure of the pattern if you use only a small range of temperatures.

13 Write down <u>two</u> things that you need to control or keep the same when you investigate the effect of temperature on dissolving.

Selecting equipment

Some choices of equipment are easy but you need to be particularly careful when you choose measuring equipment. Instruments for measuring have a **scale** on them. You need to choose the instrument with a suitable scale for your particular investigation.

For example, measuring the mass of a **small strip of magnesium** on kitchen scales would not give you a useful reading. A chemical balance would be much more useful. The choice affects the **precision** of your results.

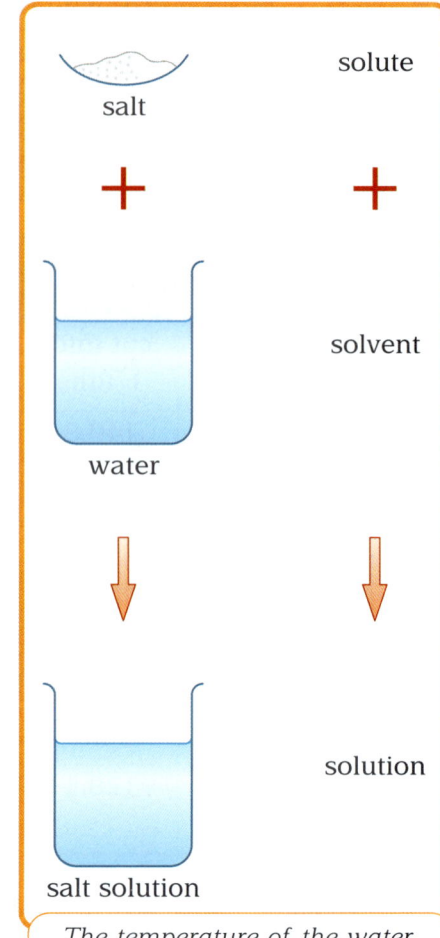

The temperature of the water, the size of the crystals and the amount of stirring all affect the time it takes for the salt to dissolve. These are all variables.

Sean is investigating the force needed to pick up objects in the lab.
He estimates that the weight of these objects varies from 5N to 45N.

14 Choose the best forcemeter for Sean's investigation.
Explain your choice.

Safety

Sometimes you need to use apparatus or chemicals that can be harmful. We call these things **hazards**. You can use them only if you make sure that you and other people are safe. You can look up some hazards in books and others on Hazcards, or you can ask your teacher for help.

Next you need to ask yourself how high a **risk** there is of the hazard causing harm. We call this a **risk assessment**. You do this to decide whether your investigation is safe enough to do. Sometimes the risk assessment helps you to see how to make your investigation safe, for example by wearing eye protection.

15 Where can you find out about possible hazards?

16 What must you do if you are not sure that your investigation is safe enough?

Obtaining and presenting evidence

Before you start an investigation, you need to know exactly:
- what you are going to do;
- what results you are going to record;
- how you are going to record your results, for example in a table on paper or using a datalogger.

Collecting appropriate data

You don't always get the same results from the same experiment. To find out what is really happening, you have to:
- do your experiment several times;
- work out the average result. You find the average by adding together your results and dividing by the number of results. This is sometimes called the **mean**.

Often you can use a range of sources of information and data in an investigation. The more data you have, the easier it is to be confident about your conclusion. A whole class set of results produces even more accurate and reliable data.

17 Why is it more accurate to have several sets of data?

Hazardous chemicals have warning labels. You need to be able to recognise them.

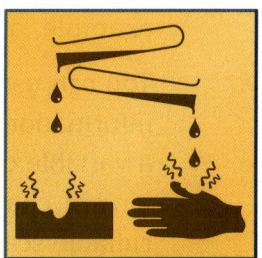

CORROSIVE

This is the sign for an irritant.

This is the sign for a harmful substance.

Presenting results as bar charts or graphs

Often you need to show results in ways that will help you to see any trends and patterns. For example, as a **bar chart** or a **line graph**.

You can use a bar chart to compare one piece of information with another. A line graph shows how a variable changes. You need to choose the best kind of chart or graph for your data as well as a suitable scale for each axis.

Usually when you are plotting a bar chart or a line graph, the variable that you changed goes along the bottom (x-axis) and the one you measured goes up the side (y-axis).

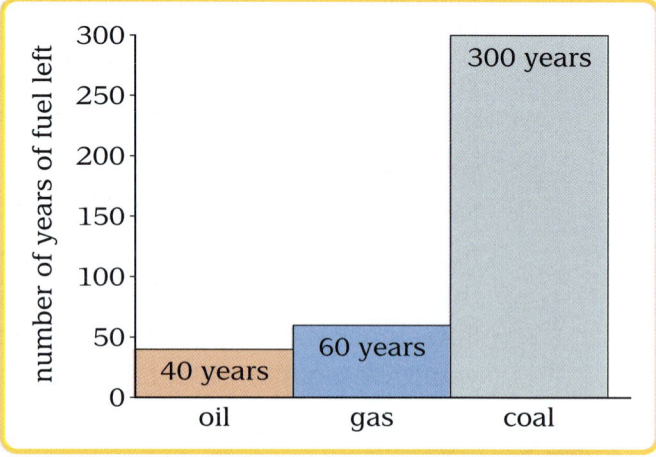

Using computers to collect data and present results

The Internet is a source of information for some investigations. You can also use a computer for **data collection** and **presenting results**.

You can use dataloggers with sensors to record different sorts of environmental changes, for example temperature, amount of light and amount of dissolved oxygen. You can also use them to log the times of readings. So data can be collected over 24 hours without you having to remember to take readings or having to stay up all night.

You can plot the results of experiments, whether collected by hand or with a datalogger, using a spreadsheet program. Careful plotting can make results easier to read. When you get used to using a spreadsheet for plotting graphs, it will also save you time.

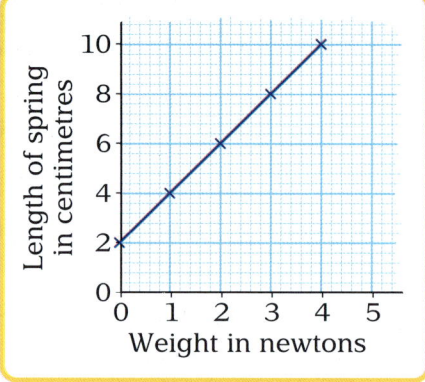

 **18** What are the advantages in using a datalogger?

Considering evidence

Identifying trends

Tables, charts and graphs allow you to identify any trends and patterns in your data and to pick out results that do not fit the pattern.

Coming to conclusions

The **conclusion** is where you say what you have found out, so it is an important part of your investigation. You need to describe any trends or patterns and the evidence that supports your conclusion. You should also try to use scientific ideas to explain why you got the results that you did.

Evaluating evidence

Measurement and observation are part of the process of collecting **evidence** to support an explanation or theory. The last part of any investigation is to carry out an **evaluation**. You need to look at the evidence and decide:

- whether there is enough evidence to support a conclusion;
- how you could improve your investigation to increase the strength of your evidence;
- whether or not things presented as evidence are <u>actually evidence</u>.

For example, perhaps you could have:

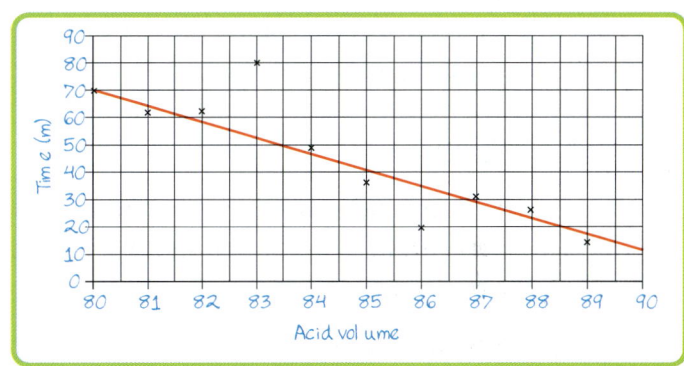

- taken readings more accurately;
- taken more readings;
- repeated readings.

You also need to try to spot any results that do not fit the general pattern. These are called **anomalous results**.

Look at the graph showing a line of best fit.

19 Some points on the graph do not lie near the line of best fit. What can you do to improve this set of readings?

Sometimes people give their **opinions**. They may have no evidence for their ideas. Their opinions may be **biased**. They are conclusions that, if correct, would benefit them in some way.

In experimental investigations, you are probably used to evaluating the number and accuracy of readings and know how to deal with readings that don't fit the pattern. You assume that the work of other people who contributed results is accurate and honest. In some other investigations, for example life-style surveys, people don't always tell the truth.

20 a Sometimes smokers deny that they smoke. Suggest reasons.

  b Write down three other life-style or health issues where people sometimes hide the truth.

So, sometimes evidence is gathered inaccurately and sometimes it is incomplete. When your evidence is incomplete, you may find that your explanation turns out to be wrong. This shows just how careful you have to be when you consider and evaluate evidence.

Glossary/Index

Words in *italics* are themselves defined in the glossary.

A

absorb, absorption   when an object or substance takes in another object or substance, for example when living *cells* or *blood* take in *dissolved* *nutrients* or *oxygen*   59–60, 63–64, 75, 78, 93, 123, 129, 131, 148

accurate, accuracy   correct, *precise* and without any mistakes; accurate *evidence* is gathered using accurate measuring instruments with *precision*   42, 154, 157, 159

acid, acidic   a *solution* that *reacts* with many metals to produce a *salt* and *hydrogen*, and with *alkalis* to produce a salt and water   62, 82, 86

acid rain   rain that is more *acidic* than rain normally is because it has *sulphur dioxide* or *nitrogen oxides dissolved* in it   137

adaptation, adapted, adapt   when plants or animals have *characteristics* which make them suitable for where they live   25–28, 30–33, 36, 91, 102

addict   a person who can't do without [is dependent on] a *drug*   115, 118, 125, 128

addictive drug   a *drug* on which people can become dependent   118, 123

adolescent, adolescence   a person who is no longer a child, but is not yet an adult; a time of physical and emotional change   22–24

aerobic respiration   using *oxygen* to break down food to release *energy*   66, 71, 74, 78

air   a *mixture* of *gases*, mainly *nitrogen* and *oxygen*   26, 67, 69, 71–78, 86, 117

air sacs   small sacs made of groups of *alveoli* at the end of air tubes in the *lungs*   72, 119

alkali, alkaline   chemicals that *neutralise acids* to produce *salts*   62

alcohol   a chemical that can be used as a *drug*   19, 122–125, 128

alveoli   tiny round parts that make up the *air sacs* in the *lungs*; one is an alveolus   72–73

amino acids   *carbon compounds* that *proteins* are built from   61, 63, 65, 78, 140

amniotic fluid   the *liquid* that surrounds and supports the *fetus* in the *uterus*   19, 24

amphibian   a *vertebrate* that lives on land and in water but has to lay its eggs in water   49, 52

anomalous results   results that do not fit the general pattern   159

anther   part of a flower which makes the *pollen*   10

antibiotic   *drugs* used to kill *bacteria* in the body   82, 87–88, 90, 122

antibodies   chemicals made by *white blood cells* to destroy *bacteria* and other *micro-organisms*   87, 89

anus   the opening at the end of the *digestive system*   60–61

Aristotle   (384–322 BC)   1, 46

arteries   blood vessels that carry *blood* away from the *heart*   68–70, 78, 126

arthropod   an *invertebrate* with an outer skeleton with jointed legs   50–52

asexual reproduction   reproduction in which only one parent is involved and the offspring have the same *genes* as the parent   112–114

atmosphere   the layer of air above the Earth's surface   136–138

atom   the smallest part of an *element*

B

bacteria *micro-organisms* that are *cells* without true *nuclei*; one is called a bacterium 63, 79–80, 83, 85–90

bar chart a way of *presenting results* 158

biased, bias in the case of an *opinion*, based on someone's feelings rather than all the facts 154, 159

Bichat, Xavier (1771–1802) 1

bioaccumulation when a substance such as a *pesticide* accumulates along a *food chain* 148

biodegradable made of *materials* that *micro-organisms* can break down or decay 149

biomass the *mass* of the *materials* that plants and animals are made of 129–130, 138

bird a *vertebrate* with feathers 14, 46–47, 52

blood a *liquid* in animal circulatory systems 8, 19, 59–60, 63–72, 78, 87, 118, 121

blood system the *heart, arteries, capillaries, veins* and the *blood* that *circulates* through them 68

breathing, breathe taking *air* in and out of the *lungs* 7, 56, 67, 72–74, 76, 78, 86, 116–119, 128

bronchitis an infection of the air tubes in the *lungs* 119, 128

Brown, Robert (1773–1858) 2

burning when substances *react* with *oxygen* and release *energy*; also called *combustion* 66, 136

C

calcium a metal *element*; a *mineral nutrient* that living things need 56–57, 64, 121

camouflage colouring to hide something against its background 25, 27, 32

cancer a disorder in which *cells* grow out of control 115, 118–120, 123, 128

capillary a narrow blood vessel with walls only one *cell* thick 67–70, 72–73, 78

car exhaust emissions waste *gases* from car exhausts 118

carbohydrates *carbon compounds* used by living things as an *energy* source, for example *starch* and sugars 53, 55–59, 64, 120, 128, 141–142

carbon a non-metallic *element* 119

carbon dioxide a *gas* in the *air* produced by living things in *respiration*, in *combustion* or *burning* and when an *acid reacts* with a carbonate 19, 66–68, 72–78, 81, 107, 116–117, 126, 129–130, 136–138, 140, 143, 149, 151

carbon monoxide a poisonous *gas* 118

carnivore an animal that eats flesh 33–34, 36, 43, 99, 102, 139

cell (in biology) building block of plants and animals 1–2, 4–9, 12, 16, 23, 53–55, 61, 63–69, 71–72, 74, 76, 80, 106, 116–117, 119, 123, 133–135, 140–141, 149

cell membrane the outer layer of the living part of a *cell* 6, 12, 105, 134

cell sap a *solution* of sugars and other substances found in the *vacuoles* of plant *cells* 6, 12

cell wall outer supporting layer of a plant *cell* 6, 9, 12, 57, 80, 134–134, 140

Chain, Ernst (1906–1979) 88

characteristics the special features of any plant or animal 37–38, 40–42, 44–52, 103–110, 113–114

chemical reaction, change a *reaction* between chemicals; it produces a new substance 66, 71

chlorophyll the green substance in *chloroplasts* which traps *light energy* 129, 131–132, 138, 143

chloroplasts tiny structures inside a plant *cell* which contain *chlorophyll*; where *photosynthesis* happens in plant cells 6, 12, 129, 131, 138

chromosome   structure made of *genes* found in the *nucleus* of a *cell*   105–106, 114

cilia   tiny beating hairs on the surface of some *cells*   7, 119

ciliated epithelial cell   a *cell* with tiny hairs called *cilia*, for example found lining the windpipe   7

circulate, circulation   the flow of *blood* around the body through the *heart*, *arteries*, *capillaries* and *veins*   68–70

classification   sorting things into groups   46–48, 50, 52, 91–92, 102

climate change   changes in climate patterns such as those caused by *global warming*   137

climatic stress   difficult *environmental conditions* caused by the climate   30, 36

clone   a group of genetically identical living things   112–114

combustion   when substances *react* with *oxygen* and release *energy*; another word for *burning*

community   all the plants and animals that live in a particular place   94, 97–98, 100, 102

compete, competition   when several plants or animals are all trying to get the same things   35–36, 151

compound   a substance made from the *atoms* of two or more different *elements* joined together

concentration   the strength of a *solution* or the amount of a substance in a *mixture*   11, 67, 144

conclusion   what you have found out   98, 157–159

conservation   preserving or taking care of living things and their *habitats*   137, 146

consumer   an animal that cannot make its own food, but eats plants and other animals   34, 36, 98–99, 102, 109, 139

contract   become smaller: *solids*, *liquids* and *gases*

do this when they cool; *muscles* become shorter and fatter when they contract   117, 125

control   the part of an experiment that is needed to make a test fair, where certain *variables* are controlled or kept the same while one variable is varied; it is needed so that we can be sure of the cause of a change or a difference   77, 132, 153, 156

coronary heart disease   disorder of the coronary *arteries* that take *blood* to the *heart muscles*   126, 128

crop   amount of food or other useful *material* produced by the animals or plants that we grow   134, 143–151

cuttings   parts of plants cut from an older plant and grown into new plants that are *clones* of the old plant   112

cytoplasm   the contents of a *cell* excluding the *nucleus*; the place where most *chemical reactions* happen   6, 12, 105, 134

D

data   information, for example facts or numbers   94, 153–154, 157–158

data collection   gathering *data* by any method   158

deficiency disease   a disorder caused by a lack of a particular *nutrient* in the diet; *scurvy* is an example   121

diaphragm   a sheet of *muscle* that separates your chest cavity from your abdomen   117

diffusion, diffuse   the spreading out of a *gas* or a *dissolved* substance because its *particles* are moving at *random*   67, 72, 78

digestion, digest   the breakdown of large, *insoluble molecules* into small *soluble* ones which can be *absorbed*   59, 61, 63–65, 78

digestive system   all the *organs* which are used to *digest* food   56–57, 59–62, 64, 66, 116

disease when some part of a plant or animal is not working properly   20, 35, 56, 79–80, 82–84, 86–90, 100, 121, 127, 150

dissolve when the *particles* of a substance completely mix with the particles of a *liquid* to make a clear *solution*   134–135, 156, 158

drug a substance that can change the way that your body works; to treat a *disease*   19, 88, 118, 122–123, 125–126, 128

E

egest get rid of *faeces* from the *digestive system*   63

egg cell female *sex cell*; also called an *ovum*   13–18, 24, 105–106

element a substance that can't be split into anything simpler by *chemical reactions*

embryo a baby in the *uterus* before all its *organs* have started to *grow*   16–19, 22, 24, 106

emphysema a disorder in which a person doesn't take in enough *oxygen* as a result of damage to the *air sacs* in the *lungs*   119, 128

energy energy is needed to make things happen   53–67, 71–78, 81, 101, 116, 121, 129, 132–134, 136, 138–142, 149

environment the surroundings or conditions in which plants and animals live   91, 93, 102, 104, 107, 114, 137, 149–151

environmental conditions conditions such as light level and *temperature* in the *environment*   25–27, 29–30, 36, 41, 91, 94, 97–98, 102, 107, 109, 149

environmental variations differences within a *species* caused by the *environment*   40–42, 52, 104, 114

enzymes *protein* substances made in *cells*; they speed up *chemical reactions*   61–62, 64

epidemic an outbreak of a *disease* affecting a large number of people   84–85

Erasistratus (about 304–250 BC)   70

evaluation considering whether there is enough *evidence* to support a *conclusion* and whether an investigation can be improved   159

evidence *observations* and measurements on which theories are based   41, 85, 108, 120, 127, 130, 132, 137, 154–155, 157–159

F

faeces undigested waste that passes out through the *anus*   60, 63–64

fair test a test in which one *variable* is varied and other variables are controlled or kept the same   11, 107

family tree a diagram to show how people are related to each other   40–41, 52

fats part of our food that we use for *energy*   32, 53, 55, 57–59, 61, 63–64, 120–121, 126

fatty acid one of the building blocks of *fats*   61, 63–64

fertile able to *reproduce*   37, 52

fertilisation when a male *sex cell* nucleus joins with a female sex cell *nucleus* to start a new plant or animal   10, 13–18, 24, 106, 108, 111, 114

fertilisers you add these to soil to provide the *minerals* that plants need to grow   143–144, 149–151

fetus a baby in the *uterus* whose *organs* are all *growing*   16, 19, 22, 24

fibre undigestible cellulose in our food; it prevents constipation   57–58, 63–64, 120

fish a group of *vertebrates* that lives in water and gets *oxygen* through its gills   49, 52

fit, fitness able to do a lot of exercise without tiring   115–116, 120, 126–128

Fleming, Alexander (1881–1955)   88

Florey, Howard (1898–1968)   88

food chain   a diagram showing what animals eat   34–36, 98–99, 101–102

food web   a diagram showing what eats what in a *habitat*   35–36, 99–100, 102, 140

fuel   a substance that *burns* to release *energy*   66

fungi   a group of living things including *micro-organisms* such as moulds and *yeasts* which cannot make their own food; one is called a fungus   79–80, 82–83, 87, 90, 97

fungicide   a substance that kills *fungi*   148

fuse   join together; the *nucleus* of a *sperm* fuses with the nucleus of an *egg cell* during *fertilisation*   13, 24

G

Galen, Claudius   (about 130–200)   70

gas   a substance that spreads out (*diffuses*) to fill all the space available, but can be compressed into a smaller volume   72, 75, 132, 137

gas exchange   taking useful *gases* into a body or *cell* and getting rid of waste gases   72–73, 78

genes   parts of *chromosomes* that control the *inherited characteristics* of plants and animals   105, 112, 114

global warming   an increase in the average *temperature* on Earth   137

glucose   a *carbohydrate* that is a small, *soluble molecule* (a sugar)   59, 62, 65–67, 71, 78, 116, 129, 131, 133, 138, 140

glycerol   one of the building blocks of *fats*   61, 63–64

greenhouse gases   *gases* such as methane and *carbon dioxide* that stop some of the heat escaping from the *atmosphere*   137

growth, growing   becoming bigger and more complicated   9–12, 14–19, 22–24, 26, 31–32, 53–55, 63–66, 78, 81–82, 87, 101, 121, 133, 135, 143–144

H

habitat   the place where a plant or animal lives   25–27, 35–36, 91, 93–94, 96–97, 102

Harvey, William   (1578–1657)   69–70

hazards   things that are harmful or dangerous and might cause damage   157

heart   an *organ* which pumps *blood*   32, 56, 68–69, 78, 118, 123–124, 126–127

herbicide   a chemical that kills plants   148

herbivore   an animal that eats plants   33–34, 36, 99, 102, 139

hibernation, hibernate   when animals go into a deep sleep through the winter   25, 32, 36

Hooke, Robert   (1635–1703)   2–3

Hopkins, Sir Frederick Gowland   (1861–1947)   120

hormone   one of a group of chemicals secreted in small amounts that controls the *growth* and activities of living things   18, 23–24

hydrogen   a flammable *gas*; it *burns* to form water

hydrogencarbonate indicator   an *indicator* that detects *carbon dioxide*   76

hypotheses, hypothesis   an idea, theory or explanation for something, but which has not been tested   152

I

Ibn-al-Nafis   also known as Al-Quarashi (1213–1288)   70

immune, immunity   able to resist an infectious *disease* as a result of *immunisation* or of having had the disease   87, 89–90

immunisation   an injection given to give the patient *immunity*   89–90

implantation   the settling of an *embryo* in the lining of the *uterus*   16, 18, 24

indicator a substance that changes colour to indicate whether a substance is an *acid*, an *alkali* or *neutral* 76–77

infect, infection when *micro-organisms* get into your body and cause a *disease* 21, 83–84, 88

inhale *breathe* in 74–75, 117

inherit, inheritance passing on of *genes* from parents to offspring 16–17, 24, 103–114

inherited characteristics, variations features or differences that are *inherited*, or passed on, from parents to offspring 40–42, 52, 103–104, 107, 114

insect an *arthropod* with two pairs of legs and two pairs of wings 25, 28, 32, 44, 47, 51–52

insecticide a chemical which kills *insects* 148

insoluble a word to describe a substance that will not *dissolve* 59, 131

insulation *material* that does not conduct heat; it prevents heat loss 32

invertebrate an animal without a backbone 48, 50–52, 91–92, 102

iodine solution a test for *starch*; presence indicated by a blue-black colour 131–132

iron a metal *element*; a *mineral nutrient* that living things need 56–57, 64, 121

irrigation supplying water to a *crop* 150–151

J

Janssen, Hans and Zacharias 2

joint where two bones meet 125–126

joule, J the unit used to measure *energy* or work

K

kilojoule 1000 *joules* 56

L

large intestine the wide part of the intestine between the *small intestine* and *anus* 60, 62

Leeuwenhoek, Antonie van (1632–1723) 2, 9

ligament *tissue* that holds bones together at *joints* 125–126

light energy *energy* that luminous objects give out 6, 12, 140

limewater a *solution* used to test for *carbon dioxide*; carbon dioxide turns the clear solution cloudy 74, 76–77

line graph a way of *presenting results* 158

liquid a substance that has a fixed volume but takes the shape of its container 69, 86

liver large *organ* in the lower part of your body that makes bile and stores *energy* 60, 63, 123

lungs *organs* for *gas exchange* between the *blood* and the *air* 7, 25, 67–68, 72, 78, 86, 117–119

M

malnutrition eating a diet with too much or too little of particular *nutrients* 121, 128

Malpighi, Marcello (1628–1694) 70

mammal a *vertebrate* with fur and whose young develop inside the *uterus* 14–15, 21, 49, 52

mammary glands milk-producing glands; in the breasts in humans 21, 24

mass the amount of stuff something is made of 129, 154–156

material substances from which objects are made 53–55, 64–65, 133, 141

mean an average; found by adding together a group of results and dividing the total by the number of results 157

menstrual cycle the monthly cycle in the human female reproductive system 18, 24

menstruation a monthly bleed in women when the lining of the *uterus* is lost; also called a *monthly period* 18, 24

microbe another word for a *micro-organism* 79

micro-organism a microscopic living thing; some cause *disease* 21, 25, 79–83, 86–87, 90

microscope an instrument for magnifying 1–6, 11–12, 15

migrate what animals do when they move to other places with the *seasons* 32, 36

minerals simple chemicals that plants and animals need to stay healthy; the chemicals in rocks 53, 56–57, 59, 63–64, 82, 107, 120, 128, 135, 138, 143–145, 149, 151

mixture different substances which are mixed but not joined together 118

model in the mind, it is a group of ideas and pictures 59

molecule the smallest part of a chemical *compound* and the smallest part of an *element* that can exist in nature 59, 61, 64, 71, 133

muscle cell a *cell* which *contracts* to cause movement 8–9

muscles *tissues* and *organs* that *contract* to cause movement 20, 56–57, 60, 65, 67–68, 117, 125

N

nerve cell a *cell* that carries nerve impulses 7

neutral solution a *solution* that is neither *acidic* nor *alkaline*; it has a *pH* of 7

neutralisation, neutralise when an *acid reacts* with an *alkali* to make a *neutral solution* of a *salt* in water

nitrate *salts* produced from nitric acid; important plant *nutrient* in *fertilisers* 135, 138, 143–144

nitrogen a *gas* that makes up about four fifths of the *air* 75

nitrogen oxides *compounds* of *nitrogen* and *oxygen* that help to cause *acid rain*

nocturnal active at night 28, 36

non-vascular plants a group of plants without a specialised transport or vascular system 92–93, 102

nucleus the part of a *cell* which controls what happens in the cell 2, 6, 9–13, 16–17, 80, 105–106, 111, 134, 141

nutrients the food *materials* that *cells* use 53, 57–60, 63, 98, 141–142, 150–151

O

observations records of changes, similarities, differences and other features 42, 69, 154, 159

oesophagus the tube between your mouth and your *stomach*; also called the gullet 60

opinion what someone thinks – but not supported by conclusive *evidence* 154, 159

organ structure in a plant or animal made of several different *tissues* 1, 8, 12, 14–15, 19, 61, 67, 118, 122, 131

ovary where *egg cells* (ova) are made 15, 24

oviduct the tube that carries an *egg cell* from an *ovary* to the *uterus* 15–16, 24

ovulation the release of an *ovum* from an *ovary* about once a month 15, 24

ovules contain the female *sex cells* of a flowering plant 10, 106

ovum another word for an *egg cell*; the name for more than one is ova 18

oxygen a *gas* that makes up about one fifth of the *air* 8, 19, 25, 65–68, 71–73, 75–76, 78, 81, 116–118, 121, 126, 129, 132, 134, 136, 143

P

particle a very small piece of matter that everything is made of 119

penicillin *antibiotic drug* used to kill *bacteria* in the body   82, 88

penis male *organ* for putting *sperm* into the *vagina* and for passing urine   1, 15

period, monthly period the 'bleeding' when a woman loses the lining of her *uterus* about once a month; also called *menstruation*   18

pest an unwanted plant or animal   147–148, 150–151

pesticide a chemical which kills *pests*   147–148, 150–151

pH a scale, 0–14, that tells you how *acid* or *alkaline* a *solution* is   154

photosynthesis a process in which plants use *light energy*, water and *carbon dioxide* to make *glucose*   129, 131, 133, 135–138, 139–140, 143

placenta the *organ* through which a *fetus* gets food and *oxygen* and gets rid of waste   19–20, 24

plasma the *liquid* part of *blood*   63

pollen contains the male *sex cell* of a flowering plant   10–11, 106, 111

pollen tube the tube that grows between the *stigma* and *ovary* of a flower to carry the male *sex cell*   10–11, 106, 111

pollute, pollution contamination of the *environment* with unwanted *materials* or *energy*   84

population all the plants or animals of one *species* that live in a particular place   35, 84, 95, 98, 100–102, 150

precision, precise *accuracy* of measurements and measuring instruments   154, 156

predator an animal that kills and eats other animals   33–34, 36

predict, prediction to say what you think will happen   29, 100, 153

preliminary tests tests, *trial* runs and information searches carried out to find out the best approach to an investigation   155

presenting results showing results in a way that makes them easy to read and understand   158

prey an animal which is eaten by another animal   33–34, 36

primary consumer an animal that eats plants   34, 139

producer a name given to green plants because they produce food   33–34, 36, 98–99, 102, 139

product a new substance made in a *chemical reaction*   66

proteins *nutrients* needed for *growth* and *repair*; made up of *amino acids*   53–55, 57–59, 61, 63–65, 80, 120–121, 128, 133, 135, 137–138, 140–143

puberty when boys and girls first make *sex cells* and are able to *reproduce*   23–24

pyramid of numbers pyramid-shaped diagram that shows how the numbers of living things change along a *food chain*   101–102

Q

quadrat an object, often a square frame, used for *sampling* living things   95, 98, 102, 153

R

random by chance   153

range the values between the lowest and the highest value fall within the range   25–26, 156

react, reaction what happens when chemicals join or separate   66

reactant a substance that you start off with in a *chemical reaction*   66

red blood cell a *blood cell* that carries *oxygen*   8, 55–56, 87

relax in the case of a *muscle*, becoming longer and thinner; the opposite of *contract* 117, 125

relevant suitable for, or appropriate to, something; relevant *evidence* helps to answer a particular question 154

reliable when something can be trusted; reliable *evidence* is based on sufficient and *accurate data* 154, 157

repair put back into good condition; heal a wound 53, 55, 64–65, 135

reproduction, reproduce when living things produce young of the same kind as themselves 10, 13–15, 24, 91, 106

reptile a *vertebrate* with scaly skin and eggs with tough shells 49, 52

respiration the breakdown of food to release *energy* in living *cells* 63, 65–67, 71–72, 74, 76, 78, 81, 116–117, 128, 133–134, 136, 138, 140–141, 143

risk the chance of a *hazard* causing harm 157

risk assessment considering how high a risk there is of a *hazard* causing harm 157

root hairs, root hair cells plant roots *absorb* water and *minerals* mainly through the tiny root hairs on root hair cells 8, 134, 138

S

saliva *digestive* juice made in the salivary glands 62, 86

salt a *compound* produced when an *acid reacts* with a metal or an *alkali*; the everyday name for common salt or *sodium chloride* 127, 156

sample, sampling take a small part to get an idea of the whole 95, 153–154

sample size the number of things in a *sample* 153

scale (i) something is drawn to scale when it is drawn smaller or bigger than in real life 3, 12

(ii) a series of numbers used to measure or compare things 156

Schleiden, Matthias (1804–1881) 2

Schwann, Theodor (1810–1882) 2

scurvy a disorder caused by lack of *vitamin* C in the diet 56, 121

seasons the different parts of each year (spring, summer, autumn, winter) 30, 36

secondary consumer an animal that gets its food from other animals 34

secondary data information that has been collected by other people 154

secondary sexual characteristics differences, apart from the *sex organs*, between males and females 23–24

selective breeding breeding only from the plants or animals which have the *characteristics* that we want; also called artificial selection 108–110, 114, 150

sex cells *cells* which join to form new plants or animals 10–11, 13, 16, 23–24, 105–106

sexual reproduction *reproduction* in which the *nuclei* of two *sex cells* join to start a new life 10, 13, 112–113

small intestine the narrow part of the intestine between the *stomach* and the *large intestine*; where *digestion* finishes and *absorption* happens 59–60, 62–63

Snow, John (1813–1858) 84–85

sodium chloride common *salt*; a *compound* of sodium and chlorine

sodium hydroxide a *compound* that *dissolves* in water to make an *alkali* 76

solar panel these produce electricity when *energy* is transferred to them by light 150

solid a substance that stays a definite shape

soluble   able to *dissolve*   59, 61

solution   a *mixture* formed when a solute *dissolves* in a solvent   62, 135

Spallanzani, Lazzaro   (1729–1799)   61

species   we say that plants or animals which can interbreed belong to the same species   37–39, 42, 46, 49–52, 102, 103, 107, 108

sperm   male *sex cell*   13, 15–17, 23–24, 105–106

starch   a *carbohydrate* with large, *insoluble molecules*   55, 59, 61–64, 131–133, 138, 140–141

stigma   for a flower to be pollinated, *pollen* must land on this part   10, 106, 111

stomach   an *organ* in the *digestive system*   60

sulphur dioxide   an oxide of sulphur that helps to produce *acid rain*

surveys   a way of collecting *data*, for example by asking people questions or by looking at things and recording details about them   154

sustainable development   development in a way that won't damage the Earth and will let development keep going   150–151

T

temperature   a measure of the heat energy contained in hot objects   19, 25–27, 30, 32, 77, 91, 98, 137, 153, 156, 158

testes   where *sperm* (male *sex cells*) are made in animals; one is called a testis   1, 15, 23–24

tissue   a group of *cells* with the same shape and job   1, 7, 8, 12, 67

tissue fluid   *liquid* between all the *cells* of your body through which *dissolved* substances *diffuse*   67

trials   testing of *drugs*, *crops*, *pesticides* and other chemicals before companies are allowed to sell them   88

U

umbilical cord   contains the blood vessels that carry food, water, *oxygen* and waste between the *placenta* and the *fetus*   19–20, 24

uterus   the *organ* where a baby develops before birth   14–16, 18–20, 24

V

vaccine   substance used to produce *immunity* to a *disease*   89

vacuole   space filled with *cell sap* in the *cytoplasm* of a plant *cell*   6, 12, 134

vagina   opening of human female reproductive system   15, 20

validity, of results   whether results are *accurate*, measuring instruments are *precise* and used properly   154

van Helmont, Jan Baptista   (1577–1644)   130

variable   in an experiment, something that can be changed to affect the result   77, 153, 156, 158

variations, vary   differences, for example between members of a species; to differ; to change something   29, 37–42, 52, 77, 98, 103, 106, 110, 112–114, 153, 156

vascular plants   a group of plants with a specialised transport or vascular system   92–93, 102

vein   blood vessels that carry *blood* towards the *heart*   68–70, 78

vertebrate   an animal with a skeleton made of bone inside its body   48–49, 52, 91–92, 102

Virchow, Rudolf   (1821–1902)   9

virus   a *micro-organism* that can only live and *reproduce* inside living *cells*; a cause of some infectious *diseases*   79–80, 83, 86–88, 90

vitamins   *nutrients* that we need in small amounts to stay healthy   53, 56–57, 59, 63–64, 120–121, 128

W

weed   a plant growing in the wrong place   145–146, 149–151

weedkiller   a chemical that kills *weeds*; also called a *herbicide*   146

white blood cells   *cells* in the *blood* that help to destroy *micro-organisms*; some make *antibodies*   87, 89

withdrawal symptoms   the effects on the body of not getting a *drug* on which it is dependent   123

word equation   this shows the *reactants* and the *products* of a *chemical reaction* in words   66, 71, 116, 129

Y

yeast   a *micro-organism* that we use to make alcohol and bread; a *fungus*   80–82

yield   how much food or other useful *material* a plant or animal *crop* can produce   144, 150–151

Acknowledgements

We are grateful to the following for permission to reproduce photographs:

John Adds 5cl; **The Advertising Archives** 125; **B & C Alexander** 14l; **Anthony Blake Photo Library** 58t (Phototeque Culinaire), 58c (Eaglemoss Consumer Publications), 58b (Martin Brig), 140 (Sian Irvine); **Ardea** 49tl (P. Morris); **Art Directors and Trip** 2l (M. Walker), 4t (M. Walker), 4b (M. Walker), 5l (M. Walker), 17b (M. Walker), 20br (M. Walker), 28c (M. Walker), 38t (M. Walker), 38bl (M. Walker), 38m (M. Walker), 49bl (Warren Jacobs); **Biophoto Associates** 19; **Bubbles Photolibrary** 20t; **Graham Burns** 101; **Cephas Picture Library** 107t (Ted Stefanski); **Bruce Coleman Collection** 26l, 26r, 28bl, 28tr, 32; **Corbis** 2mr (Bettmann), 71tl (JFPI Studios Inc.), 71m (Roger Ressmeyer), 103b (Rob and Sas), 104m (Henry Diltz), 108t (Tom Nebbia), 108b (Yann Arthus-Bertrand), 109br (Picimpact), 109bl (Jim Craigmyle), 113 (Najah Feanny), 115tl (Lawrence Manning), 115tm (Roy Morsch), 115tr (David Pollack), 115bm (Tom and Dee Ann McCarthy), 115br (Tim Kiusalaas), 145b (Danny Lehman), 150tr (Nik Wheeler), 150mr (Julia Waterlow); **Ecoscene** 94tr (Chinch Gryniewicz), 94br (Chinch Gryniewicz), 96tl (Chinch Gryniewicz), 97l (Sally Morgan), 97bl (Kevin King), 97br (Sally Morgan); **Greg Evans Picture Library** 38cl, 38cr, 38r; **Mary Evans Picture Library** 40 (all), 61, 70tr; **Fisher Scientific** 158; **Grant Heilman** 6b (Runk/Schoenberger); **Holt Studios** 141 (Duncan Smith), 144 (Nigel Cattlin), 145tl (Nigel Cattlin), 145tr (Nigel Cattlin), 146t (Nigel Cattlin), 150bl (Nigel Cattlin); **Jean Martin** 95, 96c, 96r, 153; **Mediscan Medical Images** 62bl; **Microscopix** 2t (Andrew Syred); **Vanessa Miles** 74l, 74r, 97mr, 143l, 143r; **Natural History Photographic Agency** 27 (Michael Tweedie), 28br (Stephen Dalton); **Nature Picture Library** 91 (Bernard Castelein), 152 (Tony Heald); **Oxford Scientific Films** 14t (Michael Fogden) 49tc (Mark Hamblin), 49tr (Konrad Wothe), 49br (David Tipling), 50l (OSF), 50rt (London Scientific Films), 50rb (OSF); **Professional Sport** 65r (Tommy Hindley), 75 (Tommy Hindley); **Science Photo Library** 1 (Alfred Pasieka), 5r (Claude Nurilsang and Marc Perenou), 5cr (Astrid and Hans-Frieder Michler), 6t (Dr. Gopal Murti), 13l (D. Phillips), 13r (CNRI), 16 (C.C. Studios), 17t (Gary Parker), 20bl, 21 (Mark Clarke), 39 (Peter Menzel), 46 (Prof. P. Motta), 54r (Peter Menzel), 55tr (Biophotos Associates), 55br (Biophotos Associates), 62r (CNRI), 65l (Cristina Pedrazzini), 66 (Jeremy Walker), 69 (Sheila Terry), 70br (Alfred Pasieka), 71br (James King-Holmes), 72 (Alfred Pasieka), 82 (R. Maisoneuve, Publiphoto Diffusion), 83 (Jane Shemilt), 87 (Noble Proctor), 88 (James King-Holmes), 93l (Dr. Jeremy Burgess), 93r (Th Foto-Werbung), 94c (Lepus), 97t (John Heseltine), 99 (Lepus); 103t (Gary Parker), 104t (Alex Bartel), 104b (Mike Bluestone), 109t (John Heseltine), 109mr (Rosenfeld Images Ltd.), 115bl (Erika Craddock), 119l (Matt Meadows), 119r (Matt Meadows), 121l (St. Mary's Hospital Medical School), 121r (Biophoto Associates), 123tr (Eamonn McNulty), 123br (C.C. Studio), 126 (Damien Lovegrove), 127t (Dave Reede), 127m (Gaillard Jerrican), 127b (Conor Caffrey), 146b (David M. Campione), 148 (B.W. Hoffman); **Wellcome Trust Medical Photographic Library** 3t, 54l (Fiona Progoff), 56, 123l; **Janine Wiedel** 37.

Picture research: Vanessa Miles and Jacqui Rivers

We have made every effort to trace copyright holders, but if we have inadvertently overlooked any we will be pleased to make the necessary arrangements at the earliest opportunity.